Paper Promises

PHILIP COGGAN

Paper Promises

*Money, Debt and the
New World Order*

ALLEN LANE
an imprint of
PENGUIN BOOKS

ALLEN LANE

Published by the Penguin Group
Penguin Books Ltd, 80 Strand, London WC2R ORL, England
Penguin Group (USA) Inc., 375 Hudson Street, New York, New York 10014, USA
Penguin Group (Canada), 90 Eglinton Avenue East, Suite 700, Toronto, Ontario, Canada M4P 2Y3
(a division of Pearson Canada Inc.)
Penguin Ireland, 25 St Stephen's Green, Dublin 2, Ireland (a division of Penguin Books Ltd)
Penguin Group (Australia), 250 Camberwell Road, Camberwell, Victoria 3124, Australia
(a division of Pearson Australia Group Pty Ltd)
Penguin Books India Pvt Ltd, 11 Community Centre, Panchsheel Park, New Delhi – 110 017, India
Penguin Group (NZ), 67 Apollo Drive, Rosedale, Auckland 0632, New Zealand
(a division of Pearson New Zealand Ltd)
Penguin Books (South Africa) (Pty) Ltd, 24 Sturdee Avenue, Rosebank 2196, South Africa

Penguin Books Ltd, Registered Offices: 80 Strand, London WC2R ORL, England

www.penguin.com

First published 2011
1

Typeset by Palimpsest Book Production Limited, Falkirk, Stirlingshire
Printed in Great Britain by Clays Ltd, St Ives plc

ISBN: 978-1-846-14510-0

www.greenpenguin.co.uk

To Helena and Catherine, with apologies for the debts left by my generation

Contents

Acknowledgements

This book was inspired by my work on the *Economist*, in particular a special report on debt that was published in the summer of 2010. While I was writing the report, I was struck both by the extraordinary rise in debt levels in recent years and by the role that debt has played in influencing economics over the centuries. Many a government has debased the coinage or devalued the currency to deal with a debt crisis. That brought the insight that economic history has been a war between creditors and debtors, with the nature of money as the battleground. The current crisis is just the latest skirmish.

The book is a work of journalism, based on my twenty-eight years in the profession and my extensive reading of the historical literature. It thus builds on the work of many excellent historians, who are extensively cited in both the footnotes and the bibliography. I am very greateful for their scholarship, which has allowed me to develop my own interpretation of events. Special mention should be given to Richard Duncan, whose books suggested the idea that the post-Bretton Woods era and asset inflation were intimately related.

In researching this book, I have been lucky to work for such an understanding employer as the *Economist*, under the leadership of John Micklethwait. Special thanks are due to Edward Carr, who initiated my hiring and who made many helpful stylistic comments on the manuscript; to John O'Sullivan, who put me right on many economic matters; my long-suffering officemate Andrew Palmer, who probably heard far too much about the book's gestation; and to Chris Young, who looked through the book while on secondment from the Bank of England. I hope that association with any heretical pronouncements in the book does not blight his career.

At Penguin, my thanks are due to Georgina Laycock for commissioning the work and to Will Goodlad and Richard Duguid for seeing it through to publication. Charlotte Ridings was an exceptionally diligent copy-editor and any mistakes that have slipped through into print are mine, not hers.

All through the book my wife, Sandie, has been an inspiration, both in terms of editorial advice and in terms of support when deadlines took precedence over family life. That is one debt that I shall endeavour to repay.

Introduction

In the midst of life, we are in debt. We must borrow to pay for our education, for our consumer durables and for our houses. And as nations, we borrow money because the taxes we are willing to pay rarely match the public spending we wish to see.

Another name for debt is credit, a word derived from the Latin *credere*, to believe. When we borrow or lend money, it is an act both of trust and of confidence. Lenders have to trust the borrower to pay the money back. Homebuyers take on a mortgage, rather than rent, because they are confident houses will rise in price. Banks allow their customers to run up credit-card debts because they are confident that they will pay back both the capital and interest.

For much of the past forty years in the Western world, that confidence has been well placed. The economy has grown, recessions have been rare and incomes and asset prices have risen. It has paid to borrow, and to lend, and we have done a lot of it. In many Western countries, the total value of debt is three to four times the value of annual economic output.

But all that has changed. Like a cartoon character that has run off the edge of a cliff, we have made the mistake of looking down. We have realized how much debt we have taken on and started to worry about how we will pay it back. We have realized that asset prices do not always go up, not even if we wait for a decade or more. Europe has an ageing population and will have fewer workers with which to grow its economy. The US, so long the dominant power, is watching nervously in its rear-view mirror as China catches up. In August 2011, America lost its coveted AAA rating that had signified its status as the world's safest borrower. In short, the confidence needed to borrow and lend is diminishing.

The result is a mess. This book is about this mess and how it will affect the global economy and the relationship between generations. But it is also about how our attitudes to money and debt have changed through history, and may be about to change again.

The massive debts accumulated over the last forty years can't be paid in full, and they won't be paid. The debt crises of Greece, Ireland and Portugal are just the start. The economic outlook for some countries, particularly in Europe, is weak thanks to deteriorating demographics: the number of retirees is growing relative to the number of workers. As a result, these countries' incomes will not grow fast enough to service their debts. Either there will be formal defaults, under which debtors pay back only a proportion of their loans, or there will be effective defaults, in which the debts are repaid in money that has lost its purchasing power through currency devaluation or inflation. Economics and politics for the next decade and beyond will be dominated by this issue, as social classes and countries debate where the brunt of the pain will fall.

THE FARMERS AND THE BANKERS

The Democratic presidential candidate was young, with just four years in Congress under his belt. He electrified his party with his powerful oratory and outshone his opponent, a military veteran, on the campaign trail. He represented a mid-west state although he had not been born there. He toured the country appealing to the common man against the interests of big business. 'The day will come when corporations will cease to consider themselves greater than the country which created them,' he declared. But, despite drawing more votes than the previous Democratic candidate, he lost. For this was not Barack Obama in 2008. This was William Jennings Bryan in 1896.

Bryan campaigned on an issue that may seem obscure now – he believed in bimetallism, the use of silver as well as gold as backing for the dollar. But Bryan was in fact championing an age-old cause: the interest of debtors against their creditors. Bryan spoke in favour of farmers, who had taken on debts to buy land and machinery and then had seen crop prices plunge. The farmers wanted higher prices and believed that adding silver to the currency would deliver them. He was opposed by bankers, who believed that sound money could only be based on gold.

In the late nineteenth century, most developed economies were governed by the gold standard, a system that tied the amount of paper money in circulation to the stock of gold. Since governments could not magic more gold out of thin air, the standard did not allow continuously rising prices. Safeguards also prevented governments from debasing the currency, the ancient trick of adulterating coins with base metal.

Between 1896 and 1908, Bryan ran for President three times and lost on each occasion. He was unlucky. Just as he was complaining about the lack of money, gold deposit discoveries in Alaska and South Africa were expanding supply. The 'American century' was about to dawn in which his country was to become the dominant economic and military power.

But the defeat of Bryan's ideas was only temporary. Within six years of Bryan's last defeat the gold standard was suspended, and the attempt to resuscitate it after the First World War failed. A world saddled by wartime debts found the constraints of the gold standard too hard to bear.

The world now operates with a system where money can be created at will or by decree ('fiat money' as it is known in the jargon). The last link to gold was severed in 1971. There is a fundamental difference between this paper money system and the metallic standard it replaced. Gold is no one else's liability; you can own it outright. Paper or electronic money is always a claim on someone else, whether a bank or a government. Modern money is debt and debt is money.

It is no coincidence that debt levels have exploded in the last forty years, culminating in the credit crisis of 2007 and 2008 from which the world is still recovering. In response to that crisis, new money was created via a tactic called quantitative easing (QE) – central bankers created money to buy government bonds (and other assets). The creation of money to finance government deficits is something that would have horrified the sound-money men of Bryan's era. But such tactics are hardly a surprise, now that governments and not just farmers have huge debts. The philosopher John Stuart Mill warned in *The Principles of Political Economy*, published in 1848, that 'the issuers may have, and in the case of a government paper always have, a direct interest in lowering the value of the currency, because it is the medium in which their own debts are computed'.

America is now the world's biggest debtor nation and the state of its finances is once more the subject of heated debate. The problem is that America is both the world's largest economy and the issuer of its most widely used currency, the dollar. The policies that the US has pursued to escape from the crisis (such as QE) are far from popular with its creditors, most notably the Chinese government.

In 2008, the US authorities feared a repeat of the Great Depression of the 1930s, when economic output plunged and unemployment soared. So they used all their available weapons, both monetary policy (the quantity of money and the level of interest rates) and fiscal policy (the balance between government spending and revenues), to ward off the threat. In addition, the banks were rescued with the government assuming some of their risks. Public debt replaced private debt.

The debate on the rescue has been highly political. The economists who follow the teachings of John Maynard Keynes have argued that such stimulus is essential to maintain demand and thus keep workers in jobs. Those Americans in the conservative 'tea party' movement counter that such a strategy expands the role of government, burdens future generations with high taxes and risks high inflation. The two sides clashed in the summer of 2011, when Congress debated a proposal to increase the debt ceiling, the amount the US government could legally borrow. Some in the tea party believed that the ceiling should not be raised under any circumstances; had they won the day, the US would have defaulted on its debts, causing chaos in the global economy.

Each camp has traditionally appealed to different constituencies. The debts of a country are ultimately those of its taxpayers, and the biggest taxpayers tend to be the wealthiest in the society. A government which runs a large and prolonged deficit will eventually raise taxes to pay for it, eating into taxpayers' income (or it will default on its debts, penalizing savers). On the monetary side, a government that expands the money supply at a rate in excess of economic growth will eventually erode the real value of taxpayers' wealth via inflation. Either way, the wealthy lose. The gainers will be the poorest, who benefit from increased public expenditure or who pay little tax.

Similarly, when a government decides to balance the budget by cutting public spending, or to eliminate inflation by raising interest rates, it is likely to penalize those employed by the public sector, those on benefits and those with debts. In short, one course of action tends to favour the creditor/rich class and the other favours the debtor/poor class. What is remarkable about the tea party is that a populist movement is taking the line normally associated with creditors, the complete opposite of the situation in the days of William Jennings Bryan. To complete the irony, the denizens of Wall Streeet, once firmly in the sound money camp, now favour the use of QE, since it props up the stock market and boosts their profits.

The argument is being fought across the developed world. In Britain, a Conservative/Liberal Democrat coalition is battling to bring down a huge deficit, inherited from a Labour government, in the face of trade union opposition to spending cuts. Their austerity programme is far more ambitious than anything planned by Mrs Thatcher.

But the crisis has been most intense in continental Europe. The region has conducted an historic experiment in monetary policy, replacing their individual currencies with the euro. In effect, the smaller countries hitched a ride on the reputation of the German Deutschmark, one of the world's strongest currencies in the second half of the twentieth century. In the early years of the euro, this seemed to bring nothing but benefits to the peripheral countries. Their borrowing costs fell, converging with those of Germany, while they avoided the exchange rate crises that had marked the 1970s and early 1990s.

However, the Europeans were running the monetary policy of Germany without the Germans' penchant for thrift or competitive industries. The result was either credit-fuelled construction booms (in Ireland and Spain) or repeated trade deficits (in Greece and Portugal). Debts built up. And even though the Irish government had a good fiscal record for many years, this was the result of an artificial banking and construction boom which boosted consumer spending and thus tax revenues; when the crisis hit, and the banks had to be rescued, excessive private-sector debts became a burden on the public sector.

As countries struggle to rescue their banking sectors, and cope with the rising debt burden, the future of the euro has been called into question. Will the most indebted European nations decide that default, or leaving the single currency, is a better option than years of austerity? Or will the Germans decide that they are unwilling to foot the bill for other countries' debts?

AN AGE-OLD BATTLE

Conflict between creditors and debtors is almost as old as money itself. John Taylor, an early nineteenth-century American thinker, said that the banking industry 'divides the nations into two groups, creditors and debtors, and fills each with malignity towards the other'.[1] One can see all of economic history through this prism – a battle between those who lend money and those who borrow it. The former want to be paid back with interest in sound money; in times of crisis, the debtors cannot afford to do so.

History suggests that periods of growing economic activity are accompanied by an expansion of the money supply and a widening of the definition of money. Confidence is high because trade and incomes are growing. Businesses are happy to accept the extra money, often in the form of debt – extending credit to customers, for example. Then something happens to shatter confidence and the definition of acceptable money narrows, which means that the willingness to extend credit declines.

In the twentieth century, each successive economic cycle tended to end with more debt being added. In 1981, Ronald Reagan managed to persuade some Republican Congressmen, rather against their will, to vote in favour of an increase in the government debt ceiling beyond $1 trillion, or one with twelve zeroes after it. It was assumed that a conservative President, who referred to government as the problem, would bring the deficit down. By the end of Reagan's time in office in 1989, the debt was $2.6 trillion.

That sum inspired a property developer named Seymour Durst to set up a debt clock in New York's Times Square to highlight the growing debt burden. By 2008, the clock had to be refurbished to add an extra digit because the debt total had reached $10 trillion. Just three years later, debt reached the previously agreed ceiling of $14.3 trillion, thanks to the massive fiscal deficits that followed the 2008–09 recession. This additional debt was more than the amount that originally alarmed Seymour Durst; indeed more debt than the US had accumulated in its first 212 years of existence.

The headline totals of government debt are only part of the picture. Politicians have also made promises to fund the retirements of ageing workers, in both the private and public sectors, to meet the cost of healthcare for the elderly and to guarantee the debts of banks and other companies. Beyond the obligations of the government, debt has also been accumulated by consumers on their mortgages and credit cards, by companies seeking to expand and by banks, seeking to speculate in the financial markets.

As these debts become due, rich creditors will be pitted against poor debtors; private-sector taxpayers against public-sector workers, young workers against the retired, domestic voters against foreign bondholders. It is impossible to forecast who will win each of these battles but one thing seems certain: not all these debts will be paid in full.

The crisis has also resulted in a debate about how to control the supply of money. In the 1970s, when money lost its link with gold, the result was much higher inflation; some thought we were heading for ruin. But the period of rapid money expansion since 1971 has also been accompanied by significant economic growth and the spread of capitalism to large parts of the ex-communist world. If these two developments are related (and it is not clear that they are), people might regard this as an acceptable trade-off. After all, credit is essential to make a modern economy function. Without it, businesses would be unable to grow and create jobs. More sophisticated societies seem to develop more complex financial systems. Banks may be the subject of much public opprobrium, but without them modern life would become incredibly cumbersome. Imagine if every prospective homebuyer had to raise the finance from their friends and acquaintances, or if we had to haul bags of gold or silver every time we went on an overseas trip.

Nevertheless, the modern monetary system creates some inherent dilemmas. When does the amount of bank lending become excessive? When does the financial system become too complex for the good of the economy? It is hard to define the 'right' level but it seems clear it was breached at some point in the last twenty years.

Credit can be used to finance trade but it can also be used to fuel speculation. By allowing banks to become so large and so central to the modern economy, the Western world acted like a parent who allowed his teenager to go on a credit-card-fuelled spending-spree. Banking turned from a rather dull profession into a glamorous world that the best and the brightest of the world's youth wanted to join. As money was lent to buy assets, asset prices soared. Trading on the financial markets became the route to riches. It is no coincidence that hedge funds and private equity companies, two industries that profit from easy credit and rising asset prices, have flourished in the last few decades. Whereas the new billionaires in the developing world still earn their fortunes from industry and natural resources, the developed world's plutocrats increasingly come from the world of finance. Luck and leverage can turn a trader into a genius.

Asset prices could not go up for ever. The crisis of 2007–08 overwhelmed the banks and governments felt obliged to step in for fear of widespread economic collapse. This has happened many times in the past. A government (or its agent, the central bank) is often the lender of last resort, since it can pay its debts out of taxes, or by printing money.

But a government's ability to fund itself is not infinite. In Greece, late in 2009, the sudden revelation of the dire state of the government's finances (after years of fudged statistics) soon sparked a funding crisis. The yield on Greek government debt rose sharply, making it more expensive to fund the government's huge deficit. The new Socialist administration announced several packages of austerity measures to try to close the gap, including an increase in the pension age and a cut in civil service benefits; the workers responded with strikes and violent protests.

The markets were unconvinced by the Greek plan and the cost of Greek borrowing rose alarmingly. So the Greeks turned to their richer European neighbours to fund a bailout plan and agreed an austerity plan with their new paymasters. This merely bought the Greeks time. They still had a debt bill that was too large – around 150 per cent of their annual economic output or GDP. Paying off that bill required the Greeks to run many years of surpluses – for the government to take in more tax revenues than it spends (before interest payments, at least) and for the country to export more than it imported. The implication was higher taxes, lower spending on benefits, lower wages and lower consumer demand: a massive dose of castor oil for the Greek population.

It was no surprise that a year later the Greeks were back asking their neighbours for more money. Investors had made their opinion clear: Greek two-year bonds were yielding 25 per cent, a level that indicated the fear that the debt would not be repaid in full. Default would bring down Greek debt to a more manageable level; say 70 to 80 per cent of GDP. But the EU was dead against default for fear that it would spread panic across the region. After a tense stand-off between the Greek parliament and demonstrators, a deal was agreed in June 2011 under which more money was lent in return for further budget cuts. But few people believe the deal was any more than a temporary reprieve, and the package was being renegotiated by October. What makes life so difficult for Greece is its membership of the euro-zone; the old trick of devaluing the currency and thus paying back foreign creditors less in real terms is not available.

Governments across the developed world may face the same choices as the Greeks in the next few years. Do they make the sacrifices needed to keep creditors satisfied? Do they default on their debt, at the risk of alienating the financial markets for a generation? Or do they try to ease the burden by devaluing, a trick not open to all governments (if one currency falls, another must rise)? For domestic creditors, the same effect can be achieved by the creation of inflation.

None of these tricks is new. Monarchs have been debasing their currencies (inflation by another name) for thousands of years. Modern history is littered with examples of default by developed and developing countries. Creditors have retaliated by demanding higher interest rates or by imposing agreements to tie down the value of currencies, for example by fixing monetary values in terms of gold.

This book will argue that we have reached another of the great crisis points in history. Borrowers will fail to pay back their debts, either through outright default or by encouraging their governments to inflate the debt away. The creditors, who are increasingly found in the developing world, will demand a new system to protect their rights. This might involve a commitment from the Western indebted countries to support their currencies and balance their budgets.

PAPER DREAMS

In 1971 President Richard Nixon abandoned the obligation for the US Federal Reserve to exchange dollars for gold at a set rate. At that time, gold was valued at just $35 a troy ounce; by August 2011, it was trading at $1,900 an ounce. That shift illustrates what those who believed in sound money feared would happen – paper money has an inherent tendency to lose its value. Some would say it is bound to decline to its intrinsic value: zero. In the critics' view, paper money is about as solid as air miles; the kind of currency that you accumulate but can never really cash in.

Nixon's decision also ushered in a new era in currency markets. From that point, most countries in the developed world let their currencies float, that is move up and down every day on the markets. The old constraints imposed by fixed exchange-rate systems, which forced governments to slam on the economic brakes when the currency was under threat, have been removed. It is no coincidence that this period has been marked by huge trade surpluses and deficits, booming asset markets and rising debts.

To be strictly accurate, the world of floating rates consists of the big economies (America, Japan, continental Europe, Britain) that let their currencies fluctuate against each other. However, economic power has been shifting to the countries of the developing world, led by China, which tend to manage their exchange rates – typically by pegging them to the dollar – rather than let them float. In recent years, that has often involved the use of policies to prevent their currencies from rising too fast and making their exports too expensive. China, for example, ensures that its currency, the renminbi, trades in a very narrow range against the dollar on a daily basis.

That policy has added to the potential for economic conflict. On one side you have the US, which is creating money to boost its economy; on the other, China, which is managing its exchange rate to keep its workers in employment. As a result the newspapers were full of talk of 'currency wars' in late 2010.

In a sense, this is just another version of the creditor/debtor battle being played out on a global stage, with China in the creditor camp and the US as the debtor. What is new this time around is that so many countries are facing debt problems at the same time, without the trigger of a world war to create them. The world is also enjoying interest rates that are lower than at any time in history, even though the risks of default and/or inflation seem high. We have interest rates fit for a gold standard era, but no limit to the ability to create more money.

This crisis follows a long period when attitudes towards debt have changed profoundly at the individual, corporate and national level. In the 1980s and 1990s, borrowing money was seen as a sign of economic shrewdness, rather than a matter of necessity. The developed world built an economic model on debt; consumers borrowed to finance their lifestyles, companies borrowed to enhance their returns, financial institutions borrowed more money to play the asset markets, countries borrowed money to tide economies over recessions. It may well be that the credit crunch of 2007–08 showed that this model had been tested to destruction. But what will replace it?

RUNNING ROUND IN CIRCLES

The Buddhists use a wheel of life to symbolize the cycle of life, death and rebirth. Religious scholars say that humans see everything from their own frame of reference, from their own point in the circle. Similarly, the economy flows in a circle, with money spent by one actor being received by the next. Arguments about economics tend to depend on the starting point in the circle chosen by the debater.

To some, the answer to the crisis is simple. We must abandon our spendthrift ways and start to live within our means. Saving is needed to finance investment. Only by investing in new technology and new equipment can the developed world hope to grow its economy over the long term. But the circular nature of the economy means that such individual decisions have collective consequences. As Keynes pointed out, money saved, rather than spent, reduces demand for goods and thus employment. The economy can be trapped in a circle where too much is saved, too little spent and too few jobs are available. What is true at a domestic level is also true internationally; if Western countries spend less, the economies of the developing world will sell fewer goods.

The same debate arises when governments opt for a fiscal stimulus, boosting an economy by cutting taxes or raising spending. Such a stimulus, say the Keynesians, will create a virtuous circle when an economy is in recession, boosting demand and creating jobs. As the economy recovers, tax revenues will increase and spending on unemployment benefits will decline, eliminating the budget deficit.

Nonsense, say the critics; government spending must come from somewhere else in the circle. In the short term, the government borrows the money, so diverting capital from businesses that might have created jobs on their own. And in the long run, deficits mean higher taxes which take spending power out of the wallets of consumers.

The international economic debate is also bogged down, because each country's perception of the issues is dictated by its starting point in the circle. Within Europe, the Germans think that other countries should adopt their export-led model. But if the Germans are exporting, someone must be importing. Those European nations currently facing a debt crisis incurred some of their debts buying German goods. If they stop buying, German industry will suffer.

In the China/America relationship, the Chinese see themselves as the virtuous party, with an economy based on manufacturing and the export of goods to other countries. They save and invest to lift their population out of poverty. Americans, in contrast, are seen to lack discipline, spending money they do not have on luxuries like widescreen TVs. To the Americans, however, it is the Chinese who must change. The Chinese only maintain their export competitiveness by holding their currency at artificially low levels. The West acquires cheap goods (but loses manufacturing jobs) while the Chinese get IOUs in return, which may or may not be repaid. This does not seem like a stable arrangement.

This dispute has immense historical importance. The ability of the developed nations to use their economic power to set the global agenda is now under question. Back in 1956, the British and French took military action against Egypt after President Nasser nationalized the Suez Canal. The action was quickly abandoned after the American government put financial pressure on the British. Will there come a time when Washington finds itself constrained by the need to keep its Chinese creditors happy?

At a more mundane level, the rules of international finance may need to be changed. The old rules were set by the Western nations in the 1940s when they had all the economic power; that does not seem appropriate for the new world. The focus is shifting from meetings of the G7 group of developed nations to the much broader G20 forum, which includes developing countries like China and Brazil. The Anglo-Saxon countries have been great enthusiasts for the free flow of international capital; the developing world, led by China, is far less keen.

DEBT AS A POLITICAL AND MORAL ISSUE

The crisis will have political, as well as economic, consequences. William Jennings Bryan was known as a populist, a label that applies to the 'tea party' movement today. Populism may seem to have migrated from the left to the right, from the Democrat to the Republican party, but the movement is not really a matter of being left or right wing but about a claim of representing 'the people' against the elite. Populism also seems to have a strong moral tinge, pitting the values of decent ordinary folk against corrupt government or corporate insiders.

In Bryan's case, 'the people' were the farmers, since agriculture lay at the heart of the national identity (ironically, some modern American commentators feel the same about manufacturing). Farmers earned their living through honest toil, financiers by idle speculation. Bryan represented a long-standing tradition of American suspicion of bankers, displayed by nineteenth-century presidents such as Thomas Jefferson and Andrew Jackson. John Adams, one of the founding fathers and the second President of the United States, proclaimed that, 'Every bank in America is an enormous tax on people for the profit of individuals.'

To this day, there is a vigorous literary debate over whether the children's classic *The Wizard of Oz* is a veiled parable on Bryan's crusade.[2] Dorothy, an archetype of American innocence from a midwest farming state, follows the yellow brick road (golden allegory) to the city of Oz, which coincidentally is the usual shorthand for an ounce, the traditional measure of the gold price. Along the way she kills the wicked witch of the east; the eastern states were seen as representing the money men. Her companions are the scarecrow (the farmers), the tin man (industrial workers) and the lion (Bryan himself). On their arrival at Oz, they find the wizard is a fraud, an old man with no power.

The populists felt belief in gold was a similar illusion. At the Democratic convention of 1896, Bryan thundered:

You come to us and tell us that the great cities are in favour of the gold standard. We reply that the great cities rest upon our broad and fertile prairies. Burn down your cities and leave our farms, and your cities will spring up again as if by magic; but destroy our farms and the grass will grow in the streets of every city in the country.

His final imagery still forms one of the most famous passages from a convention speech.

You shall not press down upon the brow of labour this crown of thorns. You shall not crucify mankind upon a cross of gold.

The religious tone was not a coincidence. A devout Presbyterian and teetotaller, Bryan ended his life as a figure of fun, appearing for the prosecution in the Scopes Monkey Trial, in which a Tennessee teacher was tried for teaching the theory of evolution. (The case was turned into a play and film, *Inherit the Wind*.) But a similar tone was taken by the other side. A Republican senator called George Frisbie Hoar proclaimed that 'A sound currency is to the affairs of this life what a pure religion and a sound system of morals are to the affairs of a spiritual life.'

In the Victorian era, failure to repay debts was a criminal offence and debtors were often sent to jail. In *Little Dorrit*, Charles Dickens focuses his plot on the Marshalsea prison, where William Dorrit is confined as a debtor, while Wilkins Micawber (in the novel *David Copperfield*) lives in constant fear of arrest. As the character famously remarked, 'Annual income twenty pounds, annual expenditure nineteen nineteen six, result happiness. Annual income twenty pounds, annual expenditure twenty pounds ought and six, result misery.'

Creditors tend to believe that a borrower should honour his debts as a matter of principle; 'they hired the money, didn't they?' as 1920s US President Calvin Coolidge remarked when faced with his allies' requests to reschedule First World War debts. The idea that borrowers should be allowed to escape is one example of 'moral hazard' in economics. Let the borrowers believe they will be rescued from their folly, the tone implies, and they will never meet their responsibilities. The concept of moral hazard persuaded the US authorities not to rescue the investment bank Lehman Brothers in September 2008, a decision that almost brought the global financial system to a halt.

The debtors also appeal to morality. They argue that creditors demand too high a price for lending money. Such income is 'unearned', in contrast to the wages received by the honest worker. Aristotle argued that money, unlike livestock, did not bear fruit in the sense of multiplying automatically. The Church developed the concept of usury to describe excessive interest rates; Islam has gone a step further and tried to eliminate interest payments altogether.

When debt crises occur, it is often argued that many borrowers have been suckered into their plight by 'predatory lenders', and that demanding full repayment penalizes the poor at the expense of the rich. In international relations there is the concept of 'odious debt', that the inhabitants of developing nations should not be required to repay debts incurred by kleptocratic or tyrannical governments. The Live 8 rock concerts in 2005 were inspired, in part, by the desire to persuade Western governments to forgive the debts of developing countries.

In a democracy, governments may well be tempted to favour the interests of debtors, who outnumber creditors. But they have to be careful. After all, the creditors have a choice over where they will place their savings. At the very least, they will demand higher interest rates of the imprudent; at worst, they may refuse to lend, except on stringent conditions.

It would also be a mistake to assume that forgiving, or inflating away, debts is simply a matter of rewarding the deserving poor at the expense of the rapacious rich. Sometimes the inflation cure can be worse than the disease. One reason why Bryan lost the 1896 election was that his campaign had little appeal to industrial workers for whom higher food prices meant a lower standard of living; outside the South (then a Democratic stronghold) Bryan carried only one city with more than 100,000 inhabitants. Inflation penalizes the thrifty. In the chaos that followed the end of the First World War, German hyperinflation, designed to erode the burden of the reparations imposed by the Treaty of Versailles, destroyed the savings of the middle class and paved the way for the rise of Hitler.

Even bankers become less concerned with the idea of sound money when their own survival is at stake. They are quick to call for governments and central banks to cut interest rates and to create as much new money as is needed to stabilize the financial system. While the farmers lost their battle in 1896, the debtors had much more power in 2008 and 2009; governments round the world moved to bail them out.

When money is too sound, economic activity can contract because consumers and companies are crushed under the burden of their debts. But when money is too weak, economic activity can also break down; there is no incentive to save and supermarket shelves are bare. When money is too active, the country gets caught in a frenzy of speculation as citizens seek to get rich by buying and selling assets within a short period. Eventually, the result is a spectacular bust as prices collapse. But when money is too idle, when it sits under mattresses or lies unused in bank accounts, then industry stagnates for lack of capital and no new jobs are created. The economist Paul Krugman has criticized the view that 'debt is evil, debtors must pay for their sins and from now on we must all live within our means . . . [And] that kind of moralising is the reason we're mired in a seemingly endless slump.'[3]

Getting the balance right is all-important. So this book will start by looking at the nature and origins of money and how it changed from solid objects to entries on a computer screen. It will then recount how empires and kingdoms rose and fell along with their money, see how individual currencies developed along with global trade and how such currencies changed from symbols of national pride to tools of economic policy. And it will also explain how debt ceased to be a matter of individual shame and became almost a human right. Finally, it will look at the modern debt crisis in the context of that history and will argue that the current position is unsustainable. Many debtors have made paper promises that they won't be able to keep.

I

The Nature of Money

'Someone mentioned the philosopher's stone. To the surprise
of all present, Law said he had discovered it. "I can tell you
my secret," said the financier. "It is to make gold out of paper."'
John Law, by H. Montgomery Hyde

'There is nothing about money that cannot be understood by
the person of reasonable curiosity, diligence and intelligence.'
J. K. Galbraith, *Money: Whence It Came, Where It Went*

Two thousand four hundred years separate the reigns of Dionysius of
Syracuse and Kim Jong Il of North Korea. But their similar financial
policies prove that you can teach a new tyrant old tricks.

When Dionysius's subjects requested repayment of the money they
had lent him, he demanded, on pain of death, that they handed over
all their coins. Then he simply re-stamped one drachma coins as being
worth two drachma, thereby cutting their value in half. With that trick,
he could return the face value of all the money he had seized and use
the remainder to repay his debts.

In 2009, the 'dear leader' of the communist state used a variation
of this approach. He announced that old won bills, worth 10,000
apiece, would be replaced with new 10 won notes.[1] Knocking a few
zeros off a currency has been done in inflation-prone democracies,
such as Mexico and France, but the North Korean dictator added his
own sneaky trick. Only amounts up to 100,000 won (later raised to
150,000) were able to be swapped. Those few folk who had managed
to put money aside in Kim's famine-ridden dystopia saw their savings

wiped out; one couple were reported to have committed suicide. Eventually the bouffant-haired bully realized that his plan was causing even more economic chaos than he had previously managed to inflict on his impoverished nation, and retreated on the policy. But, with a typical flourish, Kim executed the hapless officials deemed responsible.[2]

For thousands of years, the nature of money has been subject to change at the whim of those in power. Governments usually grant themselves the right to decide what is money and what is not, and changing that definition is a very tempting option when a government is in financial difficulties. Or a government can create money, like Dionysius, to settle its debts. The costs of such measures (printing the money) are very low, and governments do not have to pay interest on the money they create (an advantage known by the term 'seignorage' by economists).

Creating money can also be seen as an inflation tax. The tactic is a substitute for the hard and unpopular work of raising tax from the country's citizens. Since government debts are usually fixed in nominal terms, inflation reduces the cost of repaying the debt in real terms. At 8 per cent inflation, prices double in nine years; so the real cost of repaying a debt halves over the same period.

Governments through the ages have used the inflation tax as a way of raising revenue with minimal public outrage. The Greek playwright Aristophanes describes the minting of bad coins in *The Frogs*, and adulteration of the coinage was a favourite habit of Roman emperors, who were constantly in need of money to pay their soldiers. Failure to pay the Praetorian guards could turn an emperor into an ex-emperor quicker than you could say 'Et tu, Brute'. If 100 ounces of silver can be used to make 1,000 coins, diluting the silver content by half produces 2,000. The steady use of this tactic caused the silver content of the Roman coinage to decline by 96 per cent over the course of two centuries.

An alternative approach to adulteration was shaving the edges off coins to make them slightly smaller (sometimes known as 'clipping'). In modern times, an even simpler tactic became available. Instead of using precious metals (or 'specie') for coins, why not use paper?

THE STORY OF JOHN LAW

John Law (1671–1729) was a Scottish mathematician, gambler and early economist who left his homeland after killing a man in a duel. He found his way to France in the dying days of Louis XIV, the 'sun king', who was the pre-eminent European monarch. Louis had ruled for seventy-two years and was famed for the sumptuousness of his court, and the flattery of his courtiers ('What time is it?' he is supposed to have asked; 'It is whatever time your Majesty pleases' came the reply). He was a bigoted Catholic, expelling the highly productive, but Protestant, Huguenots and waging long and expensive wars against the heretic English and Dutch.

By the end of Louis XIV's reign, the monarchy was essentially bankrupt. The right to collect taxes had been sold to various aristocrats and merchants, whose depredations were deeply resented. When the king finally died in 1715, the national debt was 3,500 million livres (the French currency at the time) and the monarchy was paying a pricey 7 per cent interest on its debt.

Louis' successor, his great-grandson Louis XV, was an infant, so power rested in the hands of the regent, the duc d'Orléans. Given the country's debts, the regent was naturally attracted to the ideas of John Law, who persuaded him that the creation of a bank, with the right to issue paper money, was the way out of his problems. In effect, he believed he could create gold out of paper.

Law was the first economist to implement 'monetary easing' as a way of boosting an economy. He argued that, if his plan was adopted, 'the people may be employed, the country improved, manufacture advanced, trade domestic and foreign be carried on, and wealth and power attained.'[3]

It is important to understand Law's thinking since, though his scheme failed, he was the father of modern monetary economics. Gold and silver had previously been thought of as 'real wealth', the ultimate store of value. But Law believed the vital role of money was as the oil in the wheels of commerce. 'Money is not the value for which goods are exchanged but the value by which they are exchanged', he wrote. 'The use of money is to buy goods. Silver, while money, is of no other use.'

He thus turned previous thinking around. In the old system, you had to wait for wealth to arrive – for gold and silver to be discovered, or for it to be accumulated by earning a surplus from trading with foreign nations. But Law viewed wealth as the goods produced by the land and businesses of France. That trade was held back by lack of currency. If you created more money, more trade would occur and thus there would be more wealth.

In Law's view, it did not matter that paper money was not backed by an equal amount of gold and silver. 'The houses of Paris taken together as a capital stock surpass in value all the specie in the kingdom', he wrote. 'The lands of France are worth more than all the gold that still lies hid in the mines of Peru. Have then the houses for this reason nothing but chimerical value?' Law drew an analogy with banking, where the amount of cash kept by a bank is insufficient to repay all depositors, should they demand its instant return. But banks were able to do business, provided their depositors retained confidence in the business. The same could be true of national wealth. 'What is it that keeps up land to their lawful value, how high soever, but that they are not sold to realise them?' [4]

The Law saga covers many of the themes running through this book. Like William Jennings Bryan, he believed that money was in short supply, and more should be created. Not only would more money improve the economy, it would deal with the problem of the monarchy's heavy debts since shares in his enterprises would be sold to the public. Royal patronage also meant that Law's plan, unlike Bryan's, was actually put into practice.

The duc d'Orléans decreed that all taxes and royal revenues could be paid in the notes of Law's bank, the Banque Générale. Had the scheme been kept on a modest scale, with bank notes backed by gold and silver, French economic growth might indeed have been boosted over the long run. Trade would have increased, and so would the monarch's tax revenues, making the debts easier to service.

But the regent wanted, and Law had promised, quicker results. The aim was to repay the monarch's debt. This involved creating a joint-stock company, the Compagnie d'Occident, to exploit France's colonial possessions in the Mississippi basin. At the time, the Dutch and British were having success in exploiting the 'spice islands' through their East Indies companies. France aimed to do the same thing in America.

Again, given enough time, the Compagnie d'Occident (or the Mississippi Company, as it became known) might have been successful. After all, it had the commercial and mineral rights covering the territory of eight modern US states. But the initial land settled was a malaria-infested swamp and the early colonists died quickly. No great mineral riches were found. Shares in the company traded at par or below for two years.

So Law expanded his scheme. More of France's colonial rights were added to the company's possessions, while he himself made a much-publicized offer to buy shares at above the par price. A further capital-raising stock issue followed: 50,000 shares were issued with a par value of 500 livres. The shares were sold at a 10 per cent premium (i.e. at 550 livres) but payable in twenty instalments. An investor could buy a share by putting down just 75 livres – the premium of 50 livres plus the first instalment of 25 livres. As a result of speculative excitement, and the prospect of high dividends, the share price quickly rose, so those initial investors were extremely pleased. Subsequent share issues were at 1,000- and 5,000-livre values, again payable in instalments.

While things were going well, Law was the toast of every duchess in Paris, as people clamoured to buy shares. The effect was to create money, or, if you like, paper wealth. Shareholders all felt wealthier since they were heavily in profit. And they could maintain that feeling, as long as the share price kept going up. While the price was rising, few would want to sell – the point Law had made about the value of French land. However, this was a false analogy. French land was worth something because it produced food and offered shelter. The colonial possessions delivered nothing like enough to pay the dividends promised to those who bought the shares. Law had to pay those from the money raised in new issues – the definition of a Ponzi scheme.[5]

Law developed his system so that the bank would both collect taxes and assume the national debt. Everything seemed to add up; investors could pay for the shares with gold and silver (good), paper from Law's bank (also good), or with government bonds (another positive, since it reduced the debt). But the system depended on confidence, which in turn relied on an ever-rising share price. That required the printing of more bank notes, the ability of investors to pay for shares in instalments and the promise of generous dividends on the stock. By 1719, 1.2 billion livres of paper money had been printed and the Compagnie d'Occident had a market value of 4.8 billion livres.

This was one of the great bubbles in history. Voltaire wrote: 'They say that everyone who was comfortably off is now in misery and everyone who was impoverished revels in opulence. Is this reality? Is this a chimera? Has half the nation found the philosopher's stone in the paper mills?'[6]

It was during the Mississippi boom that the word 'millionaire' was first coined. Servants became as rich as their masters overnight. As investors clamoured to own shares, an informal stock exchange emerged in the rue Quincampoix, near Law's house. In one (probably apocryphal) story, a hunchback earned 150,000 livres by hiring out his hump as a writing desk so share contracts could be signed. At the peak of the boom, the shares reached 15,000 livres apiece.

It could not last. Some investors took their profits, reinvesting in gold, jewellery or land; the price of the latter rose three-to-fourfold in a few years. Some decided to shift their money to the English South Sea Company, a similar bubble-like structure which was developing at around the same time and also involved the creation of money to buy assets. By the end of 1720, some 500 million livres of gold and silver coins had been taken out of the country.

Law resorted to desperate measures to keep the system afloat. To convince the public that the Mississippi was being developed, a group of tramps was given tools and paraded through the streets, en route to the colonies. The use of precious metals for large transactions was banned; the export (and then the possession) of gold was prohibited. He promised to support the Mississippi share price at 9,000 livres. In this, Law anticipated the policies of modern governments, with their attempts to prop up the share prices of banks during the crisis of 2007 and 2008. He even reversed his own policy, burning bank notes and share certificates in open cages, trying to boost the relative value of gold and silver.

None of this worked; Law could not stop the inflationary impact of the extra money he created without also destroying the speculative frenzy that had supported his scheme. And the speculative frenzy was the key to Law's popularity. When the share price of his bank collapsed, he was dismissed from royal service, eventually dying in poverty. The French developed a suspicion of banks and paper money which lasted into the twentieth century. A contemporary of Law, the duc de Saint-Simon, summed up the sceptical view of his system:

They tried to convince the nation that . . . the wisest nations of the earth had been under the grossest error and delusions as to money and the metals of which it was made; that paper was the only profitable and necessary medium and that we could not do a greater harm to foreign nations, jealous of our grandeur and our advantages, than to pass over all our silver and gold and precious stones to them.[7]

So why did Law's scheme fail? To his contemporaries, the answer was obvious: he created nothing but worthless pieces of paper. But later economists have seen him as a monetary pioneer. The problem in Law's case was that the credit he created did not get used to create new businesses or trade, not even in the Mississippi basin, that Law had advertised. Instead the money was diverted to speculation.

As we move through history, this is a recurring theme. Credit creation is associated with economic growth since growth gives businesses and consumers the confidence to borrow against their future incomes; but it is also the basis of asset bubbles. Those who demand the creation of more money may promise the former but only deliver the latter.

WHAT IS MONEY?

John Law's experiment was, in essence, an attempt to redefine money. Given that mankind has been using money for thousands of years, it is perhaps surprising that money is still such a nebulous concept. The word itself comes from a title of the Roman deity Juno – Juno Moneta – the goddess of warning and advice; a suitable omen for those who rely too much on its value.

Most people spend little time thinking about the nature of money. They just get on with spending it. Over time, money has been everything from precious metals through paper to entries on a computer screen. One writer defined it quite neatly: 'Money is the belief that someone will pay you back.'[8] But perhaps a broader description is that money is something that people accept as payment for goods and services because they believe they can use the proceeds to buy goods and services from somebody else.

Early man settled deals by barter. I trade you two sheep for a sack of corn. But when you start dealing in a number of different commodities, this becomes a very inconvenient process. What if you want cows instead of sheep? Then we have to get a third person involved. Money makes these bargains a whole lot easier. The sheep, cows and corn all have a value in terms of dollars (or pounds or euros). No longer does the farmer need to arrange a direct swap. He can sell his livestock or crop and use the proceeds to buy all the things he needs, from seeds through to combine harvesters. So this is our first monetary use, as a 'medium of exchange'. In John Law's view, this was money's prime function.

As media of exchange, paper and electronic money are much more useful than precious metals. It is far easier to clear a vast spider's web of transactions between global banks, companies and consumers if they are all entries on a computer, than it is to transport bullion over vast distances. And while the Bible may say that 'the love of money is the root of all evil', the use of money is actually the root of most everyday activity. Imagine that, in order to buy this book, you had to perform a direct service for the salesman at Barnes & Noble, or the warehouseman at Amazon.com – wash his car, clean his windows, teach his children, etc. Life would be an amazingly complex and cumbersome business.

Money allows people to realize their potential. The likes of William Jennings Bryan portrayed an agricultural economy as a bucolic idyll. In fact, in most agrarian societies, people are concerned merely with producing enough food to survive. Life expectancy is short, literacy is rare, women have few rights and land is usually concentrated in a small number of hands. The shift to a more monetary economy, with all its faults, has been accompanied by a vast improvement in longevity, a drive towards democracy, greater equality of opportunity and so on. Money has helped this happen. The idea of a 'post-materialist' world in which we cease to care about the monetary value of things is a fantasy, and not a pleasant one. When money dies, economic activity is severely disrupted.

The second use of money is as a 'unit of account'. A personal computer can sell for £600 or $1,000, figures that everyone living in Britain and the US can understand. In a barter system, we need to know a computer's worth against the full range of products that might be on offer – a horse, two cows, four sheep and so on. Expressing the price of all goods and services with relation to one denominator is much easier.

The third use of money is as a 'store of value'. This is also highly useful. Imagine if you had to spend money as soon as it was earned, as was true during the Weimar hyperinflation or in modern Zimbabwe. Or, conversely, you had to earn money immediately before you visited the shops. In either case, the scope of economic activity would be much reduced.

This function of money also facilitates investment. In normal circumstances, money ought to be worth roughly as much next year as it is this. So we can save in order to make a very big purchase. In other words, money allows us to make deals that stretch across long periods of time. This is vital for economic activity. Saving and lending are essentially the same thing; when you save money in a bank, you are lending money to the bank's management. The bank then lends your money to businesses, which can then purchase new plant and equipment. That creates more jobs for workers, who earn wages that are deposited back in the bank. This process is beautifully illustrated in the film *It's a Wonderful Life*, where a harassed Jimmy Stewart points out to panicking depositors that their money has been reinvested in the local farms and town stores. Withdrawing their funds would mean impoverishing their neighbours.

As we shall see in Chapter 2, people need some compensation for delaying a purchase. Interest payments reward savers and lenders for tying up the money, for the potential loss in value caused by inflation (if you are saving to buy a car, it might cost more in a year's time), and for the risk that the borrower will not pay you back.

Two of these monetary roles – the means of exchange and the store of value – lie at the heart of the struggle between creditors and debtors.

Treat money mainly as a means of exchange and it seems obvious that we should want more of it. The more exchange (trade) we have, the wealthier we get. 'Bank notes are simply the small change of credit,' said one nineteenth-century observer. 'If you lend to borrowers with good credit, then the money will return to the bank when it is repaid.'[9]

But treat money as a store of value, and we want to restrict its supply. Indeed, part of the reason for the enduring appeal of precious metals as money is that there is so little of them to go around. If money is simply created at will, it eventually becomes worthless. And, of course, if it is worthless, it loses all value as both a unit of account and medium of exchange. So a bit like the porridge of Goldilocks, we want a money supply that is not too hot (commonplace), not too cold (scarce) but 'just right'. Mankind has tried to find that balance in many different ways.

Some politicians and voters have been tempted by money creation in the same way that the French regent was tempted by John Law. Modern economists mostly agree that monetary stimulus can be effective in reviving the economy. The twenty-first-century tactic of quantitative easing is a high-tech version of the same theory.

Imagine, however, that you are a creditor or a merchant selling goods. Your debtor or customer offers to pay you back, not in pounds or dollars, but in Monopoly money. You might not regard this as payment at all. The fundamental worry of creditors is that governments can issue as much money as they like. Indeed, the concept is built into the rules of the Monopoly board game. The rules state that, 'The Bank never goes broke. If the Bank runs out of money it may issue as much more as may be needed by merely writing on any ordinary paper.'

And in a sense, monopoly money is what we are all using. The monopolists in this case are governments, which permit the issue of notes and coins and give such currency their seal of approval in the form of seals, mottoes, or the queen's head. The practice of putting an image of the sovereign on one side of the coin was a way of advertising his power, and the first coins were introduced by the kings of Lydia around 640 BC. But coins can also provide an insight into the nature of the monarch's rule. Ethelred the Unready, an English king forever bribing the Danes not to invade, changed the coinage seven times in his thirty-eight-year reign. Henry VIII was known as 'old copper nose' because of his habit of adulterating silver coins, the base metal underneath showing through with wear.

Creating the right amount of money is an art, not a science. Gold and silver offer a discipline, but their supply is very lumpy. At various points in history, gold and silver have been in short supply – prior to the New World discoveries of the sixteenth century, for example. The resulting monetary boost to Europe involved the outright exploitation of the Aztec and Inca peoples unlucky enough to be in possession of the metals concerned. Ancient empires had a similarly direct approach. They acquired extra bullion by conquering their neighbours. This treasure was both an incentive to attack and a means of financing the campaign. The classical approach to monetary stimulus was thus to start a war.

Even in the absence of gold, people have a natural need to trade, and thus a natural desire to create and hold money, or something approximating to it. When gold and silver are in short supply, they use something else. When governments impose monetary rules that do not fit the economic needs of society, people usually find a way round the legislation. When the domestic currency becomes worthless, they start using a foreign currency.

When the American colonies were first established, they had the problem that there were no real supplies of gold and silver on the east coast, where they settled. So they had to improvise to deal with the shortage of coins. At one point, the government of North Carolina decreed that there were seventeen different types of legal tender; tobacco was one of the most popular examples. It is easy to understand how this system restricted trade, and thus economic activity. What if the buyer offered one of the seventeen forms of money that the seller did not like?

History's tug of war between monetary shortage and excess has resulted in several different, but interlinked, forms of money. One can very broadly break down these into three: precious metals, and other commodity-related currencies; bank notes created by government order, as in John Law's system; and credit, as created by the banking system.

PRECIOUS METALS

Western people traditionally regarded gold, and silver, as the only 'real' forms of money. 'For all practical purposes, for most of time, money has been a more or less precious metal,' wrote the economist J. K. Galbraith.[10] But the appeal of shiny metals was not universal. Professor Glyn Davies recounts how Fijians captured, by chance, a chest of gold coins from a visiting ship. Seeing no value in these strange objects, they played skimming stones with them, thereby depositing a small fortune at the bottom of the Pacific, much to the bemusement of their European observers.[11]

The Fijians viewed whales' teeth as a sign of both wealth and social status. Like jewellery, the teeth could be used for decoration. Other forms of early money have included cowrie shells and wampum – beads treasured by Native Americans and used as legal tender in the early days of the American colonies. Like precious metals, both were used for decoration. Cowrie shells were also impossible to counterfeit.

The problem in both cases was that the supply of currency was unlimited. When cowries were imported into Africa in the late nineteenth century, two shells were sufficient to buy a woman; by 1860, it took a thousand.[12] The early American colonists set up factories to manufacture wampum, an eighteenth-century version of quantitative easing.

An extreme example of this problem was created by the late writer Douglas Adams, in his book *The Restaurant at the End of the Universe*. He invented the Golgafrinchans, a people who decided to base their monetary system on a leaf. Very rapidly, the exchange rate required three deciduous forests to buy a single peanut. In an act of lunacy, the enterprising Golgafrinchans decided to embark on a massive policy of defoliation (burning down the forests) to deal with the issue.

Unlike the leaf, the supply of gold is very limited. All the gold that has ever been mined will fit into a cube smaller than a typical tennis court. If we still used gold, governments would be unable to create new money. And traditional forms of debasement would be hard to pull off. In a modern society, it is very easy to weigh coins and test whether they are pure.

Silver has a long pedigree as the basis for coinage; the French words for money and silver – *argent* – are the same. It is also more common than gold and that made it much more useful for everyday transactions. In his *Financial History of Western Europe*, Charles Kindleberger wrote that 'silver was the principal money in use in ordinary transactions within countries until late in the eighteenth century'.[13] And when silver was too valuable, copper coins could be used for small sums.

Precious metals are hard-wearing, so they will not deteriorate when stored. And they are, in the right hands, malleable, so they can be melted down and turned into coins. Economic history can be seen through the evolution of coinage, with those of the dominant economic power being accepted outside their states of origin. The discovery of silver deposits at Laureion in Greece allowed the city-state of Athens to expand its coinage; Athenian owls, as the coins became known, were widely used for the next six centuries. The Romans had the denarius and when that was debased, the golden solidus; the Byzantine Empire had the bezant. Some currencies derived their name from their origins. The British coin, the guinea, was named after the part of Africa where the gold was found; the word dollar comes from the German thaler, a coin minted in Joachimsthal in Bohemia (*thal* means valley). These were cut into eight. From this habit, we get the currency peso meaning 'piece', the old pirate talk of 'pieces of eight', and the term 'two bits' for a quarter dollar.

These coins circulated freely around the globe. In the early seventeenth century, some 341 silver and 505 types of gold coin were in circulation in the Dutch Republic.[14] Such a multiplicity of coins meant that individual traders could easily be confused by their value. This was an age-old problem which created the need for specialists who could distinguish between the different currency units. These were the 'money changers' that Jesus threw out of the temple. Another historic term, 'touchstone', derives from a method of assessing a coin's metallic value.

Just as the QWERTY keyboard outlasted the manual typewriter, initial choices of names and weights have had long-lasting consequences. Pepin the Short, the father of Charlemagne, the first Holy Roman Emperor, lived from *c.*715 to 768. He established that a livre or pound of silver was worth 240 denarii or pennies, while the solidus was worth 12 denarii.[15] This was the basis for the British monetary system for centuries until 1971. Sums in my primary school maths book had to be calculated under the headings l s d (livre, solidus, denarius) to signify pounds, shillings and pence. The L of livre is the basis of the modern pound symbol.

The Italian city-states were the next great economic powers. Florence's credit was so good that its currency, the florin, became widely accepted. Again this was a term that survived until 1971 as part of the British currency; a florin was a term for a two-shilling piece (one tenth of a pound). And the economic success of the Dutch Republic led to the widespread use of its coins in the seventeenth century.

However, the use of more than one metal created potential problems. Remember that money is used as a unit of account. So how should the value of a cow be expressed, in terms of gold, silver or copper? The answer to this problem is to fix the value of one metal in terms of another. In turn, however, this supposes that the ratio will be fixed for an extended period of time. But new discoveries of one metal might increase its supply relative to another; the official ratio might no longer reflect reality.

The relative attractions of coins led to the problem dubbed Gresham's Law after the Elizabethan financier Sir Thomas Gresham. People might prefer gold coins to other forms of money, perhaps because the official ratio undervalued gold. So people would hang on to the gold coins and offer other types of money (silver, paper) in exchange for goods. The gold coins would all disappear from circulation – bad money would drive out good.

I experienced a modern version of Gresham's Law in 2010 on a visit to Iceland, one of the countries that suffered most in the early stages of the debt crisis. Not wishing to end up with unwanted Icelandic krona, I took along some euros in the hope they would be accepted for cash deals (buying coffees, newspapers and the like). Shopkeepers would indeed accept the euros, but they would return krona, not euro, coins as change. The euro had a 'real' value, which made them want to hoard it. The krona they were happy to get rid of. In other words, the krona was acceptable as a medium of exchange but the euro was seen as the store of value.

The idea that precious metals were the only real wealth led to the doctrine of mercantilism, an economic policy followed by states in the late Middle Ages and early modern period. Governments were determined to hang on to as much money as possible, by prohibiting the export of precious metals, and by promoting exports and prohibiting imports. The flaws in this strategy, a precursor of protectionism, are many and varied. If countries hoard gold, how will their trading partners have enough money to buy their goods? The approach also assumes that trade is a zero-sum game, which it is not. Imagine how inefficient it would be if a country tried to produce everything it consumed, from apples to yachts. It is far better for countries to specialize and to produce what they are best at (or least worst at). Some argue that the Chinese and German governments are pursuing mercantilist policies today by piling up trade surpluses without any regard for the effect on their neighbours.

The ability to mint coins is a highly useful form of sovereign power. Traditionally, coins have been issued at a value a little above their metallic content as a way of extracting seignorage. Such profits are all the greater in an era of paper money, since $20 notes are worth far more than the cost of printing them. But as Kindleberger points out, there is a dilemma. If the state tries to earn too much from seignorage, the coins will not be accepted. If it earns too little (the coins are roughly worth their metallic value), it risks that the coins will be melted down, or exported, rather than used for domestic trade.[16]

While the gold standard worked very well for a long period, it is still slightly odd that a metal, whose primary use is for decoration, should have been seen as a source of wealth. In a Second World War debate on monetary systems, Lord Addison, a Labour peer, remarked that he was not convinced that 'to dig gold out of the ground in South Africa and to bury it, refined, in a cellar in the United States, in fact adds to the wealth of the world'. The author James Macdonald describes the process of gold storage as 'mining in reverse' and points out that the Persians actually melted down the gold they seized before burying it again.[17]

Gold and silver have a few industrial uses. Their main economic value is one of perception; we are willing to hold them because custom suggests that other people will afford them value. The Fijian preference for whales' teeth (also limited in supply) was just as logical to them.

In extreme conditions, such as the dystopia set out in Cormac McCarthy's novel *The Road*, precious metals would be pointless. We would want food and water (and guns to guard them).

Nevertheless, gold and silver have kept their real value over the centuries. However, as a means of exchange, they are less suitable: gold's very scarcity makes it impractical as a monetary unit for day-to-day use. At the time of writing, a mere speck is thus worth one pound or one dollar; there is no way one could create coins out of it.[18]

The supply of gold and silver has no relationship at all with economic activity. In the thirteenth and early fourteenth centuries, Western Europe was producing just 1 metric tonne of gold a year, not enough to sustain trade.[19] Some even suggest that the shortage of bullion was a key factor driving the exploration of the 'new world' in North and South America.

Whatever the motivation, the discoveries got rid of the shortage. The Spanish conquest of Central and South America led to an expansion of the gold and silver supply in Europe and a steady inflation (which by modern standards was very mild). Further discoveries were made in California in the 1840s and South Africa in the 1890s, the latter helping to relieve the pressure on farmers that had fuelled William Jennings Bryan's presidential campaign.

If, in an ideal world, you want the supply of money to grow in line with the economy, gold and silver alone won't do. It is no coincidence that gold and silver fell steadily out of use in the twentieth century, an era when economic growth accelerated rapidly. Whether this rapid economic growth was in any way caused by the switch to paper money is a subject of occasionally fierce economic debate.

Nevertheless, precious metals should not be dismissed lightly. Monetary systems based on gold and silver were tremendously long-lasting. From time to time, people argue that we should return to a gold-based system. After all, paper money has not played its role as a store of value. When the last link between gold and paper currencies was dropped in 1971, bullion traded at $35 an ounce; by mid-2011, the price was $1,900. In gold terms, therefore, the dollar had lost 98 per cent of its value. It is progress of a kind. The Romans took two hundred years to devalue their currency by the same amount; our generation has achieved the trick in just forty years.

PAPER MONEY

The idea of paper money has been around for more than a thousand years, having been introduced by the Chinese. The Emperor Hien Tsung, who ruled from 806 to 821, used a paper currency to overcome a copper shortage. The concept was then developed by the Mongols who took over the Chinese Empire. Marco Polo describes how the Grand Khan of the Mongols also used paper money, remarking that, 'All his majesty's armies are paid with this currency, which is to them of the same value as if it were gold or silver.'

Marco Polo's surprise was natural enough. Paper clearly has no intrinsic value so why accept it as payment? The answer was that traders had little choice. The Mongol regime had decreed paper's use and theirs was not a government one defied. In a sense, then, the value of the paper was equivalent to the citizens' belief in the stability of the governing regime.

The rule of the Mongols did not last for ever and nor did the value of the currency. The temptation to print more money was simply too great. According to economist Roger Bootle, the supply of paper money increased sixfold between 1190 and 1240, while prices rose twentyfold over the same period.[20] By 1448, notes nominally worth one thousand in cash were actually trading for three. That was one of the last historical references to Chinese paper money. The nation switched to silver, a system that lasted into the twentieth century.

Meanwhile, in the West, the early printing machines developed by Gutenberg were also adapted for monetary purposes. As Professor Glyn Davies points out, 'It is a further irony of monetary history that not long after China finally abandoned its paper currency, European banks began increasingly to issue paper money notes about which they had first learned from the writings of travellers like Marco Polo.'[21] Sweden was the first European country to issue paper money, but the reputation of the currency was severely damaged by the Law experiment. When France returned to metal coinage in 1721, the lawyer Marais remarked: 'Thus ends the system of paper money, which has enriched a thousand beggars and impoverished a hundred thousand honest men.'

But paper money was too useful to abandon altogether. John Law had stumbled on a kind of alternative truth. The eighteenth-century French monarchy could not impose its will with the intensity of the Mongols. However, what if economic activity was increasing, and with it the tax revenues and creditworthiness of the government? Then it might make sense for people to accept paper money issued by a stable regime, for the prosperity of the economy would allow it to redeem its paper promises. It is no accident, then, that the European experiments with paper money emerged in the eighteenth century, when the population and economic output of the continent began its long period of growth. The same era saw the development of the study of economics, led by Adam Smith, and the rejection of the earlier mercantilist approach. Wealth was not merely a matter of accumulating more bullion; it flowed from the rise of trade and industrial activity.

That the Law experiment did not destroy the use of paper money was perhaps due to a fundamental problem with precious metals – they are easy to steal. Goldsmiths kept a lot of gold and thus developed safes for security.[22] Other people then started to use those safes to store their own bullion. In return, the goldsmith handed over a receipt to the value of the gold; these were the earliest forms of banknotes. If you are a Briton, you can gaze at your banknotes and still see a picture of the sovereign with the legend 'I promise to pay the bearer on demand the sum of . . .' This dates from the days when you could present your note at a bank and demand the requisite amount of gold in return.

Historically, that promise created confidence that the money had a real value and, crucially, limited the amount that could be created. The history of the gold standard will be outlined in Chapter 3.

But a paper currency backed by gold (or silver) still raises a crucial question: how much backing should the currency have? For stability's sake, one might want to ensure that every single banknote could be converted into precious metal. However, the whole point of adopting paper money instead of gold was to create more money, so that economic activity was not restricted by mining output. Once you accept the idea that some paper could have no gold backing, it is hard to say what the upper limit might be.

Before the twentieth century, economists feared that paper money was too tempting a weapon to place in the hands of politicians. Adolph

Wagner, a German professor of economics, declared in 1868 that, before a system could be built on paper money, 'Men would first have to be capable of unlimited self-discipline to resist any temptation to increase money arbitrarily, even if their very existence, or that of the state, were at stake.'[23] Modern followers of William Jennings Bryan might protest that there is nothing wrong with a bit of inflation. Prices rose very fast (relative to history) in the second half of the twentieth century, a period that also saw an immense increase in the global standard of living. (Of course, this improvement was not shared equally, either within nations or between them.)

But even in the late twentieth century, the period when inflation was highest – the 1970s – was an era of economic disruption. And history has plenty of examples of the dangers of paper money. In the revolutionary war, the American states, short of gold and silver, issued continental notes as currency. These lost 92 per cent of their value, relative to gold, within six years. During the American Civil War, the Confederate states were blockaded by the north and found it difficult to raise money via taxation. So they simply printed money, starting with $200 million-worth of notes in 1861 and eventually reaching $1,555 million by the end of the war. An index of prices rose from 100 to 2,776 over the same period – in other words, prices rose nearly twenty-eightfold.[24]

In some cases, paper money can become no better than leaves. Zimbabwe illustrates the extreme; after years of hyperinflation, it was forced to issue notes with a face value of 100 trillion (1 followed by fourteen zeroes) in January 2009. At the time, each such note was worth just thirty US dollars. Money was thus worthless; a photo circulated on the Internet showing a notice banning the use of Zimbabwe dollars as toilet paper.

As money loses its acceptability, governments often become more and more draconian as they try to enforce its use. John Law was far from the first to ban the export of gold and silver; the Romans used this tactic before the birth of Christ. Desperate governments have prosecuted, and executed, traders for using the 'wrong kind' of money – usually precious metals instead of paper. But they find they are overwhelmed by events.

The revolutionary Russian government after 1917 repudiated all foreign debts and used their printing power to destroy the purchasing power of the currency; in a communist utopia, money would be of little use. Democracies have been a little more subtle about their abuse of their monetary powers. But the purchasing power of money has still declined pretty rapidly. Any system that allows net debtors (normally the majority) to outvote net creditors (usually the minority) has its potential weaknesses.[25] Thomas Hutchinson, an eighteenth-century governor of the colony of Massachusetts, which had its own inflationary problem, declared that 'the great cause of the paper money evil was democratic government. The ignorant majority, when unrestrained by a superior class, always sought to tamper with sound money.'

Inflation in the developed world has generally been much higher since the First World War, after which democracy became widespread. In the nineteenth century, there was a dispute between the bullion and the banking schools of thought. The former saw gold and silver as the only real money; the latter wanted to expand the money supply, regarding notes and coins as 'the small change' of the system. From the perspective of history, the banking school has won.

Even without hyperinflation, rising prices can cause harm.[26] Higher prices should indicate that there is an imbalance between supply and demand, either causing producers to make more of the good or consumers to switch to cheaper alternatives. But a rise in the general price level can distort these signals and thus lead to the inefficient use of resources. Producers see higher prices as a sign of demand for their goods and step up production, even though the prices are only a sign of general inflation. The result is a surfeit of unwanted goods and a shortage of others.

Once it was accepted that gold and silver were not the only forms of money, the modern financial system became possible. At each stage, the concept of money became more and more notional. Rather than swap metal coins, we swapped banknotes. Rather than swap lots of banknotes, we swapped receipts (cheques in Britain, checks in America) to prove we had money in a bank account. Finally, we have reached the stage where an entry on one computer is transferred into an entry on another computer; money is just 'bits' of data. Each stage – credit cards, debit cards, Internet transactions – has built on the last. As money has broken away from its precious metal origins, it has become harder and harder to define.

The electronic age means that governments need not actually go to the effort of creating money. Modern quantitative easing involves a central bank buying government bonds (gilts in the UK) from investors. Rather than send the investors bundles of notes in return, it electronically credits their accounts with money, a process as simple as altering a computer entry. It is as if a benign computer hacker had, instead of stealing money from your online bank account, decided to add money to it.

If people think that the value of something is equal to the cost of creating it, which in the case of paper and electronic money is virtually zero, then why do we accept it at all? We know there is no longer enough gold or silver to support it. The answer must be that we have faith in the government that stands behind it. The government can raise the taxes necessary to give the currency value. Since those taxes are raised from us, and from future generations, our willingness to accept paper and electronic money is essentially an expression of faith in our continuing prosperity and of the ability of governments and central banks to prevent hyperinflation. Like the *Peter Pan* audience that claps to prove they believe in fairies, our faith in paper money is the key to its survival.

However, it would be a mistake to think that modern governments can abuse our faith completely. At the extreme, they can, of course, print so much money that it becomes valueless. Short of that desperate expedient, they can only hope to influence the amount of money in the system, in part through manipulation of interest rates (when rates are low, the demand for credit will go up and banks will supply it, thereby creating more money), and in part through the reserves they require banks to hold (again, the lower the level of reserves, the more the banks will lend). But this process, as the world found in 2007–08, can be very hard to control.

BANKING MONEY

Banks are at the heart of the modern financial system. They fulfil two of the three key functions of money – as 'store of value' and as 'medium of exchange'. Most people in the developed world keep the core element of their savings in a bank and expect that money to hold its nominal value (i.e. not adjusted for inflation). Banks also are the medium through which most monetary exchanges are made; cheques, debit-card and credit-card payments are all processed through the banking system and cash payments are usually withdrawn from a bank.

The reason why the authorities panicked so much in the autumn of 2008 after the collapse of Lehman Brothers was that they feared the banking system was freezing up. Banks seemed unable to raise funds in the money markets (where companies and pension funds store their cash and billions are lent and borrowed on a short-term basis). Without such vital funds, banks might have become unable to perform their role as a medium of exchange; what if the cashpoint machines stopped working or businesses could no longer pay their employees? The result would have been economic chaos.

History has been dotted with a series of banking crises. That is because of an essential role that banks play in the creation of money. The goldsmiths that acted as banks did not take long to notice that they held lots of gold on a semi-permanent basis; only a small proportion of depositors wanted their money back on any given day. So the banks could lend out the surplus money at a profit.

Let us say banks reckoned the worst that could happen is for 10 per cent of deposits to be withdrawn on any given day. So with £100 million of deposits, they could hold £10 million in cash/gold and lend out another £90 million. Each borrower would rightly regard the loan from the bank as money. But that £90 million would also be regarded as money by the people who originally deposited it with the bank. New money would have come into existence. The way the maths work is that, if the bank has a cash-to-loan ratio of 10 per cent, it will end up creating ten times as much money as it has cash-on-hand.

But this apparent blessing also has a weakness. What if the bank's debtors don't repay? What if depositors get nervous and demand back more than 10 per cent of their money over a short period? The bank may find it runs out of cash. And the fear that the bank may run out of cash will be self-fulfilling; it will make more depositors withdraw their funds before their fellow citizens do the same.

There was a stark illustration of this problem in 2007 when the

BBC *News at Ten* programme reported that Northern Rock, a bank based in the north-east of England, was in talks about emergency funding from the Bank of England. The next day depositors were queuing to withdraw their money. In turn, the sight of those queues made other depositors fearful, encouraging them to withdraw their money. Meanwhile, those who banked online were attempting, and failing because of a system overload, to do the same thing. Eventually, it took an announcement by the government that it would guarantee all deposits (initially up to £35,000 and then up to £50,000) to bring the run to a halt.

The Northern Rock panic was not as bad as it might have been. Few depositors wanted their money back in the form of notes and coins. They were happy for their deposit to be switched to another bank. That is a big change from two centuries ago and indicates that we all recognize that money is not just the change we have in our pocket. Ask people how much money they have and they will include the money held in their bank current accounts, any instant-access savings accounts, money-market funds and perhaps even the unused limits on their credit cards. All of these could be counted as money, in the sense that they could be quickly exchanged for goods and services.

This very broad definition of money makes it even harder for economists to decide how much money there is in the system. For a brief period in the 1970s and early 1980s, politicians experimented with monetary targets in a bid to control inflation. The theory was simple: inflation was caused by too much money chasing too few goods; create less money and inflation would come under control.

However, the varying definitions of money caused the authorities to come up with a whole number of targets which sound rather like British motorways – M1, M2, M3, etc. (The Bank of England listed twenty-four different classes of assets that could be included in the monetary aggregates in 1982.) There were quasi-theological debates about whether the focus should be on narrow measures (those closest to notes and coins) or on broad ones, including forms of savings accounts and time deposits.

It did not help that the attempt to measure money coincided with a period when the authorities were liberalizing financial markets and credit cards were coming into widespread use. The various monetary aggregates grew rapidly; the authorities responded with their only real weapon, which was to raise interest rates. This succeeded in causing a recession in the early 1980s and the destruction of a fair chunk of the British (and American) manufacturing sectors, but had much less success in controlling the money supply numbers. A British economist, Charles Goodhart, coined 'Goodhart's Law', which was that any economic variable was doomed to misbehave as soon as it was targeted. It was like pinning jelly to the wall.

The key point, perhaps, is that the amount of money has tended to expand as each new form has been introduced. William Jennings Bryan has triumphed, albeit posthumously. Even when we had the gold standard, each paper note was not literally backed by gold. Just like a commercial bank, the authorities figured out that all depositors were unlikely to reclaim their money at once. Provided a decent portion of the currency had a gold backing, that was enough; in the US, for example, the ratio was set at 40 per cent. But once this principle was established, it is easy to see how the gold standard might eventually erode. Perhaps the authorities could get away with 30 per cent, rather than 40 per cent? If they did, they could create more money at a stroke. And if the public could be persuaded that more than half of all the money in the country had real value, even though it was only paper, might they not be persuaded that gold backing was not required at all?

To sum up: money is no longer gold, or silver, or indeed anything that has any intrinsic value. Nor indeed, with the exception of dictatorships like North Korea, is it necessarily what the government claims it to be.

Money is a medium of exchange and a store of value. In its former role, money is almost infinitely flexible; it is simply the form of payment that someone will accept for goods and services. Air miles are a good example. They are not accounted for in any of the central bank definitions of money supply. But as they can be exchanged for a flight, they certainly qualify as a medium of exchange.

If there is not enough official money to go round, but people want to trade, new forms of money will be invented; cigarettes and petrol in times of war, ration books in years of austerity, and so on. An analogous process occurs in the financial sector; if there is a demand for financial assets, new ones will be invented, as with all those complex products created during the sub-prime housing boom. While confidence is high, these assets will be traded at face value, 100 cents on the dollar; but if confidence is destroyed, then the assets will trade like debased coins, at a fraction of their declared worth.

In boom times, money and money-like assets multiply, as the medium of exchange function dominates. But in bad times, people start to worry more about money as a store of value; in other words, as a claim on wealth. When we multiply those claims, we do not expand 'real' wealth, in the form of food, energy or manufactured goods at all. But for reasons this book will go into, it can prove quite hard to make that distinction in the short term; when money is expanding rapidly, asset prices (like houses or shares) tend to rise too, so that people certainly feel wealthier.

This creates a whole new set of challenges. The easier it is to create money, the more tempting it is to do so. When the financial system froze in 2008, central banks flooded the system with money. One of the risks that the global economy now faces is that central banks will make the same mistakes as the Imperial Chinese, Confederate and Weimar Republic governments did before them. They are already creating new money, and there is no real limit in their ability to do so. Might they tip us into hyperinflation? An eighteenth-century cynic, Josiah Quincy, had his answer: 'I am firmly of the opinion . . . that there never was a paper pound, a paper dollar, or a paper promise of any kind that ever yet obtained a general currency but by force or fraud, generally both.'

But some critics look in a different direction, to the record of Japan over the past twenty years. There the government and central bank have tried all the options now being pursued in the US and Europe: they have cut interest rate to zero, expanded the money supply and increased the budget deficit by so much that government debt is now 200 per cent of GDP. Even after all this, Japan has not experienced inflation and has been stuck in a long period of slow economic growth.

As the current policy debate continues, the Weimar example is cited by the creditors' side and the Japanese case by the debtors' camp. In a historical sense, it is about time for the creditors to fight back. For much of the last forty years, the pendulum has swung in the direction of loose money, and the medium of exchange function. As the memory of the two world wars and the Great Depression receded, people started to believe that economies could make steady forward progress, that asset prices would always rise in the long run, and that any economic crisis could be managed with a slight shift of the monetary or fiscal tiller. This made people more confident about lending, and borrowing, money. And that brings us to the subject of the next chapter, debt.

2

Ignoring Polonius

'Beautiful credit! The foundation of modern society. Who shall say that this is not the golden age of mutual trust, of unlimited reliance upon human promises? That is a peculiar condition of society which enables a whole nation to instantly recognize point and meaning in the familiar newspaper anecdote, which puts into the mouth of a distinguished speculator in lands and mines this remark: – "I wasn't worth a cent two years ago, and now I owe two millions of dollars."'

Mark Twain, *The Gilded Age*

Since the time one caveman borrowed another's flint axe, mankind has been in debt. Historical records show that debt agreements precede coins by around two thousand years.[1]

Ever since those first debts, there have been disagreements about how that debt should be paid back. The verb 'to pay' comes from the Latin *pacare*, meaning to pacify or appease. When it comes to livestock, payment could come in the form of offspring – the Sumerian word for interest, *mas*, means calves. The Roman word for a herd of animals, *pecua*, was the basis for the word *pecunia* for money, a word that survives in the form of 'pecuniary interest' today.

Loans that were secured on land could be serviced by paying the lender the 'first fruits' of the harvest. No doubt there were plenty of loans that were repaid without interest but simply by the return of the good in question, as modern man might borrow his neighbour's lawnmower. But the idea of interest seems as old as loans themselves. The question was really not whether interest should be paid, but how much. Hammurabi, the ruler of Babylon around 1800 BC, set a limit of 33.3 per cent for loans of grain and 20 per cent for those of silver. The Romans also imposed a maximum rate for loans; Julius Caesar's assassin Brutus was rebuked for charging a rate of 48 per cent for a loan to the city of Salamis when the official ceiling was 12 per cent.[2]

Jewish custom forbade the charging of excessive interest to fellow religionists ('Thou shalt not lend upon usury to thy brother', Deuteronomy 23:19), so they had to turn to Gentiles when they needed to borrow money. Jews also developed the concept of a jubilee every fifty years, at which point all debts were written off, a good moment for a celebration.[3]

The idea that interest is in some way unnatural, or an unfair imposition, is also ancient. Aristotle argued that, since coins did not bear fruit, interest should not be paid on monetary debt. Christians adapted the concept of usury from the Old Testament, with the Council of Nicea in 325 prohibiting clerics from the practice. Usury was condemned outright, even though Deuteronomy allowed the practice of usury with 'strangers'.

What the Church did not do is make it entirely clear what usury meant. One definition, from St Augustine, was 'to expect to receive something more than you have given'. This statement did not mean that interest should not be paid at all, but that creditors should only be compensated for the loss incurred from lending. This could be defined as the 'opportunity cost': what the lender might have done with the money if it had not been lent. Profitable investment was clearly not ruled out. After all, the parable of the talents suggests that some form of interest was acceptable. The lazy servant who buried his master's money is told that 'You ought therefore to have deposited my money with the bankers, and at my coming I should have received back my own with interest' (Matthew 25:27).

The Bible is full of such contradictions. Nevertheless, the restriction on usury was real and undoubtedly the development of credit was restricted as a result. Ways were found round the injunction. The business of pawn-broking, for example, continued through the Middle Ages. Usurers were sufficiently common for Dante to condemn them to the seventh circle of hell. This dislike of money-lenders has lasted through the centuries, with particular prejudice against the Jews, as epitomized in the character of Shakespeare's Shylock. This was monstrously unfair since in many countries Jews were not allowed to own land or enter respectable professions. Money-lending was one of their few remaining options. (Modern immigrants often face a similar catch-22; condemned either for being idle, or for taking people's jobs, and usually both at the same time.)

Since trade depends on credit, credit was provided. The historian Charles Kindleberger concluded that, 'The usury laws of the Church did not so much cut down the amount of lending and borrowing as complicate them by the necessity to disguise the state of affairs.'[4] Similarly, while Islam forbids interest payments in theory, ways are found around the injunction in practice. The underlying idea is that the lender should share in the profits with the borrower – for example, if a loan is made against a house, then a lender should share in the benefits of a rise in price.

The Reformation of the sixteenth century led to a decisive break in Christian tradition. The Protestant clerics, such as John Calvin, were noticeably more favourable to the lending of money at interest. Calvin edged back to the Roman principle of setting a maximum rate, in his case 5 per cent. Some saw the change in doctrine as explaining the economic success of the Northern European Protestant nations (England and Holland) relative to the Southern Catholic nations. The Protestant work ethic also explained the rather harsh attitude towards debtors, which saw many sent to prison. But there were at least some loopholes. Daniel Defoe, the author of *Robinson Crusoe*, was known as the 'Sunday gentleman' because he only appeared in polite society on the Sabbath, a day when debtors were traditionally immune from arrest.[5]

The Pope formally accepted that interest was a legitimate charge in the nineteenth century. Nevertheless, the Catholic writer Hilaire Belloc was still forthright in condemning usury as late as 1931.[6] He proclaimed that:

Usury is at once very wicked and – in pure economics and merely as a mathematical statement, it can be proved to proceed in action to the ultimate ruin of the community.

The effort to gather harvest from a barren land, to draw water from a dry well, to seize tribute from those who cannot give it from true revenue but must provide it from stock, begins by ruining the mass of men to the profit of a few.

Belloc does not argue that lenders should not charge interest; he distinguishes between productive and unproductive loans. Demanding interest from a loan to a sick man, to help pay for an operation, is immoral. But if one lends money for the purpose of developing a gold mine, it is perfectly reasonable to demand a return in excess of the amount lent. However, that return should not be greater than the economic return on the asset against which it is lent. So if one lends money against the security of land, and the rental income on the land is 4 per cent, the interest rate should not be 5 per cent. Where rates do exceed this economic return, Belloc argued that the result is gradually to transfer all wealth into the hands of the investor class.

Adam Smith had also made a distinction between productive and consumptive loans. It made sense, in his view, for someone to borrow money if they thought they could earn a higher return than the interest they paid; for example by starting a business. It did not make sense to borrow money to finance immediate consumption. By this standard, Smith would not have approved of buying a flat-screen TV on credit. A version of this distinction was also put forward in the nineteenth century as the 'real bills' theory. This argued that an expansion in the money supply was acceptable if it was being used to finance trade, or the purchase of inventories, but not if the loan was made for the purpose of financial speculation.

Again, this is the debate between money's store of value and means of exchange functions. If economic activity requires more money, it should be created. But how does one know whether the extra money will stimulate trade or simply increase prices?

THE FUNCTIONS OF INTEREST

The Belloc argument ignores some important economic realities. When Fred lends Jim money, he takes the very severe risk of not being paid back. He also has to manage without the money in the meantime. If there is no compensation in the form of interest, he will not lend at all. Without lending, investment will be minimal and without investment, economic growth will be slow.

Indeed, the laws of usury have often made it very expensive for poor people, and small businesses, to borrow money. The legal limits were usually insufficient to compensate lenders for these borrowers' increased risk of default. So that forced potential debtors into the arms of illegal lenders who had to charge a rate that compensated, not just for non-payment, but for the risk of prosecution. And a lender who is willing to break the law may be unscrupulous in other ways; borrowers could find that, however much they paid in terms of interest, the debt was never discharged. As with illegal drugs today, or Prohibition in the 1920s, criminals are the main beneficiaries when governments ban things that people desperately want. However, the moralists would not have worried that usury laws restricted the options of borrowers, as well as lenders. They argued that an avoidance of debt was good for the soul. Having to defer gratification was a way of instilling self-discipline. Debt was the road to ruin: 'He who goes a borrowing goes a sorrowing,' as Benjamin Franklin wrote.

The distinction between productive and unproductive loans is hard to make absolute. Many people might make a loan to a friend or family member without being paid back; they might also make loans to strangers as an act of charity. But if the loan is made for business, not charity, the rate is surely a matter of negotiation between borrower and lender. The lender should charge a rate that reflects his risk. It is for the borrower to decide whether the loan is worthwhile; whether having the flat-screen TV now, rather than later, is worth the extra cost.

Similarly, it is up to the business borrower to decide whether the return from his planned investment will be greater, or less, than his interest cost. If it is not, then he shouldn't make the investment. Of course, the borrower might misjudge the return, just as the lender might misjudge the risk of default. Equally, however, the borrower might earn a return far in excess of the cost, and reap all the profit for himself.

Imagine a Bellocesque world in which interest would be restricted to the economic return on the asset. Who would decide on this return? If it were down to the borrower, the incentives would be rather skewed. Jim might borrow money from Fred to buy farmland, allow the land to be overgrown with weeds, and then claim that his economic return was nil so no interest would be paid. Or Jim might initially work hard, and then lapse into drunkenness; why should Fred bear all the costs of his irresponsibility? The need to repay creditors must surely act as a spur to effort.

Nevertheless, Belloc's distinction between productive and unproductive loans points at a wider truth. The flow of credit is vital to an economy; it allows businesses to invest and expand. But when the authorities seek to expand credit, as they often do at times of economic crisis, there is no guarantee that the result will be the creation of new factories, research into drugs, high-speed railways and the like.

It is just as likely that the new credit will be poured into the property market. Clearly, investment in property is not entirely wasted in the economic sense. People need places to live and offices to work in. But in a boom, lots of buildings will be thrown up for speculative reasons. One only has to drive around Ireland to see empty houses that were built on the hope of a quick profit, and might never be occupied. While those houses were being built, Irish labourers had jobs and the result was rapid GDP growth. But from the point of view of the long-term health of the Irish economy, this was a disastrous strategy, leaving the country with houses that no one wants and debts that cannot be repaid.

Predicting which loans will be used productively, and which will not, is far from easy. Accordingly, lenders need to be paid a return that reflects the risk of default. In modern times, investors have the option of lending to their government, a choice that has often been regarded as 'risk-free', even though that term looks rather hollow in the light of the sovereign debt crisis. Still if a country goes bust, it is likely that its consumers and companies will also be in trouble; it is rational for creditors to demand a higher rate from private-sector borrowers than from their government.

Lenders also need to be rewarded for the time value of money. It is natural to prefer having $1,000 today to having $1,000 in a year's time, not least because the price of goods might rise in the interim. Interest rates will thus naturally be higher when inflation is high. This need not necessarily be bad for the debtor, since their incomes will be growing rapidly as well in inflationary times. In addition, the effective burden of repaying the loan capital will be reduced by inflation. Economists accordingly focus on the 'real' interest rate – the part of the return that is in excess of inflation. Many governments now issue inflation-linked bonds. The interest and repayment value of these bonds rises in line with prices. The interest rate on such bonds is thus truly 'real' and is quite small, often less than 2 per cent a year.

As well as inflation, the rate of interest will also be affected by the legal rights of the creditor. Rates are likely to be lower if a country has well-established processes – bankruptcy codes, for example – for settling debts. The more debtor-friendly the regime, the more the creditor will need to charge to compensate not just for the likelihood of default but also the reduced prospects of recovering any sums when the borrower fails to repay.

The interest rate can also be reduced if the creditor is given security over some asset, such as a mortgage on a house. Baldwin II, the twelfth-century king of Jerusalem, even offered his beard as security for a loan. The Babylonian ruler Hammurabi decreed that land and goods could be pledged against debt, as well as the debtor's wife, concubine, children and slaves. In extremis, the person of the debtor himself would be forfeit, although Hammurabi generously decreed that the resulting period of slavery should be limited to three years.[7]

Skip forward a millennium to the world of ancient Greece and the Athenian statesman Solon, who was forced to deal with a debt crisis in c.600 BC. The problem of bad debts had led to a lot of people being forced into slavery. Solon freed these unfortunates and abolished the practice of slavery for defaulting debtors, cancelled some debts, reduced others, abolished ceilings on interest rates and devalued the coinage by a quarter.[8] Modern Greece may yet end up following a very similar programme.

The ancients were rather fond of setting limits on the amount of interest that could be charged. The Romans started with a limit of 8 per cent, which seems rather low; it was later increased to 12 per cent, a figure that lasted all the way to the reign of Emperor Constantine in the fourth century AD. During the Roman Republic, the general Lucullus, anticipating the arguments of Hilaire Belloc, decreed that creditors should receive an interest rate of no more than 1 per cent a month and should receive no more than a quarter of a debtor's income.[9] It is likely that many lenders simply ignored these limits.

Virtually all loans back then would have been personal. Even with the threat of severe sanction (such as slavery) for non-payment, there was a fair degree of risk to the lender; life expectancy was short and the dominant activity was agriculture, the fruits of which were highly variable. The concept of the corporation had not really developed. There were bankers, but not of the modern type; money-lenders is a better description. Nor did creditors have the 'safe' option of investing in government debt. As the economic historians Homer and Sylla remark, 'States were not in high credit standing. They were not often able to pledge the private resources of the people. They had not learned the principles of deficit financing.'[10]

Lending was a risky business for both borrower and lender, as Polonius reminded Hamlet. The ultimate sanction against high rates was that debtors wilted under the effort of meeting the interest burden. In such cases, creditors suffered as well, since they would lose their capital. Indeed, one of the central arguments of this book is that the wipe-out of creditors is a frequent historical event (starting with Solon's reforms), usually following a long period of debt growth.

These philosophical arguments are still familiar today. Many US states imposed maximum interest rates (6 per cent seemed to be the norm), with such rules surviving into the 1950s.[11] Some debtors still like borrowing money but not paying it back; they try to wriggle out of their obligations, or limit the power of the creditors. When the creditors lose money, new lenders have to be found, and they insist on harsher conditions (higher interest rates, more security) to protect them against the risk. This makes life more onerous for the debtors, who find new ways of defaulting.

BAD KINGS AND BAD DEBTS

After the Roman Empire fell, economic activity seemed to decline. The continent was besieged by Arabs from the south and east, and by Vikings from the north. The Church, which frowned on credit, was the only unifying force. It is perhaps unsurprising that Homer and Sylla find there is virtually no record of credit or interest rates until the twelfth century.

After that point, the Italian city-states started to emerge as economic powers. As well as producing high quality coins like the florin or the ducat, the city-states developed their own credit markets. Venice raised loans that, since they were compulsory, were really taxes on the city's wealthy. But the republic's steady service of the debt created a thriving capital market.

It is important to remember that the medieval state was quite unlike its modern equivalent, providing nothing in the way of welfare, education or health benefits. The state's main role was defence and it was the cost of war that drove sovereigns into debt, while failure in war was the most likely cause of default. The Middle Ages also saw a steady increase in monarchical power, and an accompanying tendency for kings to borrow money. When your debtor can make or change the laws on a whim, lending is a dangerous game. As would often be the case, the French displayed the most arbitrary treatment of creditors. Philip IV, who ruled from 1285 to 1314, borrowed heavily but forced his bankers into exile rather than repay them. Just to put icing on the *gâteau*, he then decreed that the principal on all other debts must be repaid to the crown. The result was the ruin of his main creditor, the Order of the Knights Templar.[12] Edward III of England also defaulted in the course of the Hundred Years War with France, although his latest biographer declares that the sums involved were trivial, and not enough to ruin the Italian banks, as some historians have suggested.[13]

The Spanish monarchy borrowed money to help finance the re-conquest of Granada (1482–92) from the Moors, who had ruled parts of the Iberian Peninsula since the eighth century. It often raised money in the form of perpetual annuities – financial instruments that paid interest for the remainder of the buyer's life. (Similar instruments are still bought by retirees today.) Annuities proved to be a very expensive form of borrowing as Queen Isabella subsequently realized; she recommended that her successors repay the money. They did not and Philip II, the monarch who launched the Armada against England, turned into a serial defaulter. In France, similar instruments were sold and were known as *rentes*; the word *rentier*, used to describe those who live off investment income, derived from this root. The term is not often used in a positive sense; John Maynard Keynes even quipped about the 'euthanasia of the rentier' in later years.

European monarchs had a constant need for finance, driven by their lavish court spending and military ambitions. Taxes were generally in the form of custom duties and subject to widespread evasion. The French monarchy struggled to meet its bills well before John Law; Francis I of France, a rival of Henry VIII of England, defaulted on his debts in the sixteenth century. Later monarchs fell into the temptation of selling the right to gather taxes to collectors round the country. This tactic brought in cash in the short term, but was a long-term mistake. The monarchy did not have direct control of its revenue stream but still incurred the unpopularity associated with the tax bill.

In England, this sovereign debt crisis was brought to a head in the seventeenth century as Charles I battled to raise revenue from a hostile Parliament. The subsequent civil war and the 'Glorious Revolution' of 1688 resulted in the decline of monarchical power; henceforth Parliament controlled the finances. The 1688 Revolution installed the Dutch William of Orange (the 'King Billy' of Irish history) on the British throne, and saw the adoption of Dutch financing techniques. The Bank of England was set up in 1694 as a way of financing William's battle against the profligate Louis XIV of France.

In James Macdonald's view, the triumph of Parliament in both Britain and the Netherlands was vital to both countries' economic and political success.[14] In effect, the merchant and financier class had won. It was thus possible to put state finances on a sound footing, with the government borrowing money from the ruling classes. Investors could accordingly be certain that the government would not default on its debts, since this would cripple its own supporters. In contrast, the absolute monarchs of France and Spain combined a failure to generate tax revenue with an arbitrary treatment of creditors. When it came to financing wars, the British and Dutch were ahead of their rivals.

The French national debt tripled between 1774 and 1789, with the result that interest payments consumed half the budget. A crop failure in 1785 increased political discontent while the state's financial difficulties forced the king to call the Estates General (the French parliament) in 1789, starting the process that led to revolution.

The new government faced the same financial problems. Its answer was to seize land from the aristocracy and the Church, and issue bonds, known as *assignats*, with this land as security. In a sense, this was an eighteenth-century version of mortgage-backed bonds. But what was the value of French land, and how could it be realized? Unlike with the gold standard, people could not really exchange their notes for a half-acre in Provence. As more and more bonds were issued, their face value declined; the *assignats* traded as paper money for a while and then became worthless.

Elsewhere, the development of a national debt provided a new home for the savings of the bourgeoisie. The medieval Italian city-states had had some success in raising finance from their middle classes, but the big nations – Britain, France and Spain – had relied on loans from bankers. Once national governments had established a reputation for repayment, savers had an alternative to land and jewellery as a store of wealth. In John Galsworthy's series of novels, the *Forsyte Saga*, the elderly family members relied on their income from Consols, a form of perpetual government debt.

Britain has not formally defaulted since 1672, although this record does not apply to its European neighbours. In the nineteenth century, for example, the Austro-Hungarian Empire defaulted or rescheduled its debt five times. In their magisterial study of the subject, *This Time Is Different*,[15] Carmen Reinhart and Kenneth Rogoff describe a cycle of sovereign defaults, with peaks in the Napoleonic Wars, the 1820s through to the 1840s, the 1870s to the 1890s and the Great Depression of the 1930s. Clearly, wars often played their part in this cycle, with defeated nations highly likely to renege on their debts. But economic and banking crises, often associated with the rise and fall of commodity prices, also played a big part.

The new American Republic, destined to become the world's

greatest economic power, began its life in a heavily indebted state after it achieved independence in 1783. It issued continental bonds to finance its war expenditure and paid its soldiers with IOUs. The phrase 'not worth a continental' illustrates the contempt with which such paper was regarded. Many of the founding fathers were in debt to English creditors (a good motivation for revolt). Indeed, one could describe several of the Republic's leading politicians as proto-Bryanites, being as they were farmers or plantation owners who naturally gained from rising prices.

John Adams, the second President, declared that 'I continue to abhor and shall die abhorring . . . every bank by which interest is to be paid or profit of any kind made by the deponent.' Thomas Jefferson, his successor and frequent rival, described the banking business as 'an infinity of successive felonious larcenies'. One early Virginia planter swore that 'he would no more be caught going into a bank than into a house of ill fame'.[16]

A key political battle in the early history of the Republic was that between Thomas Jefferson, the third President, and Alexander Hamilton, the Secretary of the Treasury and founder of the Federalist party. Hamilton wanted to establish a sound banking system as a way of expanding trade within the former colonies; he opted to repay soldiers' IOUs at par, even though many had been acquired by speculators. Hamilton kick-started the process of turning the US dollar into the world's most acceptable credit. 'There is scarcely any point in the economy of national affairs of greater moment than the uniform presentation of the monetary unit,' he declared. 'On this, the security and steady value of property essentially depend.'[17]

But the development of the US monetary system was far from smooth. Farmers continued to resent the 'money power' of eastern bankers. The licence of Hamilton's central bank, known as the First Bank of the United States, was allowed to expire and a successor, the Second Bank, was destroyed by President Andrew Jackson in 1833. Jackson was a Southerner who was suspicious of eastern money interests. He appealed to the small farmer and shopkeeper. But he was the opposite of a Bryanite in his monetary beliefs. He disliked the bank because it was a rival to presidential power, and he believed in gold and silver, not paper money. When the Second Bank failed, there was an explosion of note issuance by local banks, which no longer had any supervision. This may have been what the people who voted for Jackson wanted. However, it was not what he wanted.

Jackson's actions were followed by a monetary free-for-all. An 1839 Supreme Court judgment declared that 'the right to issue bank notes was at common law an occupation open to all men'. By 1862, 1,496 banks were circulating notes in 29 states, in around 7,000 varieties, with another 5,500 fraudulent notes also in issue.[18] Bank failures were a regular occurrence. It was only the civil war that persuaded the northern states to regulate issuance in the form of the 'greenbacks' that modern citizens know so well.

The examples of revolutionary finance in America and France illustrate the book's longer-term theme. Both republican governments had debts that they struggled to pay. Short of gold and silver, they issued paper money in respect of those debts, which was akin to not paying those debts at all since the paper eventually became worthless. In each case, the rights of creditors, whether they were British investors or aristocrats of the *Ancien régime* could be safely ignored. Things worked out rather better in America than France because of the booming nature of the former and the bellicose nature of the latter. Galbraith wrote, 'If the history of commercial banking belongs to the Italians and of central banking to the British, that of paper money issued by a government belongs indubitably to the Americans.'

The rival histories of America and France also give some clues to the central question of whether money creation enhances trade, or whether more trade forced men to find ways of expanding the supply of money. It is fairly clear from the history of France that the initial paper money experiments were failures. In America, however, the creation of money and debt may have been desperate expedients but were justified by the country's future growth.

Just as governments tried to tap the wealth of their growing middle and industrial classes, so industry itself developed its own means of finance. Businessmen had always relied on short-term finance to fund their ventures; witness Bassanio's loan from Shylock in *The Merchant of Venice*. It is possible to argue that trading systems were an early form of our modern economy, with its layers of debt and reliance on paper money. A merchant might extend credit to his customers; in turn, he would need such credit from his own suppliers, who might only have bought the goods with money borrowed from someone else. The default of one party would ripple through the system.

This system was formalized in the form of bills of exchange, promissory notes offered as payment from one trader to another. The recipient might then use the bill as collateral to raise cash from a bank or other lender. The bill would be accepted at a discount, depending on a number of factors, most crucially the creditworthiness of the merchant concerned. This was, in effect, a paper money system outside the government's control.

DEBT AND THE INDUSTRIAL AGE

Consumers have always borrowed money from friends, neighbours and relatives. Merchants would not exist without credit; the habit of making debts on a 'slate' in the local butcher or greengrocer was still common in the middle of the twentieth century. But the local merchant would normally offer credit only to a known, local customer; serial defaulters, or those deemed to be untrustworthy, would be refused business. In *David Copperfield*, Mr Micawber's failure to repay merchants required him to cadge off his friends.

But the modern idea of widespread consumer credit (in the form of national lenders, credit cards, etc.) really dates to the Industrial Age. A peasant's income is unlikely to grow over the long term; at best, it will be highly variable, with bumper harvests in good years giving the peasant sufficient income to pay off debt incurred in bad years. But two or three bad harvests in a row could be ruinous.

This point illustrates a wider truth already mentioned. The granting of a loan requires both the creditor and the debtor to be confident that the latter's income will grow sufficiently to repay the debt. Think of a retailer that sells a washing machine, or television, in instalments. Clearly the customer does not have the money now; otherwise he or she would pay upfront. Moreover, the overall bill, including interest, will be greater than the cash price. So the debtor must be confident that he will stay in employment to pay the larger sum. In addition, he or she will probably be confident that their future income will rise so as to offset the additional interest.[19] A growing economy makes that calculation all the more likely.

The Industrial Revolution changed the pattern of human civilization. It allowed economic growth to expand at a much faster rate than ever seen before. This was probably down to the use of carbon-based fuels (wood, coal and, eventually, oil) to power technologies to replace human and animal labour. This resulted in a substantial increase in productivity.

Think of an economy as a business with inputs and outputs. An agrarian economy is often dubbed a subsistence economy; it takes all the energy of the workers (and their livestock) to produce the food necessary to live. A bull may plough a field, and reduce the effort of the farmer, but it takes a lot of land to feed the bull. The economy (business) does not produce a profit. Carbon-fuelled machines transform the situation. Initially, man naturally exploited those fuels that were easiest to reach; chopping down trees, getting coal nearest the surface and so on. So the output, in terms of goods and energy produced, was much greater than the effort put in.

The movement of people from the land to the new industrial cities also required an agrarian revolution. Those remaining on the land had now to produce a surplus, enough to feed the industrial workers as well as themselves. Fortunately, this happened, thanks to the consolidation of smallholdings, new farm machinery, crop rotation and a host of other small reforms. In turn, these improvements allowed the population to grow.

So we now had economic growth and population growth. The next stage emerged as workers gathered in factories. Initially, the conditions were terrible – long hours, low pay (albeit better than a farm labourer's income) and non-existent safety standards. In the crowded towns, sanitation was poor, disease spread quickly and life expectancy was severely restricted. But factories made a big difference in that they grouped workers together and made it easier for them to organize in their own interest. That was very difficult for geographically dispersed agricultural workers. Steadily over the nineteenth century, trade unions grew in membership and workers flexed their muscles through strikes. Governments started to recognize their power and buy them off. Bismarck, a hard-headed pragmatist, introduced old-age pensions in

Germany as a way of recruiting worker support for the Hohenzollern monarchy.

Competition for skilled workers also drove wages up, creating a new, more prosperous category within the working class. Those with skills and above-subsistence pay were more attractive to lenders.

At the same time, the Industrial Revolution was creating a greater need for credit. Arguably, it started with the farmers. Larger farms, new machinery, new crops – all this required investment, which in turn required borrowing. Farmers would take on this risk if the extra production was sufficient to offset the interest costs. But their calculations depended on modestly rising, or at least stable, commodity prices. It was falling commodity prices in the US in the late nineteenth century that created the support for Bryan's populist crusade.

Industrial workers also required credit. A house in town, however humble, required furniture – beds, tables and chairs. Few could afford the expense upfront. In his excellent history of US consumer credit, Lendol Calder dates the development of instalment plans (or hire purchase) to the early years of the nineteenth century. [20] Cowperthwaite & Sons, a New York furniture retailer, was one of the first to adopt the practice. The Singer sewing-machine company took up the idea with enthusiasm later in the century.

The idea of instalment plans was far from new; after all, as we saw in the last chapter, John Law sold shares in the Mississippi Company in instalment form. But a system based on regular payments was suited to an industrial age where workers received regular income. Instalment selling greatly widened the potential market for a retailer's goods, and the financing charges more than offset any bad debts. In practice, one wonders if the approach was really that much different from the old habit of allowing customers to buy 'on the slate'. Presumably such retailers marked their prices higher to allow for both the time value of money and the occasional bad debts. Psychologically, however, it was an important step forward. Consumers liked the ability to get their goods upfront and found the prospect of a series of small payments easy to swallow, even though they ended up paying more for the goods in the end.

Instalment credit had other advantages for the retailer, especially when compared with outright credit. On those occasions when they did default, buyers had usually made several payments, ensuring any loss was limited. In addition, the law made it clear that the seller retained the rights to the goods until all the instalments were paid. For the same reason, buyers were reluctant to default, knowing as they did that they would lose both the goods and their cash.

The need to meet the regular payments required by instalment plans also imposed a discipline on consumers. They were far less likely to achieve the same effort of discipline had they been required to save in advance of the purchase; some other need would always have absorbed their cash. But the threat of legal action, or the removal of the goods, helped them to keep up with a repayment plan.

In the twentieth century, manufacturers joined retailers in the instalment credit club. The car industry led the way. Houses aside, a car would be most families' biggest single purchase, and manufacturers would have limited their market had they sold only to those with ready cash. Selling cars via instalments had two other advantages. People are naturally cautious when it comes to buying new products – they don't want to be the family on the block that buys the unfashionable or unreliable model. They will thus pay careful attention to what their friends and neighbours buy. A manufacturer that offers easy purchasing terms may thus establish his product as the main brand; the first buyer will bring in imitators.

In addition, increased production will bring economies of scale. Lower costs can be passed on to consumers in the form of lower prices, allowing the market leader to undercut its competitors. One reason why the Ford motor company lost ground in the 1920s, despite the early success of its Model T, was that General Motors used instalment selling to establish itself as the leading brand. A rival Ford plan which gave consumers the chance to save up to buy a car – a sort of 'pay now, buy later' – proved to be a flop. Ford was eventually forced to follow GM's lead and set up its own financing arm. The link between consumer finance and manufacturing was established, and has never gone away. By the mid 2000s, the financing arms of General Motors, Ford and General Electric were among the largest, and most profitable, parts of the companies' business.

(Legend has it that Henry Ford followed an alternative approach to gain market share of paying his workers well, so they could afford to buy his products and expand his market. That seems an unlikely business model, akin to the ancient quip about the retailer who lost $5 on every sale, but hoped to make it up on volume. The more likely motivation for Ford was a desire to head off industrial trouble and prevent his workers from joining unions.)

Factories also led to the wider use of money. While a village might get by with barter, things were much harder in the town. Some workers were given tokens to spend at the factory shop and made to buy overpriced goods; Britain banned that practice in the Truck Act of 1831. But most workers received a cash wage. In America, where there was a shortage of coin, this accelerated the use of paper money; one estimate is that the money supply grew from $28 million in 1800 to $2.4 billion by 1900.

THE MORAL MAZE

In the early twentieth century, the use of instalment credit was seen as a sign of the moral decline of America, and a departure from the traditional values of thrift – what Lendol Calder describes as 'the myth of lost economic virtue'.[21] In particular, critics harped on about the distinction made by Adam Smith between productive and consumptive credit – borrowing to invest and borrowing to consume. This is a complex issue. In the standard model of the economy, saving must equal investment. But investment often involves borrowing. The borrower could not exist without the thrifty saver, who is, if you like, the enabler of his debt.

Investment is good, since it allows the economy to expand. In an ideal world, the money that we leave in the bank on deposit is lent to businesses, which invest in new factories, creating more jobs and giving us more money to put in the bank.

But under this model, is there such a distinction between productive and consumptive credit? When a consumer buys a car on instalment, which he could not have paid for upfront, the auto manufacturer is able to step up production and thus can hire more workers, who can buy more cars and so on. Indeed, Keynes warned of 'the paradox of thrift'. If consumers stop spending and start saving, then demand for cars will fall. The manufacturer will lay off workers. Their incomes will fall, giving them less scope to save. So the paradox is that the understandable desire of individuals to save may result in lower aggregate savings, as output and incomes fall.[22]

Some have seen this link between production, consumption and demand as a kind of hamster wheel of fruitless activity. In his elegantly written book, *The Affluent Society*, first published in 1958, the economist J. K. Galbraith argued that economics had traditionally been obsessed with production. More output was deemed to be a good thing. But as society developed, the basic needs of the vast majority of citizens (food, warmth, shelter) were satisfied. So citizens had to become consumers and be persuaded by advertising to desire goods they did not really need. Often these needs were dictated by status, the need to have as good a car as one's neighbour. In turn, this led to the growth of consumer debt. Galbraith wrote that: 'It would be surprising indeed if a society that is prepared to spend thousands of millions to persuade people of their wants were to fail to take the further step of financing these wants.'

Galbraith's views have echoes in the modern environmental movement which sees the endless pursuit of economic growth as self-destructive, given the finite nature of the earth's resources. Some environmentalists talk of the 'no growth' economy; the debt crisis may mean that this prospect is closer than they think.

MONEY AND DEBT

The last chapter was about money; this whole book is about debt. But the key fact is that debt and money are two sides, not of the same coin, but of the same bank note. That would not be true of a currency consisting entirely of precious metal. Such metals have one defining characteristic: they are no one else's liability. But as we have seen, there is not enough precious metal to go round. Even coin-based systems were forced to use token coins for small amounts.

As soon as goldsmiths and banks started storing gold and issuing receipts (bank notes), money and debt became interchangeable. Early bank notes were proof that the bank owed the holder money; they were thus a claim on the creditworthiness of the bank. Modern bank notes are a claim on the creditworthiness of the government. They are 'legal tender' because a government proclaims them to be so. They lose their value (as in the case of Zimbabwe) only when faith in economic policy breaks down entirely.

A credit-card limit is money in the sense that the consumer can instantly use it to buy goods and services. But it is clearly also debt. Banks can create money simply by extending an overdraft; adding an entry on a computer. Again, this money is clearly also a debt.

As we have seen, paper money was created by the Chinese in the ninth century AD. The supply was at first restricted, and backed entirely by precious metals. But when the Chinese government started to run a budget deficit (its expenditure exceeded its revenues) it was inevitably tempted to issue paper money to cover the difference. Essentially, this was the same scam as had been practised by Dionysius of Syracuse and several Roman emperors; debasing money to repay debts.

The link goes a lot deeper. Think of money as a claim on wealth (remember the 'I promise' bit on a British bank note that dates back to the days when customers could exchange the notes for gold). We have already established that printing more money becomes pointless in the end. Each bank note becomes worth less and less. It is a bit like dividing a pizza into ever smaller slices. The process does not create any more food; printing money does not create any more real wealth unless for some reason there is such a shortage of money in the economy that activity has ground to a halt.

If debt is money, then the same principle applies. The rising debt-to-GDP ratios we have seen over the last fifty years have simply created more claims on wealth. These claims cannot all be satisfied at once. The key problem is that the creditors – those who are lending the money – expect the borrowers to pay them back. But that clearly depends on the borrowers having enough income, and wealth, to do so. If the claims are very large relative to the size of the economy, it seems likely that many creditors will be disappointed. A related issue is that only a small proportion of the creditors can be repaid at the same time. Just as a bank is vulnerable to a run by depositors, an economy is vulnerable to a loss of confidence in debtors' ability to repay. The bigger the debt pile, the more earth-shaking these crises of confidence will be.

In essence, that is why the debt crisis of 2007–08 was so alarming. Pumped up by debt, the banks had become so large relative to the rest of the economy that they simply had to be rescued, at a huge cost. The resulting recession delivered such a blow to government finances that the bank crisis was followed by a sovereign-debt crisis.

The finances of banks are highly counter-intuitive. Customer deposits are a liability, not an asset, since they may have to be repaid at any time; the assets of a bank consist largely of the loans made to companies and individuals since they too will eventually be repaid. But those debtors may not (and probably will not) have the cash available to repay the loan immediately, so any run on the bank will create a potential problem for its debtors. The bank may demand immediate repayment of loans, refuse to refinance loans when they become due, or simply charge a higher interest rate and impose more stringent conditions when the loan is renewed. This explains why problems for the banks ripple throughout the economy.

If we think back to John Law's reasoning, we can see why this must be so. If money creation encourages trade by giving people more incentive to purchase goods, then money destruction must discourage trade. For nineteenth-century economists, however, John Law's experiment was a classic example of economic folly. They knew that the only way of ensuring sound money was to base it on gold, and that is the subject of the next chapter.

3
Going for Gold

'Precious metals alone are money. Paper notes are money because they are representations of Metallic Money. Unless so, they are false and spurious pretenders. One depositor can get metal but all cannot, therefore deposits are not money.'
Lord Overstone, Victorian banker and politician, quoted in *A Financial History of Western Europe* by Charles Kindleberger

'It is an absurd and silly notion that international credit must be limited to the quantity of gold dug up out of the ground. Was there ever such mumbo-jumbo among sensible and reasonable men?'
Lord Beaverbrook, quoted in *Lords of Finance: 1929, the Great Depression and the Bankers Who Broke the World* by Liaquat Ahamed

Every minute of every day something miraculous happens. People and businesses round the world accept the currencies of other countries in return for goods and services. As they trade the value of those currencies, in terms of the purchasing power in the seller's home country, is changing by the second.

Previous chapters have shown how mankind gradually moved away from the idea that gold and silver were the only real form of money. This was partly for convenience and partly because the surge in economic activity and the creation of new forms of activity seemed to go together.

Far enough back in history, countries did not really need exchange rates. Their coins were made of gold or silver and circulated freely, for many hundreds of years, on the basis of their intrinsic value. This made it pretty easy for merchants in one country to take payment from customers in another; all they needed was a way of assessing the gold or silver content of the coins handed over (although there was the 'Gresham's Law' problem that people would hoard the best coins and pass on the worst).

In the twenty-first century, shipping over boat-loads of coins is just not practical; electronic transfer is the only option. But it is one thing to accept that all transactions within an individual country might be conducted in a denomination decreed by that country's government – in a democracy, the majority of people have some faith in the governing system by definition, and in a dictatorship, they have little choice. It is quite another to accept on faith the paper issued by someone else's government in a country one may never have visited, and in which one has no stake. Indeed, it might appear that other countries have an incentive to pay for goods in 'funny' or rapidly depreciating currency. Fixed exchange-rate systems were established to get round that problem.

What would happen if other countries refused to accept one nation's currency? To see the results, we only have to think back to the late 1940s. Britain was virtually bankrupt after the Second World War. Its debts were well known. When it wanted to buy raw materials, it needed dollars, not pounds. Since dollars were scarce (and therefore expensive), the results were economic hardship and rationing on a scale even greater than that imposed in the war years. Consumers could not get the meat, sugar, eggs, bread, etc., that they wanted.

The same effect results from linking a nation's currency to that of another, as with Europe's single currency, the euro. No longer can the home government or central bank create more money at will. If the country runs a trade deficit, it must borrow the money from abroad. If foreign creditors demand too high an interest rate, as has happened in Greece, Portugal and Ireland, then the country faces a severe crisis; cutbacks, if not rationing, will be required.

There would be no need to choose between fixed and floating exchange rates if there were a global currency that was accepted everywhere. Trade and tourism would be much easier. But the idea, akin to the spread of global languages like Esperanto, while attractive in theory, is unlikely to be adopted in practice. Governments would lose a lot of independence in monetary policy, as Europeans have discovered; capital flows would be much harder to control if a single currency was accepted worldwide, something that would upset the Chinese, for example.

Why are companies and individuals willing to take the risk of accepting another country's paper money, which that country is free to devalue? In part, it is because they have no choice; if they want to sell goods and services abroad, this is what they will get in return. In some cases, such as commodities, it has become the custom for them to be priced in dollar terms, still the most acceptable global currency. Indeed, in many countries, consumers and business may have more faith in money issued by the US government than in paper printed by their own. Faith in the American economy thus greases the wheels of global trade. Sellers also have ways to get some certainty about their foreign receipts, by locking in the exchange rate in the financial markets. Nevertheless, over the long term, companies face the business risk that changes in currency levels will affect either their profitability or their market share.

The history of paper money is the history of exchange rates. An exchange rate simply sets the value of one currency in terms of another. Each currency must have a price in terms of all the others: the dollar versus the yen, pound, peso, etc. The process of setting such prices generates a staggering $4 trillion of trades each day, according to the Bank for International Settlements.

Countries can decide to fix their exchange rate in terms of gold, silver or another currency. Or they can let the markets decide and let their currencies 'float'. Each choice has economic and political impli-cations and ends up favouring one or more groups in society. It is very hard to say what the 'right' exchange rate should be. Nor is it easy to make blanket statements, along the lines of the comic history book *1066 and All That*, saying, 'Rising currency is a Good Thing, falling currency is a Bad Thing.' Countries may wish for different outcomes at different times.

Broadly speaking, the first seventy years of the twentieth century saw most countries attempt to maintain fixed exchange rates, initially against gold and then against the dollar. When those efforts failed, the world divided into two; the developed world has been largely floating, the developing world has used a mixture of fixed, managed (where the government attempts a measure of control over the extent of fluctuation) and floating rates. Within the developed world, there has of course been the European experiment of a single currency, which eliminated fluctuations within the zone but not against outside currencies like the dollar and Japanese yen.

The choices made by countries have generally reflected the theme of this book – the preference for sound money or easy money. Fixed exchange rates have generally been favoured by creditors who want to be repaid in 'real money'; as a creditor nation, Germany has been in favour of a strong euro. Floating rates have been favoured by those whose priority is economic expansion, rather than stable prices.[1]

The rules of fixed exchange-rate systems have generally been set by the creditor country. Britain moved accidentally on to a gold standard in the early eighteenth century. Its financial success encouraged others to follow suit and indeed encouraged others to take the ideas of its leading economists seriously. They tended to favour free trade and sound money. Since Britain was the leading exporter of manufactured goods and a leading creditor, the adoption of these policies by other countries worked in Britain's favour.

When the First World War destroyed both Britain's economic position and the classic gold standard, the balance of power moved to America. The inter-war period saw a failed attempt to return to the gold standard, hampered by the lack of international co-operation that had marked the pre-war period. After the Second World War, it was the US that set the rules of the Bretton Woods system, a mechanism that clearly recognized the primacy of the dollar, the currency of the world's largest economy and creditor. As we shall see, attempts by Keynes to impose restrictions on creditors were rejected by the Americans, a decision that the US may be starting to regret, given China's financial power.

The collapse of Bretton Woods in the 1970s seemed to favour the debtor countries, not the creditors. Countries were now free to depreciate their currencies on a regular basis. Many governments attempted to dash for growth now that they were free of the old shackles; a period of worldwide inflation followed. Once again, it was the Americans, still at that stage a creditor nation, who led the way to a new system in which central banks acted to bring down inflation and thereby protect the interest of creditors.

But the debate has evolved over the years. Go back a century and the banking establishment would have been firmly in favour of fixed exchange rates and sound money. In practice, however, the banking sector has benefited hugely from floating exchange rates, which have created a highly liquid trading market and a desire for financial products that insure against exchange-rate risk. And the abandonment of fixed exchange rates has led to a huge expansion of cross-border capital flows, from which the finance sector has taken a very large bite. The seeds of the financial crisis of 2007–08 were sown in the exchange-rate revolution of the early 1970s.

THE TRILEMMA

Economists have described the choice of exchange-rate system as a 'trilemma', in which countries can choose two out of three options, but not all three. Those options are a fixed exchange rate, free capital movements, and national control of the level of interest rates.

Fix the exchange rate, and speculators may try to target it, attempting to buy and sell at a different rate. One can either prevent them from doing so, via capital controls, or discourage them from doing so by adjusting interest rates to attract capital. But a rate increase might be bad for the domestic economy. So countries can face the choice of defending the exchange rate or supporting economic growth.

Given these varying options, the preferences of countries have changed over time. Many of the key moments of economic history over the past one hundred years have revolved around changes in exchange-rate systems, from the abandonment, re-adoption and then re-abandonment of the gold standard, through the Bretton Woods agreement of 1944 and its failure in the early 1970s, to the creation of the European Exchange Rate Mechanism, which was followed by the adoption of the single European currency in 1999. The debt crisis that began in 2007 will probably lead to a new exchange-rate regime, the outlines of which will be explored in Chapter 12.

Under the gold standard, countries fixed their exchange rates and money flowed round the globe. But, as we shall see, they were at times forced to adjust interest rates to defend the standard, regardless of domestic economic conditions. Under Bretton Woods, exchange rates were fixed, interest rates were set domestically, but capital did not flow freely. This stopped speculators from exploiting interest rate differentials between countries. China still follows this approach, managing its exchange rate within tight bands and limiting the scope for foreigners to build up renminbi holdings.

Since the failure of Bretton Woods, developed countries have stopped trying to fix their exchange rates, allowing them to let capital flow freely and to set their own interest rates. At times of economic difficulty, they have opted to let both their interest rates and exchange rate decline. Both moves transfer pain to creditors in the interest of economic growth.

THE GOLD STANDARD

Once currencies became paper notes that were backed by gold and silver, exchange rates started to become important. Those who accepted the notes as payment from a foreign creditor naturally wanted information on the soundness of the guarantee. If they wanted to exchange their notes for precious metal, would the bullion be supplied? This confidence depends very much on the decisions discussed in Chapter 1. If the currency was based on gold or silver, what proportion of the currency was backed by precious metal? It was natural for creditors (and trade suppliers) to prefer payment in currencies with the soundest backing.

The sirens were figures of Greek myth, famed for luring sailors on to the rocks with their sweet songs. Odysseus stopped his crew's ears with wax and had himself tied to the mast so he could hear their song but not steer the ship to disaster. In the minds of many bankers, the gold standard played the same role. They had seen what happened in France where two eighteenth-century experiments with paper money had ended in disaster. The power to create money was simply too tempting to politicians and would quickly be abused. Tying the value of money to gold was like tying Odysseus to the mast.

Besides, the monetary system was too complicated for men to manage. The British bullion committee of 1810 concluded that:

The most detailed knowledge of the actual trade of the country, combined with the profound science in all the principles of money and circulation, would not enable any man or set of men to adjust, and keep always adjusted, the right proportion of circulating medium in a country in the wants of trade.

The simplest answer was to fix the rate at which paper money could be converted into gold or silver. Provided every country published this rate, it was then fairly simple to calculate the rate at which each paper currency could be exchanged against another.

This was the great strength of the gold standard. Creditors and traders could be sure of the value of money; this encouraged them to lend and to trade. To some this was a metaphorical, as well as literal, golden age of the global economy, although this view is a bit of an exaggeration. Not all countries were on the standard; some mixed gold and silver together. The system developed in a higgledy-piggledy fashion with different countries adopting the metal at different times; it was not set up by some eighteenth-century equivalent of the United Nations.

Indeed, you could argue that, like the British Empire, the gold standard was a result of a 'fit of absent-mindedness'. In Britain, the system came about thanks to a decision by Sir Isaac Newton who, as master of the Royal Mint, was in charge of the nation's currency. Both gold and silver were in circulation at the time and a conversion rate had to be set between the two. In 1717, the great physicist set the conversion rate at a level that seemed to undervalue silver. Gresham's Law duly kicked in. Britons were unwilling to exchange their silver for gold at an unfavourable rate; they withheld their silver coins from circulation.

At that stage, Britain was still vying with France for military leadership and with the Netherlands for economic power. So there was no incentive for other countries to follow suit; indeed, at the start of the nineteenth century, Britain was the only leading power to have the gold standard. Most countries, including America, opted for bimetallism. It was not until later in the nineteenth century that the gold standard became truly international. The process was gradual, with the final kick coming from Germany, not Britain, when the country became united after the Franco-Prussian war of 1870–71. However, the example of Britain, which had used its financial strength to battle Napoleon and which had a long tradition of stable finances, undoubtedly encouraged other countries to believe the gold standard was worth adopting. The full gold standard, with the major economies of the world linked to bullion, only lasted for forty years or so.

The standard 'worked' in the sense of keeping prices stable. It is hard to imagine today but, outside times of war, long-term inflation did not exist in the British economy in the eighteenth and nineteenth centuries, although prices did fluctuate, usually in response to changes in the supply of food: a bad harvest forced up the price of wheat one year, whereas a glut forced down the price in another. In his book *The Death of Inflation*, economist Roger Bootle cites the cost of a taxi ride, or Hackney carriage, as it was then known.[2] In 1694, the same year the Bank of England was founded, the cost was set at one shilling (a twentieth of a pound) a mile. Two centuries later, the rate was at the same level. In 1932, the average level of prices in Britain was slightly below what it had been in 1795, during the Napoleonic Wars.

Low inflation also meant low interest rates. In 1888, George Goschen, the British Chancellor of the Exchequer, converted Consols (then the name for government debt) paying 3 per cent into bonds paying 2.5 per cent, reducing the government's interest bill. In 1896, while William Jennings Bryan was leading his campaign for debtors on the other side of the Atlantic, the yield on Consols fell to its lowest level in history – 2.2 per cent.[3] Creditors had no inkling of the problems to come in the twentieth century; they would never be so complacent again.

What the gold standard also helped to create was the first great era of globalization. This was particularly true in Great Britain which had an empire stretching round the world, a navy that protected trade routes, a sound currency in sterling, and a willingness to invest its savings overseas. Low yields on British government debt (gilts) caused the prosperous middle classes to buy bonds in Argentine railways in search of higher incomes (an early version of the 'search for yield' that would be seen in the current era). The quaintly named Foreign & Colonial Investment Trust, founded in 1868 but still around today, was a fund designed to offer Victorians a diversified portfolio; it acquired investments in Argentina, Brazil, Chile, Russia, Spain and Turkey. The initial yield was 7 per cent at a time when gilts offered just 3 per cent.

Trade flowed round the globe. The arrival of steamships in the mid-nineteenth century opened up the possibility of exporting wheat from the US and meat from Argentina to the hungry European markets. The result was an agricultural depression in Britain. But by shifting workers from relatively unproductive farming into manufacturing, it gave a kick-start to European growth.

In the words of Keynes,

The inhabitant of London could order by telephone, sipping his morning tea in bed, the various products of the whole earth . . . he could at the same time and by the same means adventure his wealth in the natural resources and new enterprise of any quarter of the world . . . he could secure forthwith, if he wished, cheap and comfortable means of transit to any country or climate without passport or other formality.[4]

This system tied countries closely together in economic terms. In 1910, British author Norman Angell published his book *The Great Illusion*, which argued that, as a consequence of this interdependence, war would be completely futile. He lived to be proved right, but the European nations plunged into war anyway.

HOW THE STANDARD WORKED

Let us start with the theory. Discard any modern thoughts of paper money and assume that gold is the only 'real' yardstick of wealth and that creditors expected to be paid in that form. If Britain ran a trade deficit with America (importing more than it exported) then it would have to pay gold to American merchants. There would literally be less money in the British economy and more in America. Americans would thus have more money with which to buy British goods and the British less money to buy American grain. The American trade surplus would eventually disappear.

This adjustment could also occur through prices. A larger money supply would drive American prices higher, making its goods less competitive in Britain; a smaller money supply would make prices fall. Either way, the imbalance would not last for long.

In practice, as Barry Eichengreen demonstrates in his books *Golden Fetters* and *Globalizing Capital: A History of the International Monetary System*[5] the standard worked in a rather more sophisticated way. The high seas were not awash with gold-laden boats transporting bullion from one government to another. Indeed the gold could simply stay in the vaults of the Bank of England (or any other central bank). A given portion of it could be earmarked for the overseas central bank concerned. When a country earned a surplus, it would simply have the right to a slightly bigger portion of the storage space.

If this seems all a little like a children's game, the central bankers took it very seriously. Gold might not have been shipped around the world, but the process of realignment still occurred in a roundabout fashion. Countries would cover their trade deficits by borrowing the shortfall from nations in surplus. Surplus nations would become progressively more nervous about the ability of deficit nations to pay them back, and would charge higher interest rates accordingly. Alternatively, the deficit nations would become concerned about the potential drain of gold from their reserves and would raise interest rates to attract capital. Either way, these higher interest rates would gradually reduce the deficit. That is because higher rates increase the costs of borrowers, leaving them less money to spend on imports.

Three rules helped maintain the standard, according to economist Filippo Cesarino.[6] One, the use of interest rates to attract capital when a country was suffering outflows; two, the principle that temporary departures from the gold standard (such as in wars) would be followed by the resumption of the old rate; and three, the principle that the price level was set by the amount of gold in existence.

Barry Eichengreen argues that the standard eventually reached an even higher level of stabilization. Investors (and other central banks) believed that the countries at the heart of the system, particularly Britain, would always do whatever it took to safeguard the convertibility of their currencies. Thus they would be tolerant of small trade deficits (and falls in gold reserves). That helped keep the system stable.

In a sense, this was all a confidence trick. Britain's gold reserves rarely exceeded £40 million, a figure that was only 3 per cent of the country's total money supply (including bank notes, deposits and so on). Had foreign creditors demanded the conversion of their claims into gold, Britain could not have met the bill. Like a bank, the gold standard essentially depended on confidence. Even so there were some hairy moments. When Baring Brothers, what was then called a merchant bank, came close to failure in 1890, the Bank of England had to borrow gold from France and Russia in the face of a run on its reserves.

The Barings crisis was an example of what kept the system going; there was international co-operation between central banks, which recognized that the gold standard was the best way of ensuring sound money. Central bankers were generally of a similar class (the upper or creditor classes) and would occasionally meet at international conferences. They naturally shared the view that sound money was an unquestionable good. As well as helping each other out in a crisis (the Reichsbank in Germany borrowed money from Britain and France in 1898), they did not compete for funds via interest rates; the level of rates in the big countries tended to move in tandem.

The gold standard was accompanied by general prosperity so countries were keen to see it last. Or, to qualify that statement, the leaders of those countries were keen to see it last. That qualification is important because sound money has a price. Maintaining a sound currency often required a central banker to push up interest rates, or find some other way of restricting demand, when gold reserves were falling. The lack of democracy insulated politicians and central bankers from the anger of those thrown out of work in the resulting recessions. (Such workers could strike, however, and British industrial unrest increased sharply in the run-up to the First World War.)

By and large, sound money backed by gold was a policy that favoured the governing elite. 'The ability of the rich and their acolytes to see social virtue in what serves their interest and convenience, and to depict as ridiculous or foolish what does not, was never better manifested than in their support of gold and condemnation of paper money,' wrote the economist J. K. Galbraith.[7]

Another helpful factor for maintaining the standard was that Britain, as the cornerstone of the system, ran trade surpluses. It steadily became a huge international creditor. While it may not have had much gold in its vaults, international investors had every confidence that Britain was a wealthy nation. In addition, by luck more than judgement, the volume of gold expanded in the late nineteenth century, making it easier for the monetary system to accommodate the rising industrial nations. The world's stock of monetary gold rose from £519 million in 1867 to £774 million in 1893 and £1,909 million in 1918.[8]

Nevertheless, there were still clear weaknesses in the system. By the time the First World War broke out, Britain's economic power had been overtaken by that of both Germany and America. The first was a new nation (only formed in 1871) trying to gain recognition of its place in the world; the second had no central bank until 1913 and was suspicious of foreign entanglements. International co-operation might not have continued, even without a war.

LENDERS OF LAST RESORT

Another problem had been demonstrated by the Barings crisis. As well as being the guardians of monetary stability, central banks also acted as the lender of last resort for the domestic banking system. The nineteenth century had suffered a series of panics as individual banks had gone bust. It was a time of rudimentary accounting standards, lax financial regulation and no deposit insurance; all this gave too much scope to bank executives and too little comfort to bank depositors. At the slightest sign of trouble, there would be bank runs as depositors queued to get their money out.

Such runs were quite rational. As seen in Chapter 2, banks lent out a lot more money than they had cash-in-hand; they relied on the fact that only a small number of depositors would want to withdraw cash at the same time. Their depositors had instant access to their money while the banks made loans which would only be repaid over time; in the jargon, they borrowed short and lent long.

Some bankers had lent money to friends and cronies that would never be paid back; others made genuine mistakes, lending to bad companies in good faith. Either way, if a depositor feared a problem, it made sense to get his money out before all the bank's cash was gone. And if depositors suffered losses at one bank, those who had money at other banks would become nervous. A run on an individual bank could quickly spread across the system.

Such a run could have enormous economic consequences. Desperate banks would stop lending money to businesses and recall loans from existing borrowers. The companies involved might go bust, putting thousands out of work. The resulting decline in confidence might lead to further runs on banks and so on. (All this happened, as we shall see, in the 1930s.)

Walter Bagehot, a former editor of *The Economist*, argued in his book *Lombard Street* that, in such a crisis, central banks should lend freely to illiquid but solvent banks.[9] These loans should come at a cost – the central bank should charge a penalty rate and demand collateral. But by keeping the banks going, a panic would be avoided.

However, this creates a potential dilemma. For the central bank to lend freely, it must have the money to do so. That might mean running down its reserves; it might mean creating more money. Neither approach appears compatible with the bank's duty to maintain the value of the currency against gold. In extremis, a central bank might have to choose between saving the banking system and maintaining the gold standard. This was only one of the awkward choices that faced central banks after the First World War.

In retrospect, world economies entered a thirty-year 'dark age' after 1914, roughly equivalent to the chaos that followed the collapse of the Roman Empire. The first thing to go was the gold standard. Countries clearly could not contemplate shifting gold to the nations they were fighting against. Instead of trading with each other, they were attempting to starve their rivals into submission. Nor could they allow their citizens to convert paper notes into gold; the right to do so was suspended in Britain, just as it had been during the Napoleonic Wars.

So ended a 700-year period in which gold coins were in free circulation; while some coins are still made for collectors and investors, they have yet to return to general use. Ironically, given that many denounce Keynes as the progenitor of modern inflation, he opposed the suspension of gold and silver payment at the time. It turned out to be a decisive moment in economic history. There was a short-lived return to gold in the 1920s and 1930s, as we shall see in the next chapter, but this was a weaker form of the standard, under which the right of individuals to convert paper money into gold was restricted.

The way was open for inflation at rates unknown in previous times. As Professor Peter Bernholz writes, 'all hyperinflations in history occurred after 1914 under discretionary paper money standards except for the French case during the Revolution of 1789–1796, when a paper money standard was introduced'.[10]

Paying for the war accelerated inflationary pressures. The European governments hoped that the costs of the war could be recouped from the losing side. Indeed, after the war, they attempted to pull off this trick through the infamous reparations imposed on Germany that were so denounced by Keynes. (Before we condemn the British and French politicians of the day, we should remember that the Germans would also have imposed a reparations bill had they been victorious. They made France pay an indemnity after the 1870–71 Franco-Prussian war.) In the meantime, governments resorted to the same expedients for financing the war as were used by the Revolutionary American government of the 1770s or the Confederate government of the 1860s. They printed money.

Britain made a more valiant attempt than most to finance the war through its own resources; it quintupled the income-tax rate. Nevertheless, currency in circulation rose by 91 per cent over the war period, while that of France and Germany rose by 386 and 600 per cent respectively.[11] This more cavalier approach to money-printing may have reflected the more fundamental threat faced by each nation. France had part of its territory occupied for much of the conflict, while in Germany, the Hohenzollern regime of Kaiser Wilhelm had entered the war in the face of the threat to its legitimacy from the rising Social Democratic party; it did not wish to reduce the popularity of the war by raising taxes too far.

Just creating money was not enough for most governments. They borrowed money from their citizens and their allies as well. The British national debt rose elevenfold during the First World War, compared with merely trebling during the Napoleonic Wars, which had lasted five times as long. The UK was not alone; Russia's public debt rose fourfold, Germany's eightfold, and America's by a factor of nineteen.[12]

All this would have surprised and disappointed those bankers and politicians who declared at the start of the war that it could only last a few months because nations could not afford for it to continue. The *New York Times* reported, in late August 1914, that bankers believed the war would not be financed by the unlimited issue of paper money, because 'monetary science is better understood at the present time than in those days'.[13]

Those bankers were proved wrong because of the illusory nature of money. Yes, the great powers would have quickly run out of gold had they chosen to spend it. But their gold reserves were not the only form of national wealth; they were just the petty cash. The real wealth was in the form of the factories and the manpower that the nations had built up over the nineteenth century. It was this wealth that the nations then proceeded to squander over the next four years, an event that had much more significance than the mere loss of precious metals would have done.

It is a bit like the distinction between wealth and GDP, gross domestic product. The latter is a measure of annual economic activity. The earthquake and tsunami that devastated northern Japan in 2011 may result in a boost to GDP when the rebuilding occurs. Nevertheless, the wealth of Japan was still reduced. Frédéric Bastiat, a nineteenth-century French economist, referred to this as the broken window syndrome; breaking windows may create work for glaziers but we cannot achieve prosperity by smashing all the windows in our houses.

The First World War destroyed the cosy arrangements that had kept the gold standard in place. As we shall see in the next chapter, after the war, all the central bankers' horses and all of their men were unable to put the system back together again in the same robust form.

4

Money and the Depression

'*The sound internal economic system of a nation is a greater factor in its well-being than the price of its currency.*'
President Franklin D. Roosevelt, message to the World
Economic Conference in London, July 1933

Nostalgia is a dangerous thing. As the world's developed countries emerged from the First World War, they understandably reflected on what a waste it had been, of resources as well as human life. Surely there was a way to get back to the pre-war era when nation traded, rather than fought with, nation and life was kinder and gentler: 'Stands the Church clock at ten to three? / And is there honey still for tea?' as the poet Rupert Brooke wrote before the conflict.

From a modern perspective, it seems clear how much had changed. Three great ruling dynasties had fallen: the German Hohenzollerns, the Austrian Habsburgs and the Russian Romanovs. Russia was fighting a civil war which would be won by the communists; the Austro-Hungarian Empire had been dissolved into a host of constituent countries, based roughly on nationality; and in the Middle East, a similar fate was befalling the Ottoman Empire.

The First World War showed that the old aristocratic elites were capable of immense folly and destruction; no longer would they be trusted to do the best for their social inferiors. The war also required a lot more government planning than had ever been seen before, and if that could be justified in a military emergency, why not in an economic one?

Whereas war had once been fought by professional soldiers in

79

far-away places, it was now total, involving the complete mobilization of the economy and mass-conscription armies. The sacrifices made by the ordinary people during 1914–18 meant that many did not want a return to normal, if normal meant rule by the upper classes. Electoral franchises were generally extended to include most men (although not always women). Politicians accordingly needed to appeal to those voters; even the most conservative recognized the need to placate the working classes, given the example of the Russian revolution.

This appeal had its positive and negative aspects. In Britain, the 1918 General Election was won by Lloyd George's coalition on a slogan of 'Homes fit for heroes', so that returning soldiers would get improved accommodation. But there was also a determination to make the Germans pay for the cost of the war: a feeling reflected in the French saying *le Boche paiera* ('the Hun will pay'). The issue of German reparations was to dog economic relations for the next fifteen years.

The old economic order had been disrupted as well. The US only joined the war when it was three-quarters over, confining its activities until 1917 to financing the Allies. Therefore the cost to America in terms of men and materials was far smaller than that borne by its pre-war rivals, Britain, Germany and France. The overseas assets of those countries had also been sold or, in the case of loans to Russia, had been defaulted. Financial power had moved to New York. By 1923, three-quarters of the world's gold was in the hands of the US.[1] Moreover, the loss of the old monarchies removed a key support for the pre-war monetary system. The revolutionary government in Russia repudiated the debts of the Tsarist era, and Keynes quoted Lenin as saying that 'the best way to destroy the capitalist system is to debauch the currency'.[2]

In retrospect, all these changes made resumption of the full version of the pre-war gold standard almost impossible. If economic activity were to recover worldwide, gold needed to be spread more evenly. But there was no question of the Americans giving up their gold. Indeed they insisted that their European allies repay their debts, which they viewed as a contractual obligation. This attitude prevented the multilateral debts from simply being cancelled. When Arthur Balfour, the British Foreign Secretary, suggested that Britain would collect no more from Germany in reparations (or from other Europeans in loan interest) than it had to pay the Americans, the suggestion was greeted with outrage in the US. It was not until a moment of desperation in 1931 that President Hoover came up with a similar plan.

Only the Americans had enough bullion to allow gold coins to operate in general circulation. Any return to the gold standard was thus bound to be partial. The Genoa Conference of 1922, attended by thirty-four countries, set out the framework for what became known as the 'gold exchange standard'. This dealt with the shortage, and unequal distribution, of gold by allowing some countries to hold their reserves in the form of foreign currencies. Those reserves would comprise the currencies of the stronger countries, which had the most gold backing. This innovation dealt with a fundamental problem of the post-1918 economy – the amount of money in circulation had expanded massively to pay for the war. In the absence of additional gold (which did not appear), paper money had to take some of the strain of supporting economic activity. It was one more step on the road to the abandonment of bullion.

At the time, however, it did not seem that way. There was a lingering belief in gold as the basis for 'real' money. As a result, European countries had to grapple with two options: returning to gold at a different (devalued) rate, or shrinking the amount of currency in circulation via lower prices and lower wages.

From a distance of ninety years, the first option seems the most logical. But politicians and central bankers still felt a sense of honour to their creditors. To devalue the currency was, in effect, to default on part of the debt. As French Finance Minister Georges Bonnet remarked, 'Who would be prepared to lend with the fear of being paid in depreciated currencies always before his eyes?'[3]

Despite his remarks, the French did follow the depreciation route. Inflation was high after the war and the government indulged in 'monetization' of its debt, by allowing the central bank to buy its bonds. Left-wing politicians called for a levy on the rich to pay for the cost of the war, a campaign that only encouraged capital flight. When France did return to gold in 1926, it went back at a vastly devalued level (around 25 francs to the dollar, or 80 per cent below its pre-war level), one which made its export industries highly competitive.

French monetary problems were mild, compared with those of

Germany. German war finance had depended more on printing money than raising taxes. The Germans were also determined to prove that they were unable to pay the reparations imposed by the Allies.

The Weimar regime faced revolutionary threats from both the left and the right, and it struggled in the face of these conflicting demands. Refusing to pay its debts risked punishment by the Allies, so it agreed to do so. But that required running a budget deficit. Balancing the budget required increases in taxes or cuts in expenditure, both of which risked unpopularity with the electorate. So the government asked the Reichsbank to print the required money. The Reichsbank duly obliged. Things came to a head in 1923 after the French occupied the industrial Ruhr area in retaliation for late payment. Having printed 1 trillion extra marks in 1922, the bank printed 17 trillion in the first six months of 1923. By November of that year, a kilo of butter cost 250 billion marks.

One can see the same process at work through the mark's value in terms of the dollar, the world's strongest currency by this stage. In 1914, the dollar was worth 4.2 marks. After the war, which Germany had financed through money-printing, the dollar was worth 65 marks. By August 1923, a dollar could buy 620,000 marks, and by November 630 billion.

Why did the central bank agree to this currency debasement? Liaquat Ahamed speculates that the head of the Reichsbank, Rudolf von Havenstein, acceded because he feared the alternative was revolution.[4] In August 1923, von Havenstein told the Council of State, 'In a few days we shall therefore be able to issue in one day two-thirds of total money circulation.' Whatever his rationale, the resulting crisis still affects German economic attitudes today.

Economic activity was massively distorted as workers spent their money as soon as it was earned. As the domestic currency became worthless, sellers demanded foreign currency; tourists could live the high life on a few dollars a day. For much of this period, the wages of skilled workers kept up with the price rises. Industrialists and aristocrats also survived, as their debts were devalued in real terms and as land values rose. But the middle classes, who relied on savings income to supplement their salaries, were ruined. The resulting loss of faith in

German democracy helped pave the way for Hitler, although it took the Depression to bring him to power.

At the end of 1923, Germany did return to the pre-war exchange rate of 4.2 marks, but this was a fiction. The new currency, the Rentenmark, was worth 1 trillion of the old currency, the Reichsmark. The move, masterminded by Hjalmar Schacht, later Hitler's finance guru, had a symbolic, confidence-giving effect. Schacht's plan, which had echoes of the French revolutionary issue of *assignats*, declared that the new currency was backed by the value of German land. This was a wholly illusory promise, but in the short term, it didn't matter; the Rentenmark was an acceptable means of exchange. In its own way, though, it set a precedent. Paper money did not have to be backed by gold for citizens to believe in it.

In the short term, however, German hyperinflation only increased the belief that politicians were not to be trusted with paper money, any more than an alcoholic should be left in charge of the drinks cabinet. It was time to return to the eternal verities of the gold standard, to reassert the rights of creditors. If the gold standard was to be restored, the key country was Britain. Even though the country's wealth had declined drastically, it was still Europe's most significant financial power. If it rejoined the gold standard, others might follow suit.

However, there had been no question of an immediate resumption of the gold standard in 1918. Britain lacked the financial strength to do so. It also suffered a very severe post-war recession, with unemployment doubling from one million to two million between December 1920 and June 1921. The political system was in turmoil, as the old Liberal party declined, to be replaced by the Labour party; four different prime ministers held office between 1922 and 1924.

For much of the immediate post-war period, the pound languished well below its old pre-war parity. This was hardly surprising, given the wartime inflation. The answer might seem obvious; return to gold but at a different level. But the finance sector, led by Montagu Norman, the governor of the Bank of England, believed that such a step would amount to cheating the country's creditors and would weaken the prestige of the City of London. To Norman, sound money was the mark of a civilized society.

A report by the Cunliffe committee at the end of the war declared that without a return to the gold standard, 'there will be grave danger of a progressive credit expansion which will result in a foreign drain of gold menacing the convertibility of the note issues and so jeopardising the international trade position of the country'.[5]

Many in Britain took this attitude in part because of its experience in the nineteenth century. The aftermath of the Napoleonic Wars looked very like the aftermath of the First World War; debt and prices had risen sharply. There was considerable debate on the issue of whether to return to gold at the previous rate. In the end, the orthodox economists in the gold camp won. Prices fell sharply, causing much economic hardship; this was the period of the Peterloo massacre, when cavalry charged a workers' protest meeting in Manchester, killing fifteen and injuring hundreds more. Nevertheless, the value of sterling was protected and the interests of creditors safeguarded. Add in the parsimony of British governments during the 1800s (balanced budgets were a matter of course) and the reputation of sterling as the world's safest currency ('sound as a pound') was created.

The decision to return to gold in 1925 fell on the unlikely shoulders of Winston Churchill, a great leader but a man who showed no interest in finance before or after his stint as Chancellor of the Exchequer from 1924 to 1929.[6] Norman and other experts argued that, with the pound only 10 per cent short of its pre-war parity, the economic adjustment involved in a return to the standard would not be too severe.

Churchill held a dinner and invited various experts to debate the issue of a return to the standard, including John Maynard Keynes for the opposition. But Keynes was undoubtedly in a minority. On top of the economic arguments, Churchill also seems to have been swayed by a mixture of national pride and a need to protect the status of Britain as a global financial centre. In a Parliamentary speech in May 1925, he declared:

If the English pound is not to be the standard which everyone knows and can trust, and which everyone in every country understands and can rely on, the business not only of the British Empire, but of Europe as well, might have to be transacted in dollars instead of pounds sterling. I think that would be a great misfortune.

What were the arguments against a move? First, a rising currency makes the nation's goods more expensive for foreigners. Exporters may respond by cutting their costs (employee wages), a process that can easily lead to a deflationary contraction in demand. As Keynes wrote in his polemic against the eventual resumption of the standard: 'Mr Churchill's policy of improving the exchange by 10 per cent was, sooner or later, a policy of reducing everyone's wages by two shillings in the pound', adding that the Chancellor was 'committing himself to force down money wages and all money values, without any idea how it is to be done'.[7]

Indeed, one key difference with the nineteenth century was that trade-union power made it harder to cut wages. According to Barry Eichengreen, British wholesale prices fell 15 per cent from the return to gold in April 1925 and January 1929, while wages fell just 1.5 per cent over the same period.[8] In the jargon of economists, wages were 'sticky'. Since the cost of labour barely fell, employers were more reluctant to take on workers and unemployment stayed high.

In addition, raising the exchange rate increased the burden of repaying foreign debt. Hence another complaint from Keynes about the 1925 return to the gold standard: 'When we raise the value of sterling by 10 per cent, we transfer about £1 billion into the pockets of the rentiers and out of the pockets of the rest of us.'[9]

In short, in the historic battle between creditors and debtors, the return to the gold standard was a victory, at least in the short term, for the former. In the medium term, however, the shift imposed too high a burden on the debtors. The effects feared by Keynes did materialize. The squeeze on the economy led to an attempt to force down wages that culminated in the miners' strike of 1926, a dispute that escalated into a general strike. To some, this was the closest Britain came to revolution in the twentieth century. The strike failed, but Britain suffered from a very disappointing economic performance in the 1920s, with unemployment remaining stubbornly high.

Nevertheless, Britain's return to the standard was followed by other nations and the pre-war economic order was seemingly restored. But it was much less robust than it had previously been. The automatic adjustments that occurred under the pre-war gold standard were no longer in place. Citizens could no longer demand gold from their banks in exchange for notes. Furthermore, central bank reserves consisted much less of gold, and much more of the obligations of other countries. The proportion of foreign exchange within central bank reserves was 12 per cent in 1913, but had risen to 27 per cent by 1925 and 42 per cent by 1928.[10] In other words there was more paper money relative to gold.

The global money supply had been expanded, one reason why money was sloshing into US equities. Author Richard Duncan views the 1920s as a credit boom on a par with that of the 1990s and early 2000s; in each case the excesses of the boom led directly to the bust.[11]

Financial leadership after the war was in the hands of the US Federal Reserve, which faced a conflict between its internal and external interests. The chairman of the New York Fed, Benjamin Strong, was a friend of Montagu Norman and sympathetic to Europe's plight. He knew that an increase in American interest rates would cause a drain of capital (and thus gold) to the US and away from Europe, putting pressure on the continent's ability to remain on the standard. However, the US economy was booming, as was the stock market, and Strong came under considerable pressure to moderate the expansion by raising rates. The result was an inconsistent policy, in which the Fed neither prevented Wall Street's excesses nor made life easier for the Europeans.

In the context of the roaring 1920s, the US authorities were unwilling, except on rare occasions, to reflate their economy. The Fed did lower interest rates in 1927, only to run into criticism since the effect was to encourage stock-market speculation. In 1928 the Fed reversed course, raising rates to curb speculation. Meanwhile France, which was recovering from its inflationary excesses of the early 1920s, also had high interest rates by international standards. Gold naturally flowed to these two countries, and away from the rest. French gold reserves quadrupled between 1926 and 1931.

The French were successful at attracting gold because their economy was in good competitive shape. And that was because the currency had been devalued. The economies of those countries that had restored the pre-war parities were less credible (in the market's eyes) than those that had devalued, since the former had had to impose harsh restrictions on their economies to maintain the parity.

This highlighted a problem that was to occur again and again in later years. The US was running a trade surplus and accumulating gold, but it was not required to adjust its policy by raising its prices to make its goods less competitive. All the adjustment was forced on to the deficit countries, a process that will seem familiar to modern-day residents of Greece and Ireland.

In 1924, a deal had been made on reparations, a running sore throughout the early 1920s. Under US leadership, German reparations payments had been lowered and extended. As the German economy stabilized after hyperinflation, US banks became willing to lend to Germany. In effect, money was being recycled round the system; US banks lent to Germany, which allowed the Germans to pay the reparations bill, allowing Britain and France to meet their US war debts. But from 1928 onwards, this lending slowed and then ceased. Initially, higher US interest rates meant that American banks wanted to keep their capital at home; then the 1929 Wall Street crash and subsequent crisis made them afraid to lend abroad, and Germany lost a key source of financing.

The effect of the gold exchange standard, whereby the world's central banks had more of their reserves in foreign exchange, now increased the fragility of the system. Doubts about the willingness of a rival central bank to maintain the gold parity increased the incentive to sell the holdings of that currency. There was a rush for gold as the share of foreign exchange in central bank reserves fell sharply to 11 per cent by the end of 1931. But as Barry Eichengreen and Peter Temin have put it, 'there was only so much gold to go round. Central banks jacked up interest rates in a desperate effort to obtain it, destabilizing commercial banks and depressing prices, production and employment.'[12] This was a deflationary surge that reversed the inflationary boom of the 1920s.

It was every bank for itself. Rather than co-operating, monetary authorities were essentially competing. As we have seen, the countries that had restored their exchange rate at pre-war parities were less credible than those that had devalued. The French economy was competitive at the devalued rate; the British economy was not. An overvalued currency required the country to impose harsh restrictions on its economy to maintain the parity – something that creditors correctly guessed would not be sustainable in the long run.

By the late 1920s, Germany faced a particular credibility problem. More than half the deposits in German banks were held by foreigners. This made Germany particularly vulnerable to a loss of confidence. But after the hyperinflationary crisis of 1923 and 1924, the government was keen to stick to its policy of monetary stability. So there was no question of leaving the gold standard.

Unemployment rose sharply and the government struggled to replace the financing it had received from America. In 1930, a new German Prime Minister, Heinrich Bruning, imposed an austerity programme and, in the absence of a parliamentary majority, decided to govern by decree. He declared that 'One must either go along with deflation or devalue the currency. For us only the first could be considered since, six years after experiencing unparalleled inflation, new inflation, even in careful doses, is not possible.'[13] Bruning cut unemployment benefits, government salaries and veterans' benefits. In so doing, he weakened the popularity of the Weimar Republic and paved the way for Hitler's rise to power. Early elections in September 1930 saw a sharp rise in the Nazi vote and increased capital flight, making the German financial situation even worse.

As prices fell and businesses went bust, banks began to get into difficulties. Remember that a bank's lending is always many times higher than its capital; it only takes a few large borrowers to default to create a problem. In 1931, the Austrian bank Credit Anstalt went bust, ironically in part because it had been forced to take over a loss-making rival, the Bodencreditnastalt, in 1929. A run on all Austrian banks duly followed and in a classic case of contagion, the crisis spread to German banks. The French did not help the process, seeking to delay an international rescue of Credit Anstalt in an attempt to block a customs union between Austria and Germany.

Rescuing the banks wasn't easy under the gold standard. Lower rates would mean a drain of capital overseas. Supplying capital to the failing banks would mean a reduction in reserves at the central bank, a worrying sign for international investors. (This potential flaw in the system had been revealed by the Barings crisis of 1890.)

A failed bank also caused problems for the rest of the system. Deposit insurance was not yet in existence; when a bank failed, ordinary depositors lost their money. This only increased the incentive for them to take their money out of any bank that might be in trouble. Of course, the very act of withdrawal made such a crisis more likely, so panic spread from bank to bank. As the banks lost deposits, they were forced to shrink the asset side of their balance sheet, their loans. This made life more difficult for businesses, leading to more failures, more bad loans, higher unemployment and so on.

A WORLD OUT OF IDEAS

The crisis of 1931 simply overwhelmed the system. Governments and central banks faced shrinking economies, fiscal crises, bank failures and attacks on their currencies, all at the same time. Anyone who has listened to a recent debate on economic policy will not have to wait long before someone mentions the mistakes of the 1930s. The politicians of the era are portrayed as wilfully blind, rather like the First World War generals who sent their troops into machine-gun fire. By attempting to balance their budgets, it is said, they made the crisis worse.

At the time, politicians were simply following standard economic theory. There was no tradition of running deficits or expanding the money supply to boost demand. These policies were associated with corrupt and failed governments of the past, such as the French revolutionary regime.

The nineteenth century had seen lots of short, sharp recessions, associated with falling agricultural prices or the overexpansion of industries like the railroads. But economies had recovered as quickly as they had collapsed. Only as the early 1930s came and went without recovery was it clear that sound money, in the form of the gold standard, had not delivered prosperity. Instead, economies were caught in what Irving Fisher identified as a deflationary trap: borrowers sold assets to try to repay their debts, forcing asset prices down and making their debt problems even bigger.

It is no coincidence that the 1930s also saw a shift towards the modern welfare state. In the old classical model, supply and demand should always balance at the right price; that was as true for labour as it was for apples. Unemployment could only be the result of idleness, and providing benefits for the unemployed would reduce incentives to work. But the 1930s saw the emergence of persistent, mass unemployment. It was implausible to argue that a generation of people had become idle, especially when many seemed so desperate to find work. After the war, it became incumbent on governments to help those who, through no fault of their own, could not find work. That encouraged governments to try to 'manage' the economic cycle, something that a nineteenth-century administration would not have dreamed of doing.

The other great mistake associated with the 1930s was protectionism. Country after country retreated behind tariff walls, with the net effect that world trade slumped.

Tariffs were the norm, rather than the exception, even before the 1930s. Britain had been the nineteenth-century champion of free trade, but its advocacy was regarded by other countries as special pleading. Britain wanted free trade so it could sell its products into other countries. Instead, countries tried to mimic Britain's industrial success by starting their own manufacturing sectors. That involved tariffs to protect them from British competition.

Trade restrictions started even before the Wall Street crash of 1929. Commodity prices started to fall sharply in 1928, in part because the US's long boom had encouraged overcapacity. Stockpiles of wheat doubled between 1925 and 1929. The producing countries found that their trade positions were deteriorating as their export incomes fell. Their natural reaction was to reduce imports, either by raising tariffs or by reducing domestic demand via monetary or fiscal policy; neither option was good for world trade.

In a sense, there were two approaches to eliminating a trade deficit. A devaluation of the currency would effectively lower export prices, allowing more goods to be sold abroad, and raise import prices, allowing domestic producers to undercut foreign competitors. The latter effect could also be achieved by an increase in tariffs. Denied the option of devaluation, those countries that stayed on the gold standard were more inclined to raise tariffs.

The problem with tariffs is that other countries do not sit idly by when their own products are taxed. They retaliate, so the volume of world trade falls. And trade is good. Adam Smith had established the benefits of specialization all the way back in 1776, with his example of the pin factory. Britain could try and produce everything it needs from bananas to xylophones. But it wouldn't produce many of those goods very efficiently. Costs would rise and the standard of living of the average Briton would fall. It is better for Britain to produce the things it is best at (where, in the jargon, it has a 'comparative advantage'), sell those goods or services internationally, and use the proceeds to buy things that it needs from other countries that, say, grow bananas easily.

Inevitably, tariffs did little to protect each nation's share of the pie; instead they made the pie smaller. So politicians were eventually forced into leaving the gold standard. Perhaps the key was the weakness of the financial system. Bank executives, believers in sound money to a man when other sectors of the economy were in trouble, became less keen on monetary purity when it came to their own survival – a theme that was to be echoed in 2007 and 2008.

Economists believed the gold standard was one of the economy's great self-correcting mechanisms. When a country had too much gold, its prices would rise and its exporters would lose competitiveness. Gold would thus flow to the countries whose prices had fallen and balance would be restored. But the post-1918 experience indicated that the system could get stuck. Gold reserves were concentrated in the US and France but this did not lead to sharp price rises, even on a relative basis. Countries that were short of gold remained so because, in a democratic society, they could not impose the huge adjustment needed to restore their reserves. The Great Depression was not a short-lived affair, like the economic downturn of 1920–21, but a prolonged journey.

In the view of Filippo Cesarino, this led to a change in attitude; economists talked of the need to manage the money supply.[14] But the gold standard was designed to be self-regulating, to stop politicians from 'managing' the currency for their own devices. Once the principle of currency management was accepted, it was not clear that gold was needed at all.

As countries abandoned gold, their currencies fell, giving them a temporary advantage over their trading partners in what became known as 'beggar-thy-neighbour' devaluations. Devaluation could be seen as a game of 'pass the deflationary parcel' in which countries passed the problem of dealing with the slump on to their neighbours.

The whole episode was perceived by economists as deeply unsatisfactory, which is why they tried to create a much more formal structure after the Second World War.

THE BANKERS' RAMP

In Britain, the crisis came to a head in a way that would affect politics for decades. It was clear that Britain had rejoined the gold standard at too high a rate, and that its financial position was much weaker than it had been before 1914. In 1929, a minority Labour government had taken power; it depended on the rump Liberal party for its survival. As economic activity fell in 1929 and 1930, the budget deficit widened. This is normal for a cycle because tax revenues fall as people lose jobs and social benefits rise.

The government, under pressure from the Liberals, took a classic British option. It set up a committee under Sir George May, the former head of the Prudential insurance company. By handing a key issue of economic policy to a leading City figure, the government effectively signed its own death warrant. It was virtually certain that May would recommend cuts in benefits; accepting his ideas would damage the Labour party's supporters, while rejecting the deal would usher in a financial crisis. And so it proved. At the end of July 1931, the May committee projected a £120 million deficit, the bulk of which should be covered by £97 million-worth of spending cuts, including a 20 per cent reduction in unemployment benefits.

The Labour government was led by Ramsay MacDonald, an illegitimate son of a fisherwoman and dressmaker from Lossiemouth in Scotland. He had shown considerable courage in opposing the First World War but was anxious, above all, to make Labour a respectable party of power. His first administration had been forced from office in 1924 after a fake letter was circulated, alleging links with the Soviet Union. MacDonald was far from a revolutionary and had 'an austere insistence that socialism could not be equated with public expenditure'.[15] The Chancellor, Philip Snowden, was a classic example of the moralist strain in British politics, strait-laced and deeply religious. He was happy to sharpen the public spending axe and, indeed, revealed that the projected deficit was £170 million, £50 million more than the May committee had assumed.

The Bank of England put pressure on the Cabinet, demanding that the budget be balanced by late August. On the other side of the argument, Walter Milne-Bailey, the head of the Trades Union Congress' research department, suggested a range of options including devaluation, tariffs or taxes on high incomes. Such suggestions were all very well but the government did not have a majority to push through such radical proposals (and Snowden, an ardent free-trader, would have resigned over tariffs).

A Cabinet meeting agreed to cuts of £56 million, including a 10 per cent cut in unemployment benefit. But the vote was only eleven to nine in favour. Among those who approved were William Benn, whose son Tony became a left-wing stalwart of the late twentieth-century Labour party, and Herbert Morrison, a future Home Secretary and grandfather of Peter Mandelson, the éminence noir of the Tony Blair administration. The split was not entirely on ideological grounds; the opponents included Lord Addison, who had been a Liberal member of Lloyd George's wartime cabinet.

Such a narrow majority did little to help the situation, neither creating confidence among investors nor giving MacDonald the authority to carry on. Arthur Henderson, the wartime leader of the Labour party, threatened to resign if the 10 per cent benefit cut was carried through. Meanwhile, the Bank of England was piling on the pressure, raising interest rates to defend sterling and warning that its foreign-exchange reserves were close to exhaustion.

The subsequent left-wing accusations of a bankers' ramp (or racket) are not without merit. Although forwarded credit by the Banque de France, the Bank of England did not use it, in order to keep pressure on the government to cut the deficit. The problems were exacerbated by the crisis in Germany, to which British banks were heavily exposed. The Bank of England stopped shipping gold overseas in early August; one historian reckons the bank wanted to retain some gold in case the standard was abandoned.[16]

In any case, the government was never able to discover the actual level of reserves in the Bank of England. They had to rely on the central bank for that information, but the governor, Montagu Norman, had gone AWOL. A sensitive soul throughout his career, Norman left work on 29 July 'feeling queer' and did not return to the bank until the crisis was over. In Norman's absence, the financial sector stuck to the orthodox line of sound money and saw a cut in unemployment benefit as a token of the government's commitment to the principle. Lord Passfield (Sidney Webb) lamented that 'we can be held to ransom and forced to make an essential change in our domestic social policy as the price of rescue for the financial interests of the City'. Some would echo his words today.

MacDonald wanted to resign both as Prime Minister and Labour leader, as he could hardly oppose cuts that he approved of. But this was an era of totalitarian regimes and revolutions and the Establishment was nervous. The leader of the Liberal party, Herbert Samuel, advised King George V that MacDonald should be kept in office 'in view of the fact that the necessary economies would prove most unpalatable to the working class'.[17] An appeal to MacDonald's vanity worked, and he became leader of a National (coalition) government, which depended heavily on the Conservatives. Only three Labour ministers, including Snowden, went with him. MacDonald was henceforth reviled in left-wing circles, seen as a class traitor who boasted to Snowden that 'tomorrow every Duchess in London will be wanting to kiss me'.[18]

With a (largely) Conservative government in power, what was radical and unorthodox under the Labour administration suddenly became possible. The coalition, which won a crushing election victory later that year, eventually cut spending by £70 million, including a 10 per cent reduction in unemployment benefits; taxes were also raised by £75 million. A protest by sailors at Invergordon in Scotland was portrayed as a mutiny, further undermining investor confidence.

Eventually, as reserves dwindled, the Bank of England abandoned the attempt to maintain the gold standard. The sky did not collapse and one former Labour minister (accounts differ as to who) remarked, 'Nobody told us we could do this.' To complete the unorthodoxy, the government even adopted tariffs within a couple of years. The decline in the pound helped Britain to avoid the worst excesses of the Depression that were seen in the US, although unemployment did remain high.

It was a momentous step. Britain, the centrepiece of the gold standard in the nineteenth century, had abandoned the metal. Strenuous attempts to safeguard the interests of creditors had eventually been abandoned in the face of economic reality.

Other nations were quick to follow suit. In 1931, forty-seven countries were on the gold standard; by the end of 1932, there were just eleven. The collective decision to leave the gold standard eventually worked in the sense that it allowed countries to pursue reflationary policies. Ironically, France, which returned to the gold standard after Britain's example, was much slower to leave it. In part, this was because of a feeling that the return to gold had solved France's post-1918 inflationary problems. But the French had more gold reserves, and thus more scope to hang on. It did them little good, and the French economy was slower to recover than the British.

In 1936 the French had one of their perennial changes of government, with a left-wing 'popular front' led by Léon Blum taking office. As is often the case with left-wing governments, it felt the need to prove its orthodox economic credentials, in this case by avoiding devaluation. Indeed, even the Communist party believed a devaluation would represent a surrender to market forces. Tricks that would have been familiar to John Law were used to stave off the inevitable, including currency controls, a prohibition of the sale of gold coins and even the prosecution of individuals for spreading 'rumours of devaluation'. But devaluation came anyway in September 1936. The inter-war experiment with gold was over.

THE US EXPERIENCE

France was the laggard in leaving gold. The world's largest economy, the US, had already devalued its currency in 1933 and 1934, and was conducting experiments in economic policy that are still significant today.

The Depression came as an enormous shock to Americans, who understandably saw their country as a land of opportunity. Many were immigrants who had fled Europe in search of a better life. America with its endless space and natural resources seemed destined for ever greater riches. How could a country with so many advantages, and with people who desperately wanted to work, end up with 25 per cent unemployment and a fall in output of almost a third? It made no sense.

Initially, many people blamed the downturn on the excesses of credit and speculation that preceded it. Americans had borrowed too much, spent too much and lived beyond their means; what was needed was a purgative to clean out the system. The role of the 1929 Wall Street crash is much debated. The drama of plunging prices and lost fortunes undoubtedly had an impact on sentiment. But attributing the Depression to the crash may be a classic *post hoc ergo propter hoc* mistake.[19] The economy had already started to turn down before the crash, and the stock market rebounded in early 1930.

Milton Friedman argued that the problem was the collapse of the banking system that occurred in the early 1930s. (This was one reason why the authorities rescued the banks in 2008.) There was a spiral effect; as businesses failed, banks suffered losses, and as banks failed, businesses lost their access to capital. As we've already noted, these were the days before deposit insurance, so customers of a failed bank lost all their money. The money supply contracted sharply, with an inevitable effect on demand.

At the time, politicians did not see things that way. Andrew Mellon, the Treasury Secretary, had, according to President Hoover's memoirs, a simple answer to the crisis: 'Liquidate labor, liquidate stocks, liquidate farmers, liquidate real estate. It will purge the rottenness out of the system. High costs of living and high living will come down, lead a more moral life.' Mellon, like many economists of the time, thought that the capitalist system would always find balance, if left to its own devices. If workers were unemployed, that was because wages were too high. Reducing wages would allow the workers to find jobs. This would not hurt the workers' standard of living because prices had already fallen. In contrast, President Hoover worried that cutting wages would reduce demand further and he tried to persuade businesses not to do so. Although Keynes had not yet published his *General Theory* (that happened in 1936), Hoover was worried about aggregate demand.

It is a mistake to regard Hoover as the reactionary conservative and Roosevelt as the liberal Keynesian. Hoover allowed the budget to go into deficit in 1931 and FDR campaigned in favour of a balanced budget in 1932. At the Democratic convention of that year Roosevelt declared that 'Revenue must cover expenditures by one means or another. Any government, like any family, can for a year spend a little more than it earns. But you and I know that a continuation of that habit leads to the poorhouse.'

But FDR was willing to try anything and had a kind of patrician disdain for orthodox views. That made him perfectly willing to abandon the gold standard if it meant the economy would revive. Instead of an economist, he listed to an agricultural expert, George Warren, who argued that there was a direct link between the gold price and other commodity prices. So the President decided steadily to raise the gold price by decree.

His conventional economic advisers were horrified, seeing this as the destruction of sound money. However, Roosevelt was channelling the ghost of William Jennings Bryan. Farmers were suffering even more than they had in the 1890s; farm income fell 30 per cent between 1929 and 1932, at a time when agriculture still employed 30 per cent of the workforce. Higher commodity prices, particularly for products like wheat and cotton, would restore their prosperity. The President began the tradition of supporting the farming community via subsidies and protectionist devices that continues to this day.

Roosevelt argued that 'old fetishes of so-called international bankers are being replaced by efforts to plan national currencies'. This was an important moment in monetary history in that it began the reaction against the idea of 'sound money' – a stable currency and a balanced budget. He did not stop there. He introduced social security (state pensions), created work programmes to get the unemployed into jobs, offered guarantees for home loans, raised taxes on the wealthy and much, much more. For liberals, he was the founder of the modern state; for conservatives, he was the man who destroyed the American dream of self-reliance.

Economic historians still debate whether Roosevelt's many programmes helped or hindered the recovery. But it is worth remembering that FDR won four successive presidential elections because he appeared willing to take decisive action; voters may not have understood the theory of economic policy but they felt Roosevelt's heart was in the right place.

This was a time when democracy, in the sense of full adult suffrage, was both newly established and under apparent threat. Many contrasted the indecisiveness of democratic politicians with the direct action of Hitler, a man with little interest in orthodox economic policy. Rightly or wrongly, Hitler's pursuit of rearmament was seen as dealing with the problem of mass unemployment. At the same time, the Depression was perceived to be the kind of crisis of capitalism that the communists had predicted. The idea of industrial planning, as pursued by Stalin, appeared to make sense.

Roosevelt, and indeed Keynes, saw themselves as rescuing capitalism from the clutches of communism and fascism. With the system under threat, it was fruitless for the classical economists to argue for laissez-faire, the policy of letting the economy find its own level. Keynes believed the government must act as 'the spender of last resort' to prevent the economy from being mired in depression. Having condemned reparations, denounced Britain's return to the gold standard, and dissected the failures of classical economics, the intellectual stock of Keynes rose sharply. When politicians came to debate a post-war international monetary system in the 1940s, it was to Keynes that they naturally turned.

5

Dancing with the Dollar

'It's our currency but your problem.'
John Connally, US Treasury Secretary under President
Nixon

The traditional gold standard evolved by a mixture of accident and imitation; other countries adopted a system that had seemed to work for Britain. The late twentieth-century monetary system was developed through a process of trial and (a lot of) error. Between those two eras was Bretton Woods. It was the world's only monetary system to be deliberately designed by a committee and agreed at a conference, held at the eponymous hotel in the New Hampshire mountains in 1944. It was only perhaps in the peculiar circumstances of the Second World War that such an agreement could be reached. There was scope to remake the system from scratch.

The men who devised the Bretton Woods system were clearly trying to avoid some of the mistakes that had been made between the wars. Countries had rejoined, and then abandoned, the gold standard in a series of competitive devaluations. Economic co-operation between the great powers had vanished as many countries had descended into totalitarianism. Protectionism had deepened and lengthened the Depression. The trick was to devise a post-war system that would boost international trade, offer some stability as to the value of money, and deal with the inevitable post-war imbalances.

It was an ambitious agenda. At the conference's opening ceremony, Henry Morgenthau, the US Treasury Secretary, declared that 'We came here to work out methods which would do away with the economic evils – the competitive currency devaluation and destructive impediments to trade – which preceded the present war.'[1] The presiding gurus were John Maynard Keynes, the British economist, and Harry Dexter White, an aide to President Roosevelt who had strong sympathies for the Soviet Union. Keynes had the intellectual heft but White had the economic muscle.

The two men had some basic ideas in common. Both believed that stable exchange rates would encourage trade flows by giving certainty to both importers and exporters. But the 1930s had showed that individual countries could be overwhelmed by the effort of maintaining their currency link. This created the need for some kind of international lender of last resort, just as individual central banks acted as the lender of last resort for their own financial sectors. Eventually, the International Monetary Fund (IMF) was born out of this need. However, Keynes and White disagreed on the size and scope of this bailout fund. Keynes wanted the fund to be large, in response to the inter-war problem that gold reserves had been concentrated in America and France, creating a permanent shortfall in the other nations. He was particularly conscious of the weakness of the British financial position, given that the country's assets had been wiped out by the cost of the war. 'We shall have no means after the war out of which we can pay for purchases in the United States except the equivalent of what they buy from us,' he said.[2]

In contrast, White recognized that the larger the bailout fund, the bigger the bill for the US, which as the biggest creditor would have to stand behind it. Indeed, even if White had been sympathetic to Keynes's ambitions, he had to deal with congressional opposition to a large US commitment. One newspaper feared that 'Uncle Sam would be treated as an Uncle Sap for the rest of the world'.[3]

The concept of a domestic lender of last resort had always been dogged by moral hazard. What was to stop a bank from taking excessive risks if it believed the central bank stood behind it? The same was true at the international level. Would the IMF act as a sugar daddy to deficit nations and prevent them from making the required policy changes to address their own problems?

The initial proposal of Keynes was for a 'clearing union' in which international trade balances would be settled. The idea seems a little strange now but it originated in a world of government-run economies and where trade deficits led directly to a drain on the reserves of central banks. Domestic banks use a clearing system in which all transactions are netted out at the end of a day. The many millions of trades – cash withdrawals from Bank A, debit-card purchases through Bank B – are offset, so Bank A needs to transfer a net amount to Bank B (or vice versa). An international clearing union would have performed the same function for trade. All the aircraft and electronics purchases, all the wheat shipments would be offset, leaving the net figure – a trade surplus or deficit.

Each country would have an overdraft with the clearing union, equivalent to half the annual volume of its trade. This overdraft would be expressed in the form of a new currency, which Keynes dubbed bancor; this would be valued in terms of gold, but not convertible into it. This device was Keynes's way of trying to reduce the world's dependence on the dollar as a reserve currency. (Bancor stayed on the drawing board. Eventually, a basket currency was to be created in 1969 in the form of the Special Drawing Right (SDR) comprising fixed percentages of the dollar, pound, yen and various European currencies. But the SDR was not to be used seriously until well after the Bretton Woods era was past.)

Under Keynes's plan, a country with a persistent deficit would run up against its overdraft limit, and would devalue its currency. That was pretty much the requirement under the gold standard as well. But Keynes also imposed obligations on the creditor nations, which would be required to revalue their currency or pay interest on the credits built up in the clearing union. The aim was to prevent a repeat of the inter-war system when all the adjustment fell on the debtor nations.

To the Americans this seemed like special pleading. It was clear that, after the war, the Americans would be a trade surplus nation and Britain a deficit nation. All this talk of special currencies and clearing unions seemed to be a device for debtor countries to get goods from America and pay 'funny money' in return – not backed by gold, not backed by anything. White accused Keynes of trying to conjure gold out of thin air.

Keynes thus had to compromise on a less ambitious project: the IMF would act as a support fund to help countries in balance of payments difficulties. Instead of an overdraft with the fund, each country would have a quota. Keynes wanted the overall level of quotas to be very large, at $26 billion; White, ever mindful of the suspicions of Congress, wanted a much lower figure. The eventual compromise was $8.8 billion, closer to White's position. Each member was required to subscribe for its quota in gold and government bonds and would be allowed to borrow against the quota when in difficulties. Much of the conference was taken up with arguments about how big the individual country quotas should be. Initially, it was perceived that only developed countries would borrow from the fund; it was only much later that the IMF began to act as a lender of last resort for the developing world. This became the subject of much controversy in the 1980s and 1990s, as the conditions imposed by the IMF were perceived to be anti-democratic and favouring the creditors.

When it came to currencies, the Bretton Woods agreement found a neat way of getting round the problem of the imbalance in the world's gold reserves; the US had 60 per cent of the world's bullion. Instead of tying currencies to gold, they were tied to the dollar. No longer were gold coins in circulation, nor could private investors convert their bank notes into bullion. Only other central banks had that privilege with the US Federal Reserve.

The original Bretton Woods agreement tried to avoid another problem associated with the gold standard – it recognized the right of nations to devalue their currencies. The idea was to give economies some flexibility so they did not have to make Britain's all-or-nothing 1931 choice between the domestic economy and an exchange-rate anchor. In fact, devaluations were far less common under Bretton Woods than might have been expected, although Britain was forced into this action as early as 1949.

How did the Bretton Woods system deal with the trilemma mentioned in Chapter 3, the incompatibility of fixed exchange rates, independent monetary policy and free-flowing capital? The Americans wanted capital to flow freely. However, the lure of independent monetary policy proved too strong. The main fear was a return of high unemployment rates and politicians wanted the flexibility to adjust monetary (and fiscal) policy to boost the economy. They no longer wanted the unemployed to be crucified on a 'cross of gold'. Capital controls protected countries from the threat that speculators, alarmed by the direction of monetary policy, might undermine exchange rate targets.

Many countries had already imposed capital controls during the war so it was not that difficult to extend them. The choice did attract contemporary criticism. Economist Frank Graham wrote:

We should know that we must either forgo fixed exchange rates or national monetary sovereignty if we are to avoid the disruption of equilibrium in freely conducted international trade or the system of controls and inhibitions which is the only alternative when the internal values of independent currencies deviate – as they always tend to do.[4]

Graham added that the system contained 'not even the slightest provision for the adoption, by the various participating countries, of the congruent monetary policies without which a system of fixed exchange rates simply does not make sense'.

In other words, countries wanted to have their cake (a fixed exchange rate) and eat it (independent monetary policy). They did not want the markets to have the ability to point out when monetary policy was incompatible with the exchange-rate target.

Establishing the Bretton Woods system evoked many of the arguments that still rage today. Graham favoured floating exchange rates, but that turned out to be a policy whose time had not yet come. His arguments (and those of laissez-faire economists like Friedrich Hayek and Ludwig von Mises) were to be taken up in the 1960s and 1970s by the Chicago economists Milton Friedman and Robert Lucas. The creation of the euro owes much to the feeling – prevalent at Bretton Woods – that exchange rates should be stable and speculation curbed. And the need to impose obligations on creditor and surplus nations is now an argument used by the Americans against the Chinese.

At heart, Bretton Woods was a system blessed by the Americans, at the time the world's leading creditor. So the fact that it was based on the dollar and committed to exchange rate stability was hardly surprising. However, one of the reasons the system weakened over time was that capital found ways of evading the controls. And the ability of countries to run independent monetary policy, often with the aim of ensuring full employment, stored up long-term trouble for the fixed exchange-rate system.

The agreement was far from popular at the time, being attacked from both sides of the Atlantic. In Britain, Lord Beaverbrook, a close friend of Churchill, declared that 'This is the gold standard all over again. And at a moment when the United States has all the gold and Britain has none of it.' In the US, Representative Fred Smith described the plan as a 'British plot to seize control of United States gold'.[5] But the system survived for more than a quarter of a century.

AVOIDING MISTAKES

Many countries were conscious of the disastrous results of the post-1918 settlement and determined to avoid the same mistakes. There was little enthusiasm for financial reparations, at least on the Western side; the Russians looted East Germany in brutal fashion. Crucially, the next twenty years were not spent haggling over the issues of war debts.

Another vital difference from the inter-war period was that the US, the world's largest economy, did not retreat into the isolationism that followed the First World War. Keen to prevent the spread of communism, the Americans were involved on the ground in Germany and more widely, rebuilding economies through the Marshall Aid programme. In addition, Western governments avoided the plunge into protectionism that marked the inter-war period. The General Agreement on Tariffs and Trade (GATT) limited trade barriers without eliminating them entirely. The result was rapid post-war trade growth, allowing European countries both to specialize and to grow.

Nor did countries seriously contemplate a deflationary programme in an attempt to restore the pre-war exchange rate, as Britain did in the 1920s. As Charles Kindleberger writes, 'France and Italy decided to adjust the exchange rate to the stock of money, rather than the stock of money to a particular exchange rate.'[6] The result was that the French franc, which traded at 5 to the dollar in 1913, and around 25 to the dollar in the mid-1920s, was allowed to slump to 119 to the dollar after the war. By 1958, a further devaluation took the rate to 500, at which point the French knocked two zeros off the currency and the 5/$ rate was restored. The effect was that the franc had lost 99 per cent of its purchasing power against the dollar in just forty-five years, and this against a dollar which had itself been devalued against gold.

The Italians followed a similar path. Like the French, they had a rate of 5 lire to the dollar before the First World War; by 1947, it took 900 to buy one greenback. Anyone who travelled to Italy in the 1980s and 1990s will recall that the simplest transactions required thousands of lire; a taxi meter was a whirling blur of figures.

West Germany was, of course, a wreck in the immediate aftermath of the war. In 1918, Germany had surrendered before its territory was invaded, but Hitler fought to the very bitter end. The value of the Reichsmark had been destroyed and cigarettes, coffee, stockings all served as currency. A bitter winter in 1946 and early 1947 led to famine. In the western zone, rather than taking reparations, the Allies quickly found that they were required to supply aid in the form of food and raw materials. As the extent of Russian domination of Eastern Europe became clear, the Allies proved keen to restore prosperity to the western part of Germany.

A successful currency reform was pushed through in 1948, with the Reichsmark being replaced by the new Deutschmark at a rate of 10:1 and the country avoided hyperinflation. The stage was set for the German economic miracle, and for the Deutschmark to be the strong currency of the new Europe. By 1956, German gold reserves already surpassed those of France, and in 1961, the Deutschmark was revalued by 5 per cent against the dollar – a sign of the country's growing economic power.

The Bundesbank Law of 1957 established the independence of the new central bank from the West German government. Bank officials, many of whom were survivors of the Nazi era, were determined to avoid the mistakes made by the pre-war Reichsbank. This independence caused some resentment among politicians, notably Konrad Adenauer, the post-war Chancellor, who declared that the bank was 'an organ responsible to no one, neither to parliament nor to any government'.[7]

Britain struggled after the war. President Roosevelt's programme of lend-lease, under which vital equipment was supplied to Britain on easy terms, was abruptly cancelled after the war by his successor, Harry Truman. The Americans still regarded Britain as a potential economic competitor and disliked its imperial pretensions. That left Britain, an island nation that had experienced heavy bombing by the Luftwaffe, desperately short of the dollars needed to pay for imports. A weak and ill Keynes was sent to negotiate a loan; his last act in the service of his country.

Almost $4 billion was borrowed on terms the Americans regarded as generous (2 per cent for fifty years), but the loan was conditional on clauses designed to break down British trade barriers, including a requirement to make sterling convertible again. When the British tried to live up to this provision in 1947, the experiment lasted just seven weeks. The British economy and financial position were just too weak.

There followed a long period of austerity in Britain, in which the post-war Labour government, desperate to conserve dollars for essential goods, imposed rationing on an even wider scale than had been seen in the war. A further problem was that British wartime spending had caused many countries to accumulate sterling, which they were eager to get rid of, and not that eager to spend on British goods.

Continental Europe was facing a similar problem. Each country needed to buy goods from outside the region, and needed dollars to pay for them. This discouraged them from 'wasting' dollars on trade with their neighbours. Marshall Aid, named after Truman's Secretary of State George Marshall, proved vital in solving the problem. The plan, which offered $13 billion of aid to Western Europe, is still seen as an example of enlightened self-interest. By allowing European countries to recover, it created vast markets for US exports and prevented many countries from descending into communism.

The Bretton Woods era is still seen by many people as an extraordinary success. This was undoubtedly true of continental Europe, which recovered remarkably quickly from the worst efforts of Hitler. In Germany, there was the *Wirtschaftswunder*, or economic miracle, in the western part of the country. In France, they talk of *les trente glorieuses*, or glorious thirty years. In each case, the old laissez-faire model appeared to have been proved wrong. Europeans could use economic management to enjoy a high standard of living, low unemployment and generous social benefits.

The picture was slightly different in the English-speaking economies of America and Britain. The US certainly enjoyed a post-war boom and the 1950s are still seen by some as a kind of golden age. But the US still had a lower level of state spending than Europe and perceived its success as due to its rugged individualism. This created a crucial difference in attitude when the system broke down in the 1970s.

In Britain, the post-war period was perceived to be a long, slow period of relative national decline, marked by the loss of empire and relegation into the economic second division. There was a mid-1950s boom, but the 1960s were marked by 'stop-go' economics as governments tried to stimulate growth only to run into inflationary constraints. The whole period was marked by the constant industrial disputes that caused Britain to be dubbed 'the sick man of Europe'.

For their different reasons, when the Bretton Woods system did break down, Britain and America were far more ready to adopt monetarist and free-market ideas than the Europeans, for whom the social model appeared to be working.

THE DOLLAR'S ROLE

As the centrepiece of the Bretton Woods system, the dollar was literally as good as gold. This dominance was natural, given that the US economy was even more important than it had been after the First World War, and that the US owned the bulk of the world's gold reserves.

In the absence of gold, other central banks naturally used the dollar as the basis for their own foreign exchange reserves. But how were they to get dollars? Immediately after the war, there was much talk of a 'dollar shortage', with European countries lacking the money to buy vital goods from the US. Over the long run, the answer was for European countries to run trade surpluses with the US, which would allow them to get dollars in exchange for exports. In turn, however, this required the US to allow its trade position to deteriorate.

The French complained that when the US ran a trade deficit, exporting countries ended up lending the dollars back to America. The system thus lacked discipline, and as the economist Jacques Rueff said, 'If I had an agreement with my tailor that whatever money I pay him, he returns to me the very same day as a loan, I would have no objection at all to ordering more suits from him.'[8] The French regarded this as an 'exorbitant privilege' granted America, which could print money and receive goods in exchange. This process also created a long-term problem for the Bretton Woods system. The system required foreign countries to have faith in the dollar but it also required the US to print dollars, behaviour that weakened their faith. This became known as the Triffin paradox after the economist Robert Triffin published a book on the problem in 1960.[9]

Another way of looking at this privilege was that the US benefited from seignorage, printing dollars at virtually no cost which it could use to buy goods from overseas. This privilege did come at a price, however. The US was required to run a policy that was credible enough to support the monetary system. It was required in a sense to be the designated driver, staying off the Keynesian booze.

But the US trade position steadily weakened. In 1946, US exports were double its imports, thanks to the total devastation of European industry. But over the next twenty-five years, the country's imports rose ninefold in value while its exports increased only fourfold.[10] In 1971, the US ran its first trade deficit in goods in the twentieth century. This was hardly a disaster. Thanks to its long period of economic dominance, the US still had a substantial income from overseas assets, totalling $36 billion in 1983. This kept the current account in surplus.

However, the European nations were losing the confidence required to maintain the dollar link. By the 1960s, US debts to foreign central banks exceeded the value of its gold stock.[11] The Europeans felt that the US should tailor its economic and financial policies to the requirements of the Bretton Woods system. That would require American politicians to subordinate domestic policies to international needs. But US presidents had to cope not only with public opinion, but with the demands of two separate houses of Congress. Lyndon Johnson, President from 1963 to 1969, was pursuing his 'Great Society' reforms at the same time as financing the Vietnam War. Government spending soared. Johnson had no desire to adopt the kind of austerity policies – raising taxes or interest rates – that might have addressed the budget deficit. The complaints of European politicians were drowned out.

The build-up of dollars in Europe led to the development of the so-called Eurodollar market, where dollars were lent and borrowed offshore. This was an immensely important development in financial history since it created a financial market outside the control of governments. Capital controls had been imposed in the Bretton Woods system, but rules governing the finance of trade flows were relaxed in 1958. European exporters to the US could build up dollar balances.

The Eurodollar market flourished as a result of various US regulations, including the Interest Equalization Tax, which restricted the scale of borrowing in New York. Borrowers found it attractive to tap the pool of European capital, particularly in the form of fixed income issues known as Eurobonds. Investors were happy to buy the issues, particularly as interest was paid tax-free. Of course, bond buyers were supposed to declare the tax received but many did not. The archetypal Eurobond investor was deemed to be the Belgian dentist, attempting to escape his home country's high taxes.

London quickly became the centre for the Eurobond market as it had the legal expertise, a welcoming regulatory regime, the English language and was deemed to be a place where American bankers were happy to settle. This allowed the City of London to rise above the long-term economic decline of Britain and establish itself as one of the world's great financial centres, a development that is still significant today.

The development of the Eurobond market was also an early sign of the international flows of capital that were eventually to help bring down the Bretton Woods system. Money was being transferred across borders and between currencies, and that meant it could switch out of currencies about which investors had doubts. After years of government control, the capital markets were slowly asserting their independence. Bretton Woods survived for just thirteen years after the first easing of capital flows.

However, governments played a bigger part in the killing of Bretton Woods than the private sector. Charles de Gaulle, the French President, had enjoyed an uneasy relationship with the American authorities during the Second World War; President Roosevelt had repeatedly attempted to sideline him in favour of less prickly generals. De Gaulle resented America's post-war leadership, particularly after the 1956 Suez episode when Anglo-French intervention in the Middle East was cut short by US financial pressure on Britain. In 1966, France pulled its troops out of the NATO military command.

The French retained an attachment to gold which arguably dated all the way back to John Law's failed monetary experiment. They had been, with America, one of the two big central-bank holders of gold between the wars and had even sent their bullion hoard overseas to keep it out of the hands of the invading Germans in 1940. Once de Gaulle took office in 1958, the French started building their gold holdings again, acquiring 400 tonnes each year up until 1966.

The link between the price of gold and the dollar meant that any rise in the former was the equivalent to a devaluation of the latter, a step the Americans were not prepared to take. So the US organized (with other countries such as Britain and Germany) a scheme known as the 'gold pool' that would keep the bullion price at $35 an ounce. France was nominally supportive of this scheme, but its continued gold purchases (which, other things being equal, pushed the price of gold higher) suggested the opposite. The French withdrew from the gold pool in 1967 and started to convert their dollars into bullion.

French choices were limited. They were in the position of depositors in a bank that they feared might fail. They did not believe US policy was sustainable, and if the US did devalue the dollar against gold, the French would lose money on their dollar reserves. They may have hoped that swapping gold for dollars would force the US to change policy. If so, they were not the first to overestimate the willingness of the US to subordinate domestic priorities to international obligations.

Pressure was slow to build. The US trade deficit was not that bad, nor was its inflation record. Between 1960 and 1967, US inflation averaged just 1.7 per cent. But foreign countries lacked confidence in the commitment of the US to monetary stability. They spent much of the 1950s and 1960s building up their gold reserves, a sign that the belief in commodity money had not been eradicated. Filippo Cesarino writes that 'central banks did not see Bretton Woods as a pure dollar standard but rather as a system hinged on the dollar's convertibility into gold. The steady expansion of official dollar holdings while the US gold stock declined was thus viewed as a fatal flaw.'[12]

The late 1960s was a period of increasing political and economic difficulty. In France itself, street protests in 1968 by the *soixante-huitards* led to the eventual resignation of de Gaulle and to speculation against the franc. The French suffered the humiliation of a franc devaluation in August 1969, after the Germans initially refused the option of a second revaluation (the Germans eventually did revalue the mark in October). In America, anti-Vietnam protests and racial strife caused a marked increase in tension, culminating in the assassinations of Robert Kennedy and Martin Luther King in 1968. In Britain, after years of stop–go economics, the Labour government under Harold Wilson was forced to devalue sterling in 1967. Inflation was also generally rising over the period as governments pursued fiscal policies that promoted expansion, and central banks (with some exceptions such as the Bundesbank) did not counter loose fiscal policy with tighter monetary policy.

The Bretton Woods system had worked very well for more than twenty years, delivering economic growth with low unemployment. Arguably, however, fixed exchange rates only played a limited part in this performance, since economies had a strong tailwind as they recovered from the destruction of the Second World War, and by the late 1960s the strains were beginning to tell. American dominance of the global economy was no longer so complete. European economies had rebounded, as had Japan's, and some of the post-war recovery had surely been driven by the need to replace the capital destroyed in the conflict and by the boost to productivity resulting from the return of soldiers to the workforce. Trade volumes improved too as the inter-war restrictions were loosened, although the Communist bloc was effectively excluded from the post-war system.

In addition, the system had not been as flexible as Keynes would have hoped. He expected that currencies would adjust occasionally in response to economic circumstances. In fact, devaluations were very rare. Governments saw devaluations as a national humiliation and strived hard to avoid them. But this rigidity built up long-term pressure on the system.

THE DEATH THROES

US gold reserves steadily declined. The only way to restore them was to push up interest rates to attract capital, a step that might have induced a recession. The crisis broke in August 1971. The president of the New York branch of the Federal Reserve wrote to Arthur Burns, its national chairman, and warned that, 'Confidence in the dollar has now become so badly eroded as to threaten a breakdown of the entire international financial system within a matter of weeks if not days.' Sure enough, within four days President Nixon had suspended the convertibility of gold, accompanying the move with a 10 per cent surcharge on imports – a blatant attempt to force other countries to revalue their currencies. The Bretton Woods system was over.

It could be argued that Bretton Woods was doomed by the attempt to combine fixed exchange rates with a full employment policy. Arguably these two aims were not compatible for all countries all the time. The switch to floating exchange rates in the 1970s was followed by much higher rates of unemployment than had occurred under Bretton Woods, and the monetarists were accused of being callous about the plight of the unemployed because of their obsession with inflation.

Another problem was that the system was insufficiently flexible. It was devised at a time when the US was dominant economically, politically and militarily; only the intellectual reputation of Keynes prevented the system from being completely designed in Washington. But by the early 1970s, Germany, France and Japan had rebuilt their war-ravaged economies and were challenging the US in global markets. The dollar had become overvalued but because the system was built on the US currency, a devaluation of the anchor currency was fatal.

Nixon's tariff hike of 1971 created some disturbing parallels with the 1930s. What if the Europeans had responded with tariff increases of their own? However, an agreement was patched together at the Smithsonian Institution in Washington in December. The dollar devalued against gold to $38 an ounce (from $35) and the import surcharge was dropped. The major currencies would now float against each other, albeit within tightly defined bands.

However, this was only a temporary solution. There is little difference in practice between managing a fixed exchange rate and maintaining a currency within a narrow band. In both cases, governments have to subordinate domestic policy to the exchange rate. The Americans weren't prepared to do this in 1972, an election year. The currency bands simply gave speculators a target to aim at. By 1973, the Smithsonian agreement had fallen apart.

It was an historic moment. Gold coins had long gone, except for collectors. Note issuance was no longer tied to a set level of gold reserves. Now the last formal link between the world's money and gold had disappeared. Paper money prevailed. Without a gold anchor, and without full capital controls, fixed exchange rates were not really feasible. Governments preferred the freedom to govern their own economies as they saw fit, using both monetary and fiscal policies to support demand.

As we shall see in the next few chapters, governments and central banks overdid it, a process that culminated in the debt crisis of 2007 and 2008.

6

Paper Promises

'Only government can take perfectly good paper, cover it with perfectly good ink and make the combination worthless.'
Milton Friedman

With the demise of Bretton Woods, money was free of its link to gold, the 'barbarous relic' as Keynes had described it. In the ancient battle between creditors and debtors, this was a victory for the latter and, as we shall see in the next chapter, it led to an explosion in the amount of debt. In the battle to define money, it was also a victory for those who believed its primary function was as a medium of exchange, not as a store of value. Paper money has no intrinsic value. A contemporary of John Law might have expected the whole system to last a few years at most. Instead, it has lasted forty.

The 1970s were a very turbulent decade. Apart from the abandonment of Bretton Woods, it also saw a battle between two very different visions of how economic policy should be run: Keynesianism and monetarism.

The hold of Keynesianism was hard to shake. During the Great Depression of the 1930s, orthodox (or classical) economists argued that the economy would eventually right itself. Unemployment was the result of an excessive price for labour: if wages were allowed to fall, workers would be priced back into jobs. Governments should balance the budget and not interfere with the market-clearing process, since any budget deficit would simply 'crowd out' private-sector spending.

But the long period of stagnation, and the massed ranks of unemployed, undermined the classical economists' case. Keynes offered a reasoned rebuttal. A recession was caused by a shortfall in demand, or to put it another way, an excess of saving (income can only be spent or saved). This led to the 'paradox of thrift'. The decision to save might make sense at the individual level but proved to be disastrous at the aggregate level at a time when business confidence was weak. Money saved by a consumer is money not spent on goods and services. The lack of demand for goods and services causes companies to lay off workers. The resulting rise in unemployment makes consumers more anxious and thus eager to save. But in aggregate they have lower incomes because they have lost their jobs. The paradox is that the attempt to save more is self-defeating.

As a result, the economy might become stuck in recession for years. To avoid this problem, Keynes argued that the government should become the spender of last resort. It could borrow money and spend the proceeds on building roads, dams, etc.; the workers thereby employed would spend their wages at local shops. This initial burst of spending would be multiplied as it rippled through the economy. As the economy grew, tax revenues would rise and social spending (on things like unemployment benefits) would fall, meaning that the budget would eventually return to balance.

From the 1940s to the mid-1970s, Keynesian economics held sway. Governments attempted to fine-tune their economies by increasing spending in the face of recession. Whether Keynes would have approved of what was done in his name is a difficult question. His remedy was devised for the Great Depression, when the economy appeared to be stuck. It is not clear he thought that governments should attempt to abolish the business cycle altogether. He argued that governments should build up surpluses in good years, like the biblical Joseph, to give them scope to run deficits in bad years.

By the end of the 1960s, as we saw in Chapter 5, the flaws in the system started to become apparent. Inflation seemed to be creeping remorselessly higher with each cycle, and it became a serious problem throughout the developed world in the 1970s. In the US, President Gerald Ford launched a Whip Inflation Now (WIN) campaign in 1974, while inflation in Britain reached 26 per cent shortly afterwards. Something had gone wrong with economic policy.

THE RISE OF THE MONETARISTS

The Keynesian consensus came under challenge in the 1970s on three grounds. First, critics argued that the Great Depression should have been attacked with monetary rather than fiscal policy. Milton Friedman said that the US Federal Reserve allowed the money supply to contract sharply in the early 1930s, as hundreds of banks failed. This would have caused a contraction in activity regardless of whether the government had balanced the budget.

Secondly, Friedman and his fellow economists at the University of Chicago argued that the use of fiscal policy to stimulate the economy was eventually doomed to failure. Money spent by the government is either raised by taxes, or it is borrowed. In either case, the money has to be taken (or borrowed) from a person or company in the private sector, leaving them less money to spend or lend. Indeed, even if the government borrows money and gives it to the private sector (via tax cuts), rational individuals will figure out that the inevitable consequence of a large deficit now will be higher taxes in future. So they will save, rather than spend, the resulting handout.

The third issue was the supposed trade-off between inflation and unemployment. In the 1950s and 1960s, the Keynesians argued that inflation tended to fall as unemployment rose, and vice versa. Since unemployment was an unalloyed evil, a bit of inflation was a price worth paying to keep unemployment down. Friedman, however, argued that this process was self-defeating. Workers would eventually demand higher wages in compensation for higher prices. The revenues of companies would go up, but so would their costs. They would have no more incentive to employ any more workers.

Politicians eventually agreed. In 1976, Jim Callaghan, the British Prime Minister, proclaimed at the Labour party conference that:

We used to think that you could spend your way out of a recession and increase employment by cutting taxes and boosting government spending. I tell you in all candour that that option no longer exists, and in so far as it ever did exist, it only worked on each occasion since the war by injecting a bigger dose of inflation into the economy, followed by a higher level of unemployment as the next step.

The first duty of governments (and central banks), in Friedman's view, was to keep inflation down by controlling the money supply. 'Inflation is always and everywhere a monetary phenomenon,' he said.[1] Just as the New World discoveries of silver had pushed up prices in the sixteenth century, the printing of paper money did so in the twentieth. Fiscal policy would have no effect on unemployment, according to the monetarists. The answer, instead, was to improve the workings of the economy by making it easier for employers to hire and fire labour. These so-called 'supply side' reforms would improve productivity.

By the early 1980s, with Margaret Thatcher in power in Britain and Ronald Reagan in America, Friedman's influence was at its peak. The government role in the economy was to control inflation and to ensure the rule of law and property rights. Otherwise, markets should be given free rein to allocate resources, which they would inevitably do in a more efficient way than bureaucrats. The Chicago school also argued that lower taxes would result in a 'supply-side boost' to economic activity, as businessmen and workers were given incentives to work harder.

The same critics argued that the government had interfered too much in the private sector by nationalizing industries and raising taxes. Economic growth would improve if regulations were reduced and taxes cut. This was the birth of the neo-liberal school of economics. Both Mrs Thatcher and President Reagan saw it as their job to face down the union power that had resulted in a wave of industrial strikes in the 1970s. Trade union membership began its long, slow decline.

Initially the freeing of markets, via the abandonment of exchange controls, helped create some anti-inflationary discipline. Countries that ran large fiscal deficits needed to turn to the markets for their financing; those that combined fiscal deficits with trade deficits needed to rely on international investors. In theory, investors could punish irresponsible governments by pushing up interest rates. Indeed, that is what happened in the 1980s when real interest rates were very high, as investors reacted to their losses of the 1970s. The 'bond market vigilantes' would keep errant governments in line, and head off an inflationary rebound.

By itself, this was a crucial difference from the Bretton Woods era. Capital controls meant that, until the late 1960s, the markets played a limited role in disciplining governments. Instead, the key role was played by trade.

An alternative explanation for the lack of high inflation relates to the advantage that can be gained by countries from having their money widely accepted. Competition prevents countries from debasing their currencies, since the miscreants would be replaced by harder currencies like the dollar or yen. Thus, central banks also played a different role after the break-up of Bretton Woods. In the absence of an exchange-rate target, they no longer had the role of defending the external value of the currency (in the developed world at least). But they did become responsible for safeguarding the *internal* value of the currency, via inflation targets. The first formal adoption of an inflation target was by New Zealand, and other central banks followed suit. (In the US, the Federal Reserve targets no particular inflation rate but has a mandate to ensure price stability.)

POLICY IN A WORLD OF FLOATING RATES

The era of floating exchange rates, ushered in by the collapse of the Bretton Woods system, brought a whole new challenge for the global economy. In one sense, it was a relief. Governments did not have to devote time and resources to defending a particular currency level. They could give other economic issues, like unemployment and growth, more priority. On the other hand, letting an exchange rate float also involved a loss of control. No longer could the government or central bank dictate what the exchange rate should be. Now it was down to the markets. But how would the markets determine the exchange rate? Would they be rational, as monetarists like Milton Friedman assumed? Or would they overshoot, leaving governments to cope with the side-effects of over- or undervalued currencies?

It was a tricky business on all sides. Once the link with gold was broken, what faith could creditors and traders place in a paper currency? The natural assumption was that pre-1971 trends would continue, and that strong currencies like the Deutschmark and Japanese yen would continue to be strong. However, plenty of countries had no track record of anti-inflationary success with which to impress sceptical investors. Many developing nations accordingly tried to continue the Bretton Woods system by other means, by pegging their currency to the US dollar. In effect, they were piggybacking on the perceived strength of the world's dominant economy. The tricky bit was convincing the markets that the peg could be maintained.

Fixed exchange rates after 1971 were often adopted as a way of importing the anti-inflationary credibility of another country. The classic example was Europe, where France and others traded off the stability of the Deutschmark. Another example was Argentina, where the country went even further than pegging the exchange rate. In the 1990s, it adopted a currency board, in which the amount of domestic currency was tied to the country's dollar reserves. It was like a gold standard, but with the dollar taking the place of gold.

The idea behind the board was that inflation is a psychological phenomenon. If workers expect inflation to be 10 per cent, they will demand 10 per cent wage increases. That will push up the costs of businesses, forcing companies to increase prices. So the expectation of high inflation will by itself create inflation. In contrast, if workers expect the central bank to control inflation because of a need to maintain a currency peg, they will demand less in the way of wage increases. And that will reduce the cost pressures on businesses.

The problem with such pegs, however, is the same one that confronted countries during the gold standard era. There may be occasions when one has to choose between maintaining the peg and avoiding a recession in the domestic economy. It needs a remarkable degree of political consensus to stick to a currency system, whose benefits can seem nebulous, when millions of jobs are at stake. Argentina failed to maintain the fiscal discipline needed to keep investors convinced that the peg would be maintained. As a result its currency board ended in failure and default on its government bonds in 2001.

A MIXED SYSTEM

Economists tend to refer to the post-1971 era as a world of floating rates. That was only true of the big currencies – the dollar, Deutschmark and yen; these traded fairly freely against each other. But the swings in these rates were much greater than most people would have anticipated in 1971. Broadly speaking, the dollar has weakened against the other two. It took 358 yen, for example, to buy one dollar in 1971; by mid-2011, it took just 80. The trade was not all one way. In some periods, such as the early 1980s, the dollar was strong. Indeed, governments agreed the Plaza accord in 1985 in an attempt to let the dollar depreciate and the yen and Deutschmark rise. It succeeded so well that another agreement – the Louvre accord – had to be cobbled together to stop the dollar from falling too far.

Economists have struggled to explain, and predict, these vast swings in currencies. By and large, exchange-rate movements seem to have been driven by three factors – trade, inflation and interest-rate differentials. But at different times in the last forty years, different factors have been in the ascendancy.

The trade explanation dates back to the gold standard days. Countries with deficits would seem likely to see their currency fall; those with surpluses would see their currency rise. When the US had a deficit, foreign merchants would accumulate dollars. They would eventually become nervous about the risks of holding so much of another currency; when they offloaded the surplus, the dollar would fall. So, instead of trading patterns adjusting to suit the exchange rate, as happened with the gold standard, the exchange rate would change to suit the trade. If a country's goods were uncompetitive, its exchange rate would decline until they became cheaper, and thus more attractive to foreign buyers. Eventually, the imbalance would correct itself in a mechanism rather similar to that envisaged under the gold standard.

What has been remarkable about the last forty years, however, is that the adjustment has not occurred. Some countries have been almost permanently in deficit; others in surplus. The US was just edging into trade deficit when Bretton Woods collapsed but it still had the advantage of the assets accumulated during the long period of post-war US strength. But by 1985, foreigners had more claims on the US than America had overseas, and by the end of the 1990s, the US was suffering a deficit on the investment-income account.[2] By this stage, America had turned from the world's biggest creditor into its biggest debtor.

Under the gold standard, the US would have run out of reserves after many years of deficits. But trade was no longer the driving factor behind exchange-rate movements. Post-1971, trade flows were overwhelmed by the decisions of international investors as they shifted money between currencies.

In the twenty-first century, currency policy has become tied up with the whole issue of global imbalances. After the Asian economic crisis of 1997–98, many developing countries followed an export-led model, aimed at trade surpluses. Their goal was to avoid the dependence on foreign capital that precipitated the crisis, and they proved extraordinarily successful. Indeed, their reserves now far exceed their plausible needs for exchange-rate protection.

To the extent that some countries run surpluses, others must run deficits, and the biggest shortfall was in the US. For a decade, there has been much debate about who was responsible for this imbalance. Was it profligate Americans, spending more than they earn? Or was it sinister Chinese, manipulating their currency? Chinese labour costs were so low that, once the country joined the global trading system, it quickly grabbed market share in low-cost manufactured goods. Americans routinely complain that everything they buy seems to be made in China. Manufacturing employment in China surged. The result was one of the biggest migrations in history as rural workers moved to the big cities.

Much of the rest of the world may have abandoned the Bretton Woods approach but China did not. The Chinese Communist party had no intention of letting their interest or exchange rates be controlled by the markets; they opted for capital controls and a managed currency, pegged to the dollar. The corollary of this policy was that they accumulated a massive current-account surplus which (being China) the government controlled. These foreign-exchange reserves were then held in Treasury bonds and bills, making it easier for the US to finance its trade deficit.

In his book *Fixing Global Finance*, *Financial Times* columnist

Martin Wolf argues convincingly that the 'savings glut' of China and others was more responsible for the imbalance than American profligacy.[3] His argument is that a low level of real interest rates indicated an excess of desired saving over investment. The Chinese (ironically for a communist state) did not provide much in the way of pensions, so their citizens saved to cover their old age; the Japanese had little desire to spend or invest because of their sluggish economy. These savings naturally ended up in the US government bond market, the most liquid in the world, and reduced the cost of US borrowing. Cheap borrowing in turn encouraged Americans to go on a speculative and spending binge.

Whatever the reason, the size of the US trade deficit no longer seemed the main force in driving short-term movements of the dollar. The US could run repeated deficits without triggering the kind of crisis that would have occurred under Bretton Woods.

Inflation

For investors, it makes sense for inflation to be a determining factor in currency markets. Inflation reduces the purchasing power of a currency; so investors should avoid currencies with high inflation rates. Roughly speaking, economists think that, over the long run, exchange rates will move in line with relative inflation rates, a concept known as purchasing-power parity (PPP). If country A's inflation rate was 5 per cent higher than that of country B, its currency would decline by around 5 per cent a year.

It has never worked quite as simply as that. At the extremes, PPP proved roughly right. Countries with very high inflation, such as several in Latin America in the 1970s and 80s, did see their exchange rates decline significantly. But for the main currencies, the dollar, yen, Deutschmark or sterling, relative inflation rates were often a very poor guide to exchange-rate movements.

In part, this was a definitional problem. The theory of PPP is that trade flows will drive currency movements, that the dollar will have to decline if American car prices get too high and Japan steals market share. But a lot of goods are not traded. This is particularly true of services. You might opt to buy a Japanese TV or mobile phone on price, but you will not go to Japan to get a cheap haircut. The indices that measure inflation include very wide ranges of goods and services, many of which will have no bearing on international competitiveness.

But even when economists looked at more specialized measures of inflation, such as producer prices, they found that exchange rates in the floating era could spend long periods being cheap or dear on a PPP basis. *The Economist* publishes a 'big Mac index' which compares the cost of burgers in different parts of the world; often, the comparison makes some currencies look very cheap or very expensive.

In short, when one looks at the economic fundamentals, trade deficits and relative prices, modern currencies can depart from 'fair value' for prolonged periods. Clearly economic fundamentals are not the only factors that determine currency movements.

Yield

Most of the trading in foreign exchange markets these days is not related to the exchange of goods and services, but to the flow of capital round the world. From the early 1980s, almost all restrictions on capital flows in the US and Europe were lifted.

Investors will choose to buy a currency for a number of reasons. In some cases, the choice may be incidental; investors in, say, Google are expressing a confidence in the growth prospects for the search engine company rather than belief in the relative merits of the dollar. And when investors buy the government bonds of another country, their primary motivation may be the soundness of the government's finances, rather than the likely exchange-rate movement.

For those who are depositing money in a foreign bank, or investing very short term, the level of interest rates is likely to be the primary consideration. In the early days of floating exchange rates, low interest rates were associated with strong currencies, and high interest rates with weak ones. That was because high interest rates were usually needed to cope with high inflation and, on a PPP basis, one would expect high inflation currencies to depreciate. The high interest rates were thus needed to compensate investors for the risk of depreciation.

By the late 1990s and early 2000s, the relationship had flipped round, perhaps because inflation was less of a global problem. High interest rates were associated with strong currencies; the extra yield lured in investors. Experience had taught such speculators that the increased yield more than compensated for the risk of depreciation. Indeed, they would borrow money in a low-yielding currency and then invest the proceeds in a higher-yielding one, a tactic known as 'the carry trade'. The carry trade was self-reinforcing since by its nature it drove low-yielding currencies down and pushed high-yielding currencies up.

There is even an index that replicates this strategy, devised by Neil Record, and launched as the FTSE Currency Forward Rate Bias Index. It uses five currencies – the dollar, euro, yen, pound and Swiss franc. Each currency is compared with each other, a total of ten pairs. Every month the higher-yielding of the pair is bought against the lower. In the thirty years to the end of 2009, this strategy generated a positive return in every year bar three, one each in the 1980s, 1990s and 2000s.

The carry trade was not necessarily good news for businesses. Instead of becoming more competitive, the exports of countries favoured by carry traders became less so. At the same time, the funding costs of those same exporters were being driven up by high interest rates. Individuals and businesses in the countries concerned would often be tempted into their own version of the carry trade, borrowing in foreign currencies, such as the Swiss franc, at lower interest rates. This created a clear mismatch; their assets were in one currency, while their liabilities were in another.

The whole process involved some risks. The country's banks would attract 'hot money' from speculators figuring they would take advantage of the high yields and take their profits before the currency eventually devalued. This led to a mad rush for the exit when the currency first started to weaken. The resulting depreciation caused financial ruin for those domestic businesses that had borrowed in foreign currencies, as the cost of repaying their loans suddenly shot up. Worse still, the hot money would usually lead to a speculative boom in the economy. Foreign money would be deposited in the banking system; the banks would then seek to make a profit by lending those deposits. Often, the money would be channelled into a domestic property boom.

The two clearest examples of this spiral are the Asian boom of the mid-1990s, in particular that of Thailand, and the Icelandic bubble of the 2000s. In both cases, hot money was attracted by high interest rates, encouraging a speculative boom in property. Thailand actually tried to peg its currency to the US dollar; all this achieved was to give false comfort to Thai businesses borrowing in foreign currencies. They thought their exchange-rate risk was limited.

Both crashes were disastrous. As sentiment turned in the face of a rising trade deficit, the Thai authorities used their reserves to defend the dollar peg. It might have seemed that the answer was to accept the inevitable and devalue the Thai currency, the baht. However, the authorities resisted the step for the obvious reason that, since so many Thai businesses had borrowed in foreign currency, a devaluation might bankrupt them by increasing the cost of repaying their debts. In the end, the Thais got the worst of all worlds: they lost their reserves, had to devalue anyway, and crippled their banking system in the process.

The Thai crisis sapped confidence in the economies of other Asian nations and 1997–98 was a period of plunging crises, failed banks and recessions. Some countries were forced to turn to the IMF for assistance – a humiliation summed up in a picture of President Suharto of Indonesia signing a loan agreement in 1998, under the headmasterly eye of IMF officials. It was a determination to avoid a repeat of those events that led Asian nations to pursue their export-led policies in the 2000s; one of the factors that led to the credit crunch.

Iceland's was an even more incredible story. A country of just 300,000 people on a remote island in the North Atlantic, best known for its fishing grounds and volcanoes, suddenly became a global financial power house. The carry trade led to an influx of capital in the 2000s; a strong currency allowed its entrepreneurs to go on a shopping spree for European businesses (including the West Ham football team and Hamleys toyshop, London's equivalent of FAO Schwarz in New York). Its high interest rates also persuaded domestic fishermen to pay high prices for houses, in mortgages denominated in Swiss franc and yen. The country's banks, hitherto obscure, expanded rapidly; Icesave, the savings brand of Landsbanki, became one of the most popular homes for British nest eggs thanks to its relatively high interest rates. At one point, the banking assets of Iceland were ten times its GDP. Again, the collapse was inevitable; the country's currency, the krona, fell sharply and the banks had to be nationalized.

The result was a nasty dispute between Iceland and Britain over how to compensate British savers who had accounts with Icesave. In theory, they were covered by the deposit insurance scheme of Iceland, under a European passport system. The rights and wrongs of the issue are too complex to worry about here. What is important, however, is to consider how absurd it was for anyone to think such a scheme could be adequate. Britain and the US both have deposit insurance schemes, in theory financed by the banks themselves. In extremis, the central bank can always create the pounds or dollars needed. But how can one country insure another's deposits? The Icelandic central bank can print krona, not sterling or euros. Even if it did print a lot of krona – in order to buy sterling with the proceeds – it would probably fail, because the krona would decline in value as fast as it was printed. It would be the equivalent of handing out monopoly money.

What lesson can be taken from the booms and busts of Thailand and Iceland? It is not just about exchange rates; after all, the Thais fixed their rate and the Icelanders let it float. But neither boom would have happened under Bretton Woods because the size of trade deficits, and the scale of capital flows, would not have been allowed.

In both cases, the core issue was hot or short-term money, which causes damage as it flows into an economy and then again when it cascades out. Free-market economists have argued that there should be no restrictions on capital movements as they allow money to be invested in the most profitable projects worldwide, and thus help the economy operate more efficiently. But it seems clear that countries are much better off if they attract what is known as foreign direct investment (factories, call centres and the like) rather than bank deposits. By its nature, such direct investment is far more likely to be long-lasting; having made all the effort of setting up a factory, a company is likely to think carefully before closing it down.

EXCHANGE-RATE CHOICES

Earlier chapters have recounted the long struggle by countries to maintain fixed exchange rates and the crises that occurred when they failed to do so. But what is the economic impact of exchange-rate moves?

When a nation's currency falls, its exporters have a choice. They can cut the price at which they sell abroad, in which case they can expect to gain market share. Or they can keep the price constant in foreign currency terms and earn a higher profit.

Say it costs BMW €20,000 to make a car, which sells for $40,000 in the US. At an exchange rate of 1.5 dollars to the euro, its sale proceeds will be €26,666, a 33 per cent profit margin. If the euro falls to 1.2 dollars, and BMW maintains the dollar price, then the proceeds of each sale will be €33,333, a 66 per cent profit margin. Alternatively, it could cut the price to $32,000 and sell more cars at the same profit margin. Either way, it gains.

But to the extent that the exporters gain, importers lose. Commodities are priced in dollars. For countries that import raw materials, this means that any fall in their currency against the dollar increases their costs. If the fall is big enough, this can lead to a rise in inflation. If workers respond by increasing their wage demands, then the cost advantage gained by exporters can quickly erode.

Similarly tourists lose from their home currency's depreciation. Britons who visited America in 2006 found that their pounds went a long way, being worth two dollars each at the time. Given that most prices seemed to be roughly the same in pound and dollar terms, the effect was a 50 per cent discount for British travellers. The subsequent fall to below $1.50 reduced the attraction, while the decline of the pound against the euro made continental Europe seem distinctly expensive for British visitors.

At its simplest, a fall in a nation's currency represents a fall in its standard of living; the citizen's money will go less far. Of course, this is not how governments tend to sell a devaluation or depreciation. British Prime Minister Harold Wilson's response to the 1967 sterling devaluation, paraphrased as 'This will not affect the pound in your pocket', is a classic example of the genre.

From the late 1960s to the early 1990s, Britain's record was one of a long cycle of inflation and devaluation, which the country found hard to escape. Inflation made its goods uncompetitive, so governments were forced into devaluation to improve competitiveness. But, by pushing up import prices, they only increased the inflationary pressures on the economy.

Nevertheless, devaluation can sometimes work, either when the economy has lots of spare capacity or when deflation is a threat. In the 1930s, Britain was one of the earliest countries to devalue and leave the gold standard. Its economy was quicker to recover than those who stuck with bullion. In 1992, Britain's exit from the Exchange Rate Mechanism allowed the government to cut interest rates from crippling double-digit levels without a significant inflationary aftermath.

Pursuing a mercantilist policy to build up trade surpluses might seem an obvious strategy to build wealth, like a miser hoarding gold. Surplus countries often prosper in the short term. But in the end a surplus country is just like any shopkeeper – very dependent on his customers' ability to pay. The relationship is symbiotic.

In *Vanity Fair*, the Victorian masterpiece of William Makepeace Thackeray, Becky Sharp and her husband, Rawdon Crawley, live entirely off credit, duping merchants into supplying goods on the basis of their supposed wealth. No doubt the merchants recorded sales to the couple as credits in their accounts, but they were being paid with paper (or verbal) promises that the couple had no intention of redeeming. (The Victorians jailed people for unpaid debts precisely to discourage this kind of behaviour.)

Similarly, those countries, such as China, with trade surpluses steadily accumulate claims on debtor nations, often in the form of government bonds. Will those claims be paid in full? If those government bonds are denominated in the debtor's currency, then there is always the option of devaluation. From the creditor's point of view, this is a partial default. Of course, the creditor could insist on being paid in his own currency or in gold, but the cost of this option could push debtors into actual default.

THE EURO

The creation of the euro was an amazing monetary experiment, involving the citizens of eleven countries adopting a new range of notes and coins overnight. Those countries also gave up the right to operate an independent exchange rate, potentially for ever; indeed there is no explicit mechanism for a country to leave the euro-zone. In mechanical terms, the launch of the euro was a great success. In 1999, the various member currencies fixed their conversion rates into the euro. In theory, over the next three years, speculators could have launched an attack on such fixed exchange rates, but they did not. And then in 2002, the old currencies disappeared and the new notes and coins appeared in pay packets and shops. By 2008, there were 15–20 per cent more euro notes in circulation than dollars, and the euro-zone comprised one fifth of global economic output.[4]

It is easy to see the appeal of the single currency; indeed there was an earlier effort in the nineteenth century known as the Latin monetary union, involving France, Italy, Switzerland and Belgium. The primary appeal is that it makes intra-zone trade much easier; the costs and revenues of businesses in different countries are in the same currency. German businesses do not have to worry that, when selling goods to Italy, the lira will fall in value by the time they get paid. Tourists travelling across Europe do not have the hassle or expense of changing currencies every time they cross a border. In theory, it should be easy for consumers to compare prices across the continent and buy the cheapest (in practice, bureaucratic barriers make this more awkward than it ought to be).

A single currency area has made it easier for companies to raise finance. Investors are far happier holding the euro, a liquid currency used by several hundred million people, than they were holding the hotchpotch of small national currencies. This should have lowered the cost of capital for European businesses, although that is hard to prove given all the other economic developments which have occurred since the euro was created.

The third motive was to strike a blow against international finance. In the aftermath of the Bretton Woods collapse, European countries made a number of attempts to set up managed exchange-rate systems. The first, known as the snake, was launched alongside the Smithsonian agreement of 1971, and allowed currencies to float in a narrow band. Even Britain joined this system, although not for long.

The snake faced a fundamental problem, one that also dogged its successor, the European Monetary System (EMS). Currencies were most likely to trade within a tight range if the economic conditions of their host countries were closely linked. But that was not true in

Europe, where inflation rates (and the attitudes of central banks) were sharply different. International investors naturally preferred to own the Deutschmark than the French franc or Italian lira and this put repeated strains on the currency bands.

One answer would have been to adjust economic policy so as to eliminate the difference with other countries. But European nations, like the US under Bretton Woods, wanted both to run expansionary policies and to have stable currencies. A classic example was the Mitterrand government that took office in France in 1981 on a left-wing platform. The markets soon forced the President to change course.

There was an underlying hope, frequently expressed in European capitals, that exchange-rate links would allow the inflation-prone countries to 'import' the sound-money approach of the Germans. The system produced occasional stability during booms, but found it impossible to survive recessions.

The EMS fell apart in the early 1990s under the strain of German reunification. Concerned about the cost of subsidizing the impoverished former East Germany, the Bundesbank raised interest rates. Other countries were forced to follow suit to keep their currencies within the system's bands, which were wider than those prevailing under the snake, but not that wide. The result was economic pain for the countries concerned, which effectively had to choose between the exchange-rate target and higher unemployment. Unsurprisingly, countries buckled under the strain, including Britain which had made another ill-fated attempt to join a European currency grouping.

Naturally enough, national governments did not like being overruled by the markets on such a crucial aspect of economic policy. By combining forces to form one giant currency, European countries would no longer be at the market's mercy (or so they thought); they had no particular exchange rate to defend.

The fourth and probably most important factor in the euro's creation was politics. The EMS had been dominated by the Deutschmark, the currency of Europe's largest economy. The result was that the Bundesbank set the tone for European monetary policy, and the Bundesbank had a fierce anti-inflationary bias, reflecting German history. For some countries, particularly France, there was a hope that a new European central bank would reflect a more balanced view of the needs of the continent's economy. In effect, the influence of the Bundesbank would be diluted.

In addition, a single currency was seen as deepening integration within Europe and thus enhancing the drive towards political union. This was why it was a dream of federalists since the 1950s, and was championed by Jacques Delors, a former French Finance Minister and President of the European Commission. For the same reason, the concept was viewed with great suspicion by British politicians.

It was also a geopolitical statement. Europe wanted to be recognized as a great economic power, like America. The US has a single currency which is the most widely accepted in the world. Europe needed its own currency to match.

However, the comparison with the US prompted a lot of debate. Unlike the euro-zone, the US is a single, sovereign nation, with a single language and legal system, allowing businesses and workers the freedom to move from one area to another. This makes it potentially an 'optimal' currency area. If the economy of, say, Mississippi is depressed, workers can head for California in search of a job. Alternatively, the federal government could grant a subsidy out of national taxes to encourage new businesses to move to Mississippi. Voters might be willing to approve this deal since fellow Americans would be reaping the benefits.

Euro enthusiasts could argue that individual US states had the right to raise taxes, and set laws, making them analogous to countries like Belgium and Luxembourg. Furthermore, the European Union did have the capacity to make grants to depressed areas like Northern Ireland. In relative terms, however, the federal government was far more powerful in the US economy than the EU administration was in the euro-zone.

European governments tried to deal with these problems in advance. They recognized that without fiscal (i.e. taxation) union, there was the danger of the currency zone breaking down. In particular, the Germans worried that they would be required to bail out the more spendthrift nations (such as the Italians) who would suddenly have the freedom to borrow in a trans-European currency. Therefore, advance conditions were set for the euro-zone. Countries would only be admitted if their inflation rates and budget deficits were under control, at 3 per cent of GDP or less. The Stability and Growth pact was created to try to keep errant countries in line, with fines for those countries that broke the rules. It was explicitly stated that one EU nation would not be bailed out by the rest, a commitment that would be broken later on.

The warning signs were apparent from the start. First, a rule that said nations would only be admitted if their total debt-to-GDP ratios were less than 60 per cent (or heading towards that level) was effectively ignored. Secondly, it was clear that some countries used dodgy accounting to qualify under the budget deficit criteria, but a blind eye was turned. Thirdly, the markets drove down the borrowing costs of all euro-zone governments down towards the German level.

This convergence trade, as it became known, had largely benign effects at first. By reducing borrowing costs, it improved the budget positions of member governments, making it easier for them to meet the deficit criteria. Lower interest rates could then be sold to voters as a reward for giving up their historic currencies and monetary independence. But convergence was also a sign that, when push came to shove, the markets did not believe the no-bailout clause. They thought governments would have to rescue their neighbours in the end. A lack of fiscal discipline was thus implied from the start.

The initial performance of the euro on the currency markets did not inspire that much confidence either. Far from challenging the dollar as the new global reserve currency, the euro steadily lost value, dropping from around $1.18 as an initial value in 1999 to be worth just 82 cents in October 2000. But those who thought the euro was doomed to early failure were proved wrong. The currency rallied from that low, established itself as a fixture in international trading and as a currency for debt issuance. No countries were forced to quit the euro-zone in its early years, quite the reverse: other nations queued up to join. At the time of writing, seventeen countries are now members, from an initial eleven.

Nevertheless, this short-term success masked some long-term strains. The penalties designed under the Stability and Growth pact were not applied, not least because the big countries like France and Germany also broke the rules. The 'one size fits all' monetary policy led to interest rates that were too low for some countries, creating property booms in both Ireland and Spain.

These booms were part of the bubble process that we shall explore in the next chapter. Low interest rates encouraged asset prices to rise in many countries. They created a feeling of euphoria that may have made economic performance look better than it was by masking underlying problems of competitiveness.

Crucially, the euro area lacked any mechanism to put pressure on countries that were running a trade deficit. Germany joined the euro at what was arguably too high a rate; to restore its competitiveness and keep its export machine going, it endured years of sluggish wage growth. But other countries seemed unwilling to suffer the same level of pain. In particular, the costs of the southern European countries seemed to rise steadily relative to those of Germany.

Under a gold standard, such countries would have seen a drain on their reserves, forcing them to take action (such as raising interest rates) to attract bullion. Under a floating exchange-rate system, such countries would have devalued their exchange rates to make their export prices more competitive. Under an optimal currency area, workers would have moved to high wage areas, like Greece and Italy, and brought labour costs down. But in the euro area, none of those things happened. Slowly but remorselessly, the southern countries became less and less competitive.

The implications were also dire because of the lack of an exit route. As we shall see, countries could not cut costs by devaluing their currency; their only option to restore competitiveness was painful austerity.

The lesson here is that exchange-rate systems can seem like an easy option. However, they do not really solve the problem of uncompetitiveness; at best they postpone it. Fixed-rate systems impose the adjustment on the real economy, workers and businesses, for the benefit of creditors. That seemed too harsh a deal, particularly in a democracy.

After 1971, floating-rate systems appeared to be the answer. But a country that gives into the devaluation option too often under floating rates eventually suffers from higher inflation and interest rates. Creditors extort their revenge over the long term. The Europeans sought to escape this problem by clubbing together in a single currency, but eventually the strains had to show.

7

Blowing Bubbles

'Stock market bubbles don't grow out of thin air. They have a solid basis in reality, but reality as distorted by a misconception.'
George Soros, hedge fund manager

Where did all the money go? My father-in-law asked that question in the aftermath of the credit crunch of 2007 and 2008, when house prices, share prices and corporate bond prices all tumbled. It seemed a reasonable point. If all the assets in the world were worth, say, $3 trillion one year and $2 trillion the next, what happened to that missing trillion?

To explain the answer, we have to turn to the career of Bernie Madoff, a convicted fraudster. Madoff was an American stockbroker who had a prominent role in the finance industry, serving as chairman of the board of directors of the National Association of Securities Dealers. On the side, he ran an investment operation, looking after the funds of clients. He claimed a near-perfect record, hardly ever losing money in a given month, and reporting steady annual returns. Investors clamoured to give him money, even though his investment strategy was never fully explained.

When Madoff's scheme was exposed as a fraud in 2008, the early estimates of the loss were $65 billion, a quite staggering amount. But this was an entirely fictional figure. It was what Madoff had *told* his clients that the accounts were worth. In reality, he had never invested any money at all. Investors did lose what they put into the scheme – somewhere between $10 and $20 billion – but all the declared profits were invented by Madoff. The extra $50 billion hadn't 'gone anywhere'; it had never existed.

The same story can be told of asset prices at the peak of the bubble. One can add up the value of all the shares and all the houses in existence and say that, at current market prices, their total value is several trillion dollars. But it isn't really. All the houses and all the shares could not be sold at that price. Who would have the money to buy them?

An old colleague, asked to explain a rising stock market, would mutter 'more buyers than sellers'. This throwaway line was both right and wrong. Every deal has one buyer and one seller, so the totals are exactly matched. But if there are more *willing* buyers than sellers at any moment, prices will rise. At any given moment, only a small proportion of the total stock of houses and shares are trading. It only takes a small preponderance of willing buyers to push prices higher. And this can happen for quite a while, *provided they don't want to realize their gains.*

In other words, a lot of people can make paper profits out of a bubble, provided they remain on paper. Madoff's clients were all happy as long as they didn't ask for their money back. Once a sufficient number of bubble investors try and spend their gains, the bubble pops. The money hasn't 'gone' anywhere; it was never really there.

Unlike a soap bubble, an asset bubble has lasting effects. As it inflates, behaviour changes. As Jeremy Grantham of the fund management company GMO has written, 'Individuals, as well as institutions, were fooled into believing that the market signals were real, that they truly were rich. They acted accordingly, spending too much or saving too little, all the while receiving less than usual from their overpriced holdings.'[1]

It is not just investors who are fooled. Policymakers can be too. As Carmen Reinhart and Kenneth Rogoff put it, 'Debt-fuelled booms all too often provide false affirmation of a government's policies, a financial institution's ability to make outsized profits or a country's standard of living. Most of these booms end badly.'[2]

FORTY YEARS OF BUBBLES

The last forty years of economic history (since the collapse of Bretton Woods) have been remarkable. Not only have they seen an explosion in debt and in money creation, unprecedented swings in exchange rates and the massive growth of the financial sector. They have also seen some spectacular gains in asset prices. And that is because William Jennings Bryan won the long-term war. No longer is there any limit set on the amount of money that can be created. Central banks do not even have to add silver to the coinage, or adulterate precious metals with copper – they can create money out of thin air. And the combination of a paper money system with asset price bubbles is no coincidence, as Richard Duncan shrewdly pointed out in his books, *The Dollar Crisis* and *The Corruption of Capitalism*.[3] Debt and asset prices are closely linked. The simple fact is that many people, for example homebuyers, borrow money to buy assets.

A greater willingness to lend quickly translates into higher asset prices. Imagine that the banks in country A were willing to lend a maximum of three times a person's income for him or her to buy a house, provided the buyer could put up a 25 per cent deposit. If the average salary was £25,000 a year, then the average house price would be £100,000.[4] Suppose the banking industry were to decide to relax its standards and allow borrowers to take out loans worth four times their income. Over time, prices would be forced higher. Some homebuyers might not want to borrow the extra money and devote more of their income to interest payments, but the more prudent would be outbid by the less prudent. The same effect would be achieved by lowering the deposit ratio to 10 per cent. That would allow potential homebuyers with just £10,000 of savings to enter the market. With the same degree of housing supply, more demand would push prices higher.

Would house prices be 'worth' more in such a scenario? At the simple level, yes; an asset is worth what people are prepared to pay for it. Even at a more sophisticated level, one might say that citizens had made a conscious decision to devote more of their expenditure to home ownership. But in no sense could a society be called richer because house prices had risen due to laxer lending standards.

Indeed, the whole notion that we can all get rich by owning houses makes no sense. What does rich mean? It means that you are better off than other people. To put it another way, you have a better claim on resources than others. If house prices go up faster than economic growth, we have inflated the claims, not the resources. If 70 per cent of the population are homeowners a rise in house prices can only make them better off than the non-property-owning 30 per cent. You get rich by owning an asset (usually a business) that the vast majority of the population does not own. And of course you can only turn your housing investment into cash by selling it; but if all (or even a significant proportion) 70 per cent of the home-owning population wished to sell, prices would collapse.

In a paper called 'Housing Wealth Isn't Real Wealth',[5] the economist Willem Buiter gave a neat analogy. A fall in the price of coconuts makes coconut exporters worse off – i.e. those who produce more coconuts than they consume – and it makes importers better off (i.e. those who consume more coconuts than they produce). But at the aggregate level, it makes no difference to the nation's wealth. A fall in house prices hurts the old – i.e. those people for whom the value of their houses exceeds the expected value of the housing services they will consume over the rest of their lifetime (the rents that they would pay were they not homeowners). But it boosts the wealth of the young, who will need to consume a lot of housing services (pay a lot of rent) over the rest of their lives.

If there is a shortage of houses, then building new ones would improve national welfare. But, except for the very rich who might want an apartment in central London, houses are not things that people from other economies tend to wish to buy. In general, economic welfare improves when we create *tradable* goods and services: pharmaceuticals, manufactured goods, video games or raw materials. Adam Smith worked all this out in *The Wealth of Nations* when he declared that, 'Though a house . . . may yield a revenue to its proprietor but it cannot yield any to the public, nor serve in the function of a capital to it, and the revenue of the whole body of the people can never be in the smallest degree increased by it.'

In short, a belief that a nation can prosper from higher house prices makes one think of the mythical island where every household earned its living by taking in its neighbour's washing. As Russell Roberts of George Mason University in Washington DC has put it, 'Having every American own a home is not the American Dream, but the dream of the National Association of Home Builders and the National Association of Realtors.'[6]

But such truths are easy to forget in a bubble. The key to asset bubbles is that the link between higher debt levels and higher prices is self-reinforcing. When people borrow money to buy a house and it goes up in price, they feel richer. They feel smart. They tell their friends. Those friends start fantasizing about the gains they would make if they bought a house. The willingness to borrow goes up.

At the same time, the banks also feel good about their lending decisions. Assuming they have lent money at a sensible rate (one that is higher than their cost of funding), the banks will make money provided the borrower keeps up the monthly payments and is able to repay the capital. Repayment normally takes place when the borrower moves house, usually after five to ten years (a long time before the official repayment date). If the house price has fallen by no more than the deposit, then the banks will be fine – and if house prices rise, the banks' margin of safety (their collateral) increases. If a house-price boom appears well established, then the banks will be more confident about their collateral, and will accept smaller deposits and offer higher multiples of income. And so prices can be pushed even higher.

These price spirals are not confined to houses. The commercial-property sector (office blocks, shopping malls, etc.) displays the same pattern. And investors can buy a whole bunch of other assets, from shares to commodities, putting little money down. Again, the more prices are rising, the easier it is to speculate (which is what buying with borrowed money involves).

Law's system, described in Chapter 1, fits the template perfectly. He printed bank notes and lent money so investors could buy shares in the Mississippi Company. While the share price was rising, the system worked perfectly; bank notes and shares were both perceived to have value. But when investors lost confidence, prices fell as quickly as they rose.

THE MINSKY EFFECT

Hyman Minsky, an American economist who died in 1996, thought these debt-fuelled spirals were inherent to financial markets. During the early stages of the boom, a typical borrower is a 'hedge borrower': he is able to meet both interest and capital repayments on the loan from his income. In the second stage, there are 'speculative' borrowers who can meet the interest on the loan but will be unable to repay the capital. They need to keep refinancing the debt to stay afloat. The final stage is dominated by 'Ponzi' borrowers who can repay neither interest nor capital; they are looking to 'flip' the asset, by selling it quickly for a profit.

Charles Ponzi was an American fraudster in the 1920s who claimed to have discovered a way of doubling investors' money within three months. The scheme was based on international postal coupons which, he said, could be bought cheaply in Europe and exchanged for stamps in the US.[7] The scheme had some basis in fact, although it would never have worked if attempted on a large scale. However, Ponzi did not try to make it work. He simply relied on his charm to entice investors. Should a few investors want to withdraw their money, he could pay them off with the money taken from new applicants. Bernie Madoff effectively used the same system without offering returns on the Ponzi scale; it was the steadiness of his returns, not the size of them, that ought to have made investors suspicious.

This kind of fraud is also known as a pyramid scheme and it is a recurrent historical phenomenon. Women Empowering Women was a British version in the 1990s. Person B pays Person A a thousand dollars; B then hopes to raise the same sum from each of Persons C and D. If he does, then both A and B are a thousand dollars ahead. In turn C and D attempt to raise money from E and F, or G and H. A giant pyramid builds on a small base. But like any pyramid that rests on its tip, it is doomed to topple over. Each layer needs more people than before, and the supply of optimists (suckers) is limited. In the Women Empowering Women scheme, each person needed to find eight new investors at every stage. At that rate, the expansion is very rapid, with successive stages requiring 8, 64, 512, 4,096, 32,768 and 262,144 investors. Five more stages after that and the scheme would require more investors than there are people on the planet.[8]

The Ponzi scheme was built on a similar epic scale. With money doubling every three months, investors would have been 16 times better off in a year and 256 times better off in two. Within five years, anyone who had invested a single dollar would have become a millionaire.

We know that pyramids must eventually collapse, and the higher the return (or promised return), the faster that collapse will come. (Bernie Madoff's scheme lasted so long because he offered reliable, rather than outlandishly high, returns.) The outright frauds have no investment justification at all. But even pyramid markets based on a genuine social change (such as the creation of the Internet) are doomed to eventual failure.

The Ponzi stage described by Minsky is often known as a 'greater fool' process. Buyers do not believe prices are justified but think they will find a gullible buyer willing to pay even more. They buy apartments sight unseen and purchase Internet stocks with no dividends or even revenues. Investors who take part in such bubbles will usually feel much more sophisticated than the naïve fools who fall for pyramid schemes, but they are making a similar mistake. Even Isaac Newton lost money in the South Sea bubble of the early eighteenth century, declaring afterwards, 'I can calculate the motions of heavenly bodies, but not the madness of people.'

In the long run, the value of an asset must be linked to the income that can be generated from it (rent in the case of property, dividends in the case of shares). It is quite possible for individual assets to shoot up in price since residential areas can become more fashionable and companies can have very successful products. But *in aggregate*, share and property prices are constrained by the growth rate of the economy, which in turn depends on the stock of productive capital (new factories and so on).

That may require some explanation. Economic activity can be measured in three ways: income, output and expenditure. So when we say gross domestic product (GDP) has risen 5 per cent in a year, that means the nation has earned 5 per cent more, produced 5 per cent more stuff and spent 5 per cent more. Companies can only pay dividends out of profits, and these profits come from revenues (i.e. the nation's spending).[9] Even if companies improve their margins (their profits rise faster than their revenues), the excess must come from the share of someone else (the workers). The profit share cannot rise for ever.

Similarly, rents cannot rise faster than incomes for long before no one can afford to rent. On the same basis, if house prices outstrip GDP, more and more of a homebuyer's income must go to service the mortgage. This cannot last.

Of course, in the short term, changes in interest rates, lending practices and the rest can cause house prices to overshoot. But look at the chart below compiled by Professor Shiller of Yale University. Real house prices were constant for around a century before jumping suddenly in the late 1990s. This was an indication that a serious distortion had appeared in the market.

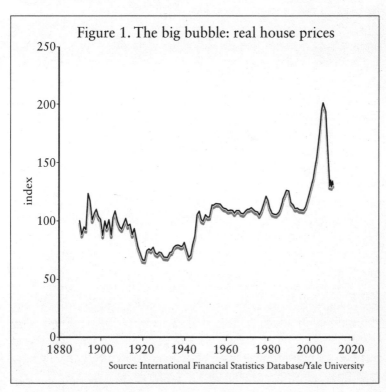

Figure 1. The big bubble: real house prices

index

Source: International Financial Statistics Database/Yale University

THE SUB-PRIME BOOM

Housing bubbles are common and particularly hard to stop. That is because such bubbles have a lot of supporters while they are inflating. Banks are making money from lending; estate agents are making money from commissions on property transactions, as are lawyers and other agents (like valuers). Homeowners feel richer because their home is worth more. In the American example, politicians welcomed wider home ownership: on the right, because property owners were seen as likely supporters of capitalism; and on the left, because the poor and ethnic minorities had previously been excluded from the mortgage market.

The Federal Reserve, the US central bank, was not minded to act in the early 2000s because the housing boom was not accompanied by general consumer-price inflation. House prices are not directly included in the consumer price index (although a version of housing costs, known as owner-equivalent rent, is in the index). Even first-time homebuyers were not put off, although the height of the first step on the housing ladder was rising. They were still able to buy, because lending standards were being relaxed.

And lending standards had to be relaxed if the boom was to be kept going. Had banks kept a lid on the amount they would lend, relative to incomes, the supply of new buyers would have run out. So they increased the income multiple – janitors were given the chance to buy $500,000 houses. This was the heyday of sub-prime mortgages, when people with poor credit records and no proof of income were able to get loans. From the point of view of a Ponzi scheme, this made sense. A scheme always needs a fresh supply of new buyers. So the proportion of homeowners in the US population increased from 63 per cent to 69 per cent, and plenty of people 'invested' in property by buying additional homes.

Loans were made with no money down. Indeed some loans did not even require borrowers to meet the full interest payment, with the shortfall simply added to the capital sum due. This was the final stage of Minsky's template. But house prices could not rise faster than incomes for ever (eventually, all of a homebuyer's income would have been taken up with servicing the mortgage).

When a bubble pops, the virtuous cycle turns vicious. Falling prices mean that those asset owners who borrowed a large proportion of the price become forced sellers. That forces prices down even further. Meanwhile banks become unwilling to lend, and indeed demand repayment of their loans, further weakening the supply/demand balance. In the case of American housing, homeowners walked away from their loans or faced foreclosure from the banks, leaving behind a glut of empty houses that weighed on the markets.

Charles Kindleberger, a great historian of bubbles, used the Minsky model to examine everything from tulip mania in the seventeenth century to John Law's system and the Asian crisis of the late 1990s. He showed they followed a template of a 'displacement' – some development like a war or technological change – credit expansion, overtrading (the final speculative phase), followed by distress (as some investors try to exit) and revulsion, as all who took part are berated for their stupidity. The sub-prime boom fits the pattern.

BUBBLES, PAPER MONEY AND THE END OF BRETTON WOODS

As Kindleberger noted, without credit expansion, it is hard to generate asset bubbles.[10] The ability to borrow money to buy houses, or to buy shares on margin, creates the temptation for investors to speculate.

Bubbles did occur during the gold standard. In the 1840s, for example, Britain enjoyed railway mania in which investors bought shares in the new transport system. Often different companies built parallel routes between the same destinations. The railways were as exotic then as the Internet seemed in the late 1990s, and investors believed the prospects for profits were limitless. The mania only collapsed when it was clear that many lines lacked sufficient passengers to make them profitable.

However, the end of Bretton Woods released the remaining brake on the system. There was no limit to the amount of money and credit that could be created. Countries no longer suffered a gold drain when they ran a trade deficit. Richard Duncan has argued that trade deficits are closely linked with credit growth, and thus with the asset bubbles.[11] He calls the post-1971 system 'the dollar standard'.

Under this standard, global foreign-exchange reserves have mushroomed. From 1949 to 1969, while Bretton Woods was still in place, the non-gold element of reserves rose 55 per cent; between 1969 and 2000, they rose 2,000 per cent (see Figure 2). These reserves expanded the money supply of the surplus countries. (This is a slightly technical point. Remember that we saw in the previous chapter that the surplus countries are selling their own currencies and buying dollars. To the extent they create currency to finance this process, the money supply is expanded.) In the US alone, the value of the broadest measure of money (known as M3) rose from just under $1 trillion in the early 1970s to $10 trillion by 2006, at which point the Federal Reserve stopped calculating the numbers.

This initially resulted in inflation, as any economist might have

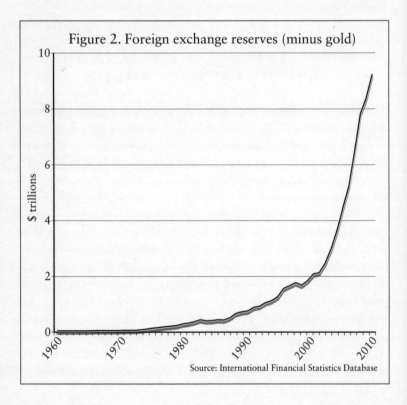

Figure 2. Foreign exchange reserves (minus gold)

Source: International Financial Statistics Database

predicted. In the US consumer prices rose more than fivefold between 1971 and 2010; in Britain, the increase was tenfold. The effect was fastest in the 1970s, when US prices more than doubled and in Britain they increased more than threefold. After that, central banks managed to get a handle on inflation. The period after 1982 has been described by economists as the 'great moderation' because economic growth was steady and recessions rare while inflation was generally low, except for a brief period at the end of the 1980s.

The great moderation was accompanied by an extraordinary boom in asset markets. Share prices had really suffered in the 1970s, under pressure from double digit inflation and falling output; the real value of US share prices fell by 42 per cent between 1972 and 1982, according to Barclays Capital. In Britain, share prices fell by 31 per cent in real terms in 1973 and by a further 55 per cent in 1974. In 1979, the cover of *Business Week* proclaimed 'The Death of Equities'.

But share prices are nearly always at their most attractive when sentiment is weakest. In 1982, the Dow Jones Industrial Average was no higher than it had been in 1965, even though economic activity was much greater. Shares offered a dividend yield of 6 per cent, as high as it had been in the depths of the Great Depression or during the Second World War. The price–earnings ratio (the relationship of the share price to current profits) was in single digits. The market was like a Labrador dog after an hour in the car, bursting to run wild. Not only did profits boom but valuations soared: moving from a 6 per cent dividend yield to a 3 per cent yield means a doubling in price, even if dividends remain unchanged. By the middle of 1987, the Dow had risen almost threefold from the low.

What followed was, in retrospect, the defining moment of the bubble era. On 19 October 1987, the Dow fell by almost 23 per cent in one day (Black Monday as it became known). Share prices round the world followed suit, from London to Hong Kong. No economic or political event seemed to be to blame. At the time, it seemed eerily reminiscent of the crash of 1929, the event popularly assumed to have ushered in the Great Depression.

Central banks, led by Alan Greenspan, the chairman of the US Federal Reserve, resolved to head off this calamity. They vowed to lend money to any bank or broker who had been caught out by this sudden plunge in prices. And they cut interest rates in order to encourage spending, discourage saving and make owning shares look more attractive than holding cash.

Investors learned an important lesson from this crisis. If asset markets fell far and fast enough, central banks would ride to the rescue. In a sense, the central banks had insured investors against enormous losses. This policy became known, in a nod to the technical intricacies of the options market, as the 'Greenspan put'.[12] In the long run, protecting investors served to encourage speculation. As Russell Roberts describes the process: 'What we do in the United States is make it easy to gamble with other people's money – particularly borrowed money – by making sure that almost everybody who makes bad loans gets his money back anyway.'[13]

Investors borrowed to buy assets. According to PIMCO, the fund management group, US economic output was $3.5 trillion in 1984 and private-sector credit was about the same amount.[14] By 2007, output had grown to $14 trillion but credit had soared to $25 trillion. Not that households were worried, since their net worth had risen from $12 trillion to $64 trillion over the same period. Output had quadrupled, asset prices had quintupled and debt had risen sevenfold.

If markets are accurately pricing in the future, the implicit message of higher asset prices is that future income streams (and thus future GDP growth) will be strong. The similar implication of high debt levels is that investors are gambling on higher growth coming true. But an era of slow growth, in the developed world at least, seems likely.

Clearly the entire rise in stock markets and house prices since the early 1970s has not been a bubble. There was a good deal of economic growth in the last three decades of the twentieth century which would justify higher asset prices. The addition of China and India to the capitalist world after around 1980 has immensely boosted global productivity. Nevertheless, it is clear that valuations of stocks rose higher than ever before. The best long-term measure of share price valuations is the cyclically adjusted price–earnings ratio. This complicated sounding statistic uses the profits made by companies averaged over a ten-year period. The aim is to even out any fluctuations in the economic cycle.

The higher the ratio, the greater the optimism of investors; they are willing to pay a high price, relative to past earnings, in the belief that *future* earnings will grow rapidly. (Just as banks are willing to lend a higher proportion of a house's value when they think asset prices are rising.) The graph below shows the data for the US market, compiled by Professor Robert Shiller at Yale University.[15] For years, many people had regarded the 1929 boom as the height of investor folly. Back then, they were willing to pay a ratio of nearly thirty-five. In effect, had profits stayed unchanged, investors would have had to wait until 1964 to get their money back. But in 2000, even that valuation was surpassed. Investors were paying forty-four times the cyclically adjusted profits of American companies. The assumption was that the Internet would transform corporate profits; actually it allowed consumers to get a better deal and destroyed some business models (recorded music, for example).

For investors, disappointment inevitably followed. The next decade

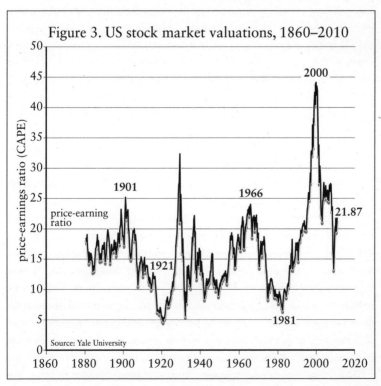

Figure 3. US stock market valuations, 1860–2010

saw not one, but two bear markets and negative returns for developed-market equity investors.

WHACK-A-MOLE

Whack-a-mole is an arcade game in which players aim to hit plastic humps with a mallet. The 'moles' pop up with increasing frequency. No sooner is one mole forced back into its hole than another appears elsewhere.

The system of money and credit creation that emerged after 1971 was like a game of whack-a-mole. The money created was bound to pop up somewhere. In the 1970s, it popped up as higher consumer prices and it took a very hard blow (in the form of higher interest rates) to force it back into its hole. But the mole reappeared in the form of higher asset prices, at which point the central banks became pacifists and refused to keep hitting. Indeed, to corrupt the analogy, they started offering the moles some juicy titbits to tempt them to the surface.

Central banks never tried to pop these bubbles, partly for ideological reasons, and partly because of the absence of consumer inflation pressures. And the rise of China (and other Asian nations) removed a further constraint.

The inflationary burst in the 1970s caused a lot of pain for investors in government bonds; the nominal value of their holdings was repaid but the real value (purchasing power) deteriorated greatly. As they spotted this was happening, the bond market vigilantes mentioned in Chapter 6 naturally reacted by demanding a higher interest rate on bonds to compensate them for the risk. James Carville, an adviser to President Clinton, was astonished to find that his administration's economic plans would have to take account of these vigilantes. 'I used to think if there was reincarnation, I wanted to come back as the president or the pope or a .400 baseball hitter,' he said. 'But now I want to come back as the bond market. You can intimidate everybody.'[16]

That was in the 1990s. By the following decade, the vigilantes seem to have fallen asleep. Alan Greenspan even talked of a bond-market 'conundrum': as the Fed pushed up the cost of borrowing over the short term, bond yields (effectively the cost of borrowing long term) actually fell. The explanation for this conundrum seems to be that the nature of bond-market investors had changed. No longer was the tone set by professional fund managers, scouring the world for the best combination of risk and return. Instead, the dominant class of investors were central banks in Asia and the Middle East.

These banks had accumulated their holdings as a result of the vast current-account surpluses generated by their parent countries. This was part of a deliberate export-oriented strategy designed to boost economic growth. China, in particular, was keen for its manufacturing sector (located largely in the coastal region) to create jobs and to absorb the surplus labour that had migrated from the inland, largely agricultural, areas.

To maintain this boom, the exporting countries needed to prevent their currencies from rising too fast against the dollar (for all the reasons explained in Chapter 6). This required them to sell their own currencies and buy dollars, which they held in the form of foreign-exchange reserves. Those reserves were invested in developed-world government bonds (mostly US Treasury bills). The system had thus created a very wealthy group of investors who were effectively uninterested in the price of, and return from, their investments. The bond-market vigilantes had been swamped. There was a savings glut that forced up asset prices.

The result was an odd system that seemed to suit both sides. The Chinese had a flourishing export market; the Americans were able to fund their consumption at low cost. There were occasional grumbles. American politicians feared that the Chinese were stealing US manufacturing jobs; the Chinese occasionally lectured the Americans on the need to safeguard the value of the Treasury bond market. In the last chapter, I will argue that this arrangement is unsustainable (although it hasn't broken yet).

McKinsey, the management consultancy group, has an alternative explanation for the asset boom.[17] It thinks that low real (after inflation) interest rates are the main driver. And it believes that those low real interest rates were the result of a shift in the patterns of saving and investment.

Economists say that savings must equal investment; it is a truism in their models. Nevertheless, most also accept that *desired* saving can be higher than desired investment. The way that the two quantities are matched is via interest rates. If desired investment is higher than desired saving, real interest rates will rise, but if the figures are the other way round, real interest rates will fall.

McKinsey calculates that the investment share of GDP fell from an average of 25.2 per cent in the 1970s to less than 21 per cent in the early 2000s.[18] This small percentage shift was the equivalent of $700 billion a year and amounted to a cumulative $20 trillion by 2008 – a figure equal to the combined GDP of Japan and the US in that year. McKinsey argued that this imbalance caused the fall in real rates, and in turn pushed up the value of shares and houses.[19]

Why did investment decline? McKinsey reckons that Europe and Japan invested heavily in the 1950s and 1960s to rebuild the capital destroyed in the Second World War. By the 1970s, this process was over. The report reckons that real interest rates may start to rise as a developing-world investment boom runs up against reduced Chinese saving, and as the People's Republic moves towards a more consumption-based model.

Another possible reason why asset markets may have been strong in the 1980s and 1990s was the influence of the 'baby boomers', those born between 1946 and 1964. As this large generation moved through the system, it competed to buy houses, and employers offered generous pension plans, which required them to invest heavily in equities. It may have been no coincidence that the markets started to crumble from 2000, as the baby boomers began to retire.

The baby boomers also had a benign effect on economic growth. There were simply more of them than in the preceding (and succeeding) generations. As a result, once they reached adulthood, a higher proportion of the population was economically active. In addition, more baby-boomer women joined the workforce, increasing the pool of potential employees.

(The addition of women to the workforce became a classic case of a feedback effect. If one family has two earners, they will be able to afford a better standard of living; for example, buying a bigger house. But that will increase the incentive for women in other families to go out to work, so they can keep up.)

Higher asset prices also helped fuel the consumption bubble. As house prices rose, people felt wealthier, and they used the opportunity to borrow against their wealth; a process known as equity withdrawal. Say that a consumer borrowed $150,000 to buy a $200,000 house. After five years, the house was worth $300,000. So the consumer refinanced the property, borrowing an extra $50,000. He still has $100,000 of equity in his home, providing a measure of security for the lending bank. But he also has an extra $50,000 which he can use to buy a new car, widescreen TV, etc.

In addition, this extra wealth seemed to relieve baby boomers of the need to save. Why stick money away in the bank when the housing market was adding to your wealth every year? Contrast the US with Germany, which did not enjoy a housing boom. In 1990, the American savings ratio (the proportion of disposable income not spent) was 7%, while the prudent Germans were saving 12.9%. By 2005, the Germans were still saving 10.6% of their income but Americans were saving just 0.4%. The British savings rate was actually negative in 2005; they spent more money than they earned thanks to borrowing on credit cards and the like. Saving was for wimps.

In demographic terms, this did not make sense. The baby boomers were in their peak earning years and should have been saving for their retirement. But rising housing and equity markets appeared to be doing the work for them. They could have their cake and eat it; spend the bulk of their incomes and still see their wealth rise.

DISGUISED INFLATION

Consumer-price inflation is noticed, and often resented, by a large proportion of the population. Most people feel, rightly or wrongly, that their wages are not keeping up with rising prices and that their standard of living has dropped.

Asset inflation also has its victims. It benefits the rich at the expense of the poor and the old at the expense of the young. It is much harder for twenty-somethings to get on the property ladder, for example. But they may not resent the process. Instead, they may simply hope that, when their turn comes, higher asset prices will make them rich.

Remember that borrowing money is an expression of confidence on the part of either the lender or the borrower (or both). Nothing is more likely to inspire confidence than economic growth, which tends to raise incomes, profits and prices both of goods and assets, making it easier for debtors to repay. So a debt spree might make sense if investors really believed that economic growth was rising; they are simply creating claims on a more prosperous future. But analysis by Jeremy Grantham of the fund management group GMO shows that belief has been wrong-headed. The bull market in assets began in 1982. In the century prior to that date, US GDP growth had averaged 3.4% a year while debt had hovered in the 100–150% of GDP range. After 1982, GDP growth has slowed to 2.4% a year, while the debt-to-GDP ratio has soared to more than 300%.[20]

To sum up, something fundamental changed after 1971, when the Bretton Woods system collapsed. Floating exchange rates allowed larger trade deficits and greater international capital movements. In turn, this allowed the financial sector to grow as a facilitator for such movements, and created a vast industry for hedging against (and speculating on) exchange-rate risk.

Liberalizing financial markets also allowed credit growth to accelerate. After the 1970s, this credit growth did not show up in consumer-price inflation but in higher asset prices. Asset prices and debt levels became locked in a virtuous circle as people borrowed money to buy assets, pushing prices higher and increasing the value of bank collateral. Central banks did not regard it as their duty to pop the resulting bubbles. Instead, by intervening when markets fell, but not when they rose, they encouraged speculation. A necessary precondition for the crisis had been established.

In the next chapter, we shall see how the financial sector prospered from the bubbles, rather like a turkey is fattened in the run up to Christmas.

8

Riding the Gravy Train

*'The banking industry is a pollutant. Systemic risk is a noxious
by-product.'*

> Andrew Haldane, executive director for
> financial stability, at the Bank of England

*'The Wall Street banks are the new American oligarchy – a group
that gains political power because of its economic power.'*

> Simon Johnson and James Kwak, *13 Bankers*

The post-Bretton Woods era has not just produced bubbles. It has also
been accompanied by another remarkable development – the phenomenal growth of the financial sector. As we read the daily headlines
about hedge fund billionaires and bankers' bonuses, it is hard to imagine that finance was once perceived as a rather dull affair.

The banking model was described as 3-6-3: borrow money at 3 per
cent, lend it at 6 per cent and be on the golf course by 3 p.m. As for
fund management, the old joke was 'Why don't fund managers look
out of the window in the mornings? Because then they would have
nothing to do in the afternoon.' J. K. Galbraith had a particularly lofty
disdain for the finance profession. 'In monetary matters as in diplo-
macy,' he wrote, 'a nicely conformist nature, a good tailor and the
ability to articulate the currently fashionable cliché have usually been
better for personal success than an excessively inquiring mind.'[1]

People who worked in the US financial sector actually earned less
than those with similar qualifications in different professions in the late
1970s. It was only in the 1980s – and in particular the 1990s – that their

wages took off. Meanwhile the finance sector's share of US GDP doubled, rising from 4 per cent in the 1970s to 8 per cent in 2007–08. Bank assets and profits were also rising relatively rapidly over this period.

Many of the best and brightest of our graduates have headed for the finance sector over the last thirty years. Their reasoning was as simple as that of bank robber Willie Sutton. Asked why he picked on banks, he replied, 'That's where the money is.' The seven-figure bonuses paid to investment bankers get a lot of attention. But the really big fortunes have been earned by those in private equity companies and hedge funds, where a vast number of billionaires have been created. It is a simple process: if you take 20 per cent of all investment returns, and you manage billions of dollars, your own wealth will climb rapidly.

The hedge fund industry consists of private funds that operate with fewer restrictions than the traditional fund management industry. It controlled just $39 billion of assets in 1990 but almost $2 trillion by 2011. Even the annual fees on such a sum translate to $40 billion a year, with performance fees on top. In 2008, the top ten hedge fund managers earned more than $10 billion between them.

This divergence in earnings has played a large part in rising wage inequality, particularly in the Anglo-Saxon economies. The period from 1940 to 1980 has been dubbed 'the Great Compression' in America since income inequality was reduced, in part due to high tax rates and the gains made by skilled workers such as those in the car industry. After 1980, tax rates were cut, particularly for those at the top end of the income scale, while the rewards for talent increased. This was true of sports stars and chief executives as well as bankers and fund managers. For the last three categories, much of this increase was due to the relationship between their remuneration and rising asset prices, thanks to share options or bonuses.

In 1973, for example, the average American chief executive earned 27 times the pay of the average worker; by 2005, the ratio was 262.[2] The fruits of economic growth went almost exclusively to the rich. The real wage of the US worker grew by just 11% over the thirty-five years from 1966 to 2001 or 0.3% a year; the wages of the top 0.1% of the population grew by 3.4% a year over the same period.[3] In 1990, the wealthiest 1% of the population had a 12% share of overall income. By 2007, their share had risen to 17%.

In terms of wealth, the concentration is even greater. The top 1% of the population owned 38.3% of all stockmarket wealth (in personal hands) in 2007. The top 5% owned 69.1%. Rising markets overwhelmingly help the already rich.[4]

In the circumstances, many workers only made ends meet by becoming two-earner rather than one-earner families, and by borrowing money to sustain their spending. It was a policy of 'let them eat credit' as the economist Raghuram Rajan memorably described it.[5] Of course, this surge in borrowing expanded the profits of the financial sector, increasing the inequality still further.

Why did these rewards flow to bankers when engineers and doctors, who also have vital skills, fared far less well? Clearly the finance sector does play an important role in the economy. Studies indicate that countries with better-developed financial systems tend to grow faster, since it is easier for business to get hold of capital and grow.[6] But it is very hard to delineate the precise nature of the sector's contribution to growth in the last decades of the twentieth century; arguably the personal computer and the rise of China were much more important.

Adair Turner, head of the UK's Financial Services Authority, argued that the finance sector played four key roles.[7] The first was payment services. Most economic transactions are settled through a bank. Even cash deals usually involve money withdrawn from a bank. The second role was the provision of insurance. This allows people to protect themselves from 'real world' risks such as fire, theft and death. The third role was the creation of futures markets in foreign exchange, interest rates and commodities. These allow businesses and investors to protect themselves against financial risks such as sudden changes in price. This ability to protect themselves against such risks makes business more secure. The final key role, according to Turner, was the channelling of funds from savers to borrowers. The deposits that you and I leave in our bank end up as loans to industry; the monthly contribution we make to our pension fund is used to buy shares and bonds issued by companies. Without such investment, the economy would not grow.

The first two functions have been around for centuries, and are highly competitive. In themselves, they should not generate huge profits, and certainly there seems no reason why profits from such activities should have increased over the last thirty years. Where banks have really made their money, and taken their risks, is in the third and fourth categories. Again, much of this is down to the end of the Bretton Woods agreement. As already noted, the post-war settlement restricted capital flows; investors mostly kept their money at home. Changes in exchange rates were also very rare. Indeed, capital controls were designed to keep exchange rates stable.

Once currencies were allowed to float, some governments gradually realized they had no need to restrict capital movements, because there was no particular level of exchange rate they had to defend. This was not true in the developing world, which still attempted to manage exchange rates, or in those countries in the European Exchange Rate Mechanism. But it was true in the 'Anglo-Saxon' economies of the US and the UK.

Both nations had leaders in the early 1980s who had an ideological preference for free markets (Ronald Reagan and Margaret Thatcher, respectively). The financial sector was generally set free. Britain unleashed the Big Bang reforms on its stock exchange in 1986, bringing foreign capital into the market. America gradually allowed commercial banks to move into the investment-banking market, reversing the strict separation that had been put in place in the 1930s. Free capital movements and floating exchange rates changed the financial sector in two big ways. First, they created the need for companies and investors to protect themselves against currency risk. The result was the development of financial futures markets, pioneered in Chicago, which traded first currencies, then fixed-income instruments, then equities. A vast, and profitable, derivatives market was born.

Secondly, these huge capital movements created the need for bigger financial institutions. Stockbrokers had traditionally linked asset buyers and sellers, in return for a commission. But the big investment institutions – pension funds, insurance companies and the like – found the service too expensive. They wanted financial companies to take their assets off their hands, and assume the risks until other buyers could be found. Such a risk-taking role was beyond the capacity of the small brokers and investment banks, many of which were partnerships in which the capital consisted of the assets of the leading employees. To play in the big league of global capital flows, these middlemen had to get bigger.

So the commercial banks moved into the business of trading and market-making, either taking over existing investment banks or creating their own subsidiaries. The remaining investment banks raised capital by floating on the stock market. Even Goldman Sachs abandoned its cherished partnership structure in 1999.

The banks could not have done this if the economy had not prospered. In a sense, the 'great moderation' of the 1980s and the boom in the financial sector were locked together. Banks make their money in three broad ways: from lending money at a higher rate than they borrow it; by owning assets that rise in price; and through earning fees for giving advice. The great moderation was thus ideal for their purposes. The infrequency of recessions meant that borrowers were both willing to take out more loans and more able to repay their debts. Buoyant economic conditions led to rising equity and property prices. They also encouraged companies to float on the stock market and to make acquisitions – activities that are lucrative fee-earners for the sector.

The bankers were like croupiers in a casino. They took a cut every time money flowed round the system. As the money flowed faster and faster, their take got bigger and bigger. The long succession of bubbles helped the process. Since asset prices were rising rapidly, investors barely noticed (or didn't mind) the finance sector's cut of their profits.

But while individual bankers profited, the potential costs to the taxpayer increased. In some instances, governments stand explicitly behind their banks, for example by guaranteeing deposits. In other eventualities the support is implicit. A collapse of the banking system will devastate an economy, as the 1930s showed. The 2007–08 crisis showed that governments will always be tempted to step in to rescue their banks, especially when the consequences of failure are so great. As Andrew Haldane, executive director for financial stability at the Bank of England, put it in March 2010: 'The banking industry is a pollutant. Systemic risk is a noxious by-product.'[8]

The effect of this governmental 'backstop' is to lower the cost of bank funding, since creditors assume the government will bail them out. A lower cost of funding thus translates into higher profits for the banks. Mr Haldane reckons that the average annual subsidy to the top five British banks in the years 2007 to 2009 was more than £50 billion, equivalent to their annual profits prior to the crisis. These subsidies are not competed away; they are taken as 'rents' by bank employees. In the US, Russell Roberts of George Mason University wrote that, 'The expectation by creditors that they might be rescued allows financial institutions to substitute borrowed money for their own capital even as they make riskier and riskier investments.'[9]

A further malign effect seems to have occurred. The financial system is not at risk when a small bank fails, but a large bank failure is a real problem. It makes sense, therefore, for banks to get as big as possible since they can earn a greater benefit from the government guarantee. The industry duly became more concentrated. According to Andrew Haldane, the share of total assets of the top four US banks rose from 10% in 1990 to 40% in 2007.[10] At the global level, the share of assets of the five largest banks rose from 8 per cent in 1990 to 16 per cent in 2008. The banks became, in the phrase of the day, 'too big to fail'.

It is not clear that the economy gains much in efficiency from this concentration. Mr Haldane suggests that the optimal size of a bank is somewhere below $100 billion in assets. But in 2008, 145 global banks, controlling around 85 per cent of the industry, had assets greater than that level. Moreover, not only did each individual bank become bigger, the aggregate size of the industry increased. In the US, the long-term average ratio of bank assets to GDP, according to Jim Reid of Deutsche Bank,[11] was around 61%. From the mid-1990s, this ratio accelerated to reach 85%. For a century after 1880, UK bank assets hovered at around 50% of GDP. From that point onwards, the ratio took off, and reached a remarkable 500% of GDP by 2007. The potential bill for the taxpayer had risen tenfold.[12]

The stock market came to be dominated by the finance sector. In America, the sector had a value equivalent to just 8.8% of the S&P 500 index in 1989. By early 2007, that proportion had risen to 22.3%.[13] At one stage, the sector was contributing a third of all US domestic profits.

This huge expansion owed a lot to a greater willingness of the banks to take on risk. Banks held less capital against their assets or, to put it another way, they used more leverage. When things go well, higher leverage translates into higher returns for shareholders.[14] The change in bank governance structures from that of partnerships to public companies also made a difference. The men who built up the great Wall Street firms in the first half of the twentieth century (like Sidney

Weinberg at Goldman Sachs) were more cautious about taking risks because it was their own money that was at stake; taking risks with other people's money is always more appealing.

In the late nineteenth century, US banks had capital ratios (equity as a percentage of assets) of around 25%; by the first decade of the twenty-first century, this had fallen to less than 10%. In Britain, the ratio fell from 15% to around 5% over the same period.[15] All this reduces the margin of safety in the system. A relatively small loss can still threaten the financial health of the bank.

The relationship between central banks, markets and debt levels has already been mentioned; when markets falter central banks cut interest rates, thus encouraging investors to take more risk. There is also another spiral at work involving banks and governments. Governments support banks, so banks get bigger, requiring more government support. One study found that deposit insurance schemes increased fourfold, relative to GDP, in the wake of a financial crisis.[16] This leads to a 'moral hazard' problem. Depositors have no incentive to monitor the health of their banks since governments stand behind them and will guarantee their deposits. That was how British savers became exposed to an Icelandic bank. Banks ceased to compete on safety. Instead they competed to attract shareholders by the size of their profits, creating the incentive to take more risk. The banks profited when their bets paid off, but the taxpayer ended up with the bill when the bets were unsuccessful.

Regulators were aware of these problems and tried to control them via international agreements on capital, set out in the Basle accords. But as we shall see later in the book, banks found ways to get round the rules, moving risk off their balance sheets, and the regulators did not seem able to keep up with their better-paid counterparts in the private sector. This may relate to a problem well enunciated by Simon Johnson, a former chief economist for the IMF. In his book *13 Bankers*, co-written with James Kwak, Johnson remarks that developing countries used to be notorious for having governments that were in cahoots with, or controlled by, a few powerful businessmen. But now that could be said of the US.

The Wall Street banks are the new American oligarchy – a group that gains political power because of its economic power, and then uses that political power for its own benefit. Runaway profits and bonuses in the financial sector were transmuted into political power through campaign contributions and the attraction of the revolving door [between Wall Street and government].[17]

Suspicions about this cosy relationship were aroused when Hank Paulson, a former chief executive of Goldman Sachs, was in charge of the US Treasury during the financial crisis. Remarkably, he was the second Goldman Sachs alumnus, after Robert Rubin, to be Treasury Secretary within a decade.

The recruitment of Wall Street titans to government is likely to have a more innocent, albeit equally revealing, explanation. The success of the Wall Street firms, and the intellectual complexity of modern finance, meant that finance executives were generally perceived as the smartest people in the country. (Similar reasoning persuaded John F. Kennedy to recruit Robert McNamara from Ford Motor Company to be his Defense Secretary, back when the US auto industry ruled the world.)

Nevertheless, regardless of the reason, the effect is probably the same. An ex-Wall Street boss is unlikely to impose stringent regulations on the finance industry. Alfred Sloan, head of General Motors, once proclaimed that 'What is good for General Motors is good for America.' It was easy, in the 1990s and early 2000s, for officials to assume that what was good for Goldman Sachs was good for America.

The finance industry was also a huge taxpayer, once one allowed for income taxes on bonus payments, capital-gains tax on share-price gains, stamp duty on property and share deals and all the rest. In Britain, even the Blair/Brown Labour governments pursued a light-touch regulatory regime for fear of driving the big banks away to foreign countries. They trumpeted the fact that London appeared to be catching, or even overtaking, New York as a global financial centre.

The prospect of regulatory arbitrage – companies migrating to countries where they would be treated more leniently – may also explain why regulators were unwilling to crack down on the banks and why post-crisis reform programmes have been so mild. In the US, the 1929 crash was followed by the passing of the Glass–Steagall Act, which separated commercial (deposit-taking) banking from investment banking. Nothing so radical has been attempted this time round. The US did pass a massive financial-reform act – the Dodd–Frank bill – but it envisaged neither a break-up of the biggest banks nor a radical separation of activities. Much of the detailed implementation was left to a vast number of study groups – a classic bureaucratic device for kicking reform into the 'long grass' – whereby the reforms can be conveniently forgotten or emasculated. The chances of substantial reform were further diluted when the Republicans took control of the House of Representatives in 2010. In Britain, an independent banking commission report in 2011 recommended the 'ring-fencing' of retail from investment banks, but the proposals are likely to be implemented slowly. The banks might yet persuade a future government to ditch them altogether.

The danger is that the finance sector has become what economists call a 'rent-seeker', charging excessive prices for its services. These rents may emerge from a lack of competition, since the government guarantee may create a barrier to entry for new firms. Or it may result from a lack of transparency. Financial products are often complex with the result that the effective price is obscure; clients may be paying over the odds without realizing it. The prices charged by the industry represent a transfer of wealth from the rest of the economy. This is a 'principal-agent' problem in that the interests of the client and those of the people who handle their money are not aligned.

Paul Woolley, a former fund manager, has set up a centre to study what he calls 'capital market dysfunctionality' at the London School for Economics. He describes his former industry in harsh terms. 'Why on earth should finance be the biggest and most highly-paid industry when it's just a utility, like sewage or gas? It is like a cancer that is growing to infinite size until it takes over the entire body.'[18]

EFFICIENT-MARKET THEORY

The reluctance of central banks to intervene in asset bubbles owed something to the feeling of euphoria induced by higher asset prices. Central bankers did not wish to lose their much-cherished independence by alienating the public. However, the main motivation was ideology. Alan Greenspan, the head of the US Federal Reserve, was a disciple of Ayn Rand, a philosopher and cult novelist whose 'objectivism' glorified the elite at the expense of the dull masses and interfering bureaucrats. Howard Roark, the hero of her novel *The Fountainhead*, is an architect whose ambition to create modernist buildings is frustrated by lesser beings. (You know the sort. The people who don't want to live in concrete tower blocks.)

In the Rand world, we should be grateful for such heroes who have the drive and vision to get things done. This self-chosen elite is what drives society forward, not governments or the popular will. In economic terms, this philosophy means that the markets should always be trusted, and that governments should keep out of the way. It was not for Alan Greenspan to second guess the decisions of smart fund managers – the Howard Roarks of their day – who had spent their lives analysing the data.

This analysis reflected the general reaction against the Keynesian consensus of the post-war period, which seemed to end in significant parts of industry being under government control. An academic fight back was led by Milton Friedman of the Chicago school of economics, who argued that governments were poor at allocating capital. The free market view certainly had some justification; government projects are often marked by bloated spending and 'white elephants' such as Concorde. Bureaucrats are unlikely to devise such popular products as the iPod or the Nintendo Wii. Markets are inherently better at innovating since they can respond to pricing and demand signals sent every day by individual consumers.

Quite separately, finance academics had developed 'efficient-market theory', which suggested that current prices were always likely to be a better reflection of the fundamental state of the market than the view of a government official or central banker. Efficient-market theory dovetailed with an observation common to many investors: that it was difficult to beat the market. In one sense, this is a truism. The FTSE 100 index in Britain, or the S&P 500 in America, are groups of stocks that represent the bulk of the market's value. The performance of the index must therefore resemble the performance of the average investor since, collectively, investors own the entire market. But the index does not bear the costs of trading shares, while the average investor does. So the typical investor should under-perform the market.

Professional fund managers charge fees for managing money; for retail investors, this fee is usually more than 1 per cent a year. So the average retail investor should under-perform the market by the extent of those fees. Lo and behold, that is pretty much the case.

Aha, you might say, but surely it is possible to pick an above-average fund manager. Such managers undoubtedly exist. But if they could be reliably identified, then investors would give them all their money, while giving no money to the below-average fund managers. That would leave the market purely in the hands of above-average managers. Since, by definition, not all managers can beat the average, some would start to under-perform.

The same insight applies to any strategy that might appear to beat the market on a consistent basis – buying the shares of companies with better profit prospects, for example. If such a strategy could be identified, everyone would use it, thereby driving the share prices of such companies to levels from which only average returns could be generated.

This academic insight behind efficient-market theory has been very useful. It led to the development of low-cost tracking funds that give retail investors exposure to the stock market. These funds simply attempt to mimic the index. They are doomed to under-perform the index slightly because of costs, but the best index-trackers such as Vanguard (a mutually owned group) keep those costs as low as possible. Pick an index-tracker and you do not have to worry about the star manager leaving the firm, or having a brainstorm and investing the entire fund in Canadian diamond mines.

But rival academics have been chipping away at the efficient-market hypothesis ever since it was developed. The theory assumes that news is automatically reflected in share prices, that there are no constraints on investors and that the market is populated (or at least dominated) by rational investors poring over each company's accounts.

In fact, investors can be shown to have a number of biases, such as selling their winning stocks and hanging on to their loss-makers. Efficient markets would allow investors to be able to sell short (i.e., bet on falling prices) as easily as they can bet on rising ones, but in fact regulators impose a host of restrictions on short-selling. History is also full of market anomalies, such as the over-performance of stocks in the month of January or the better performance of smaller companies.

It is also hard to argue that markets are always efficiently priced when stocks were worth 23 per cent less on 20 October 1987 than they were worth at the start of trading the day before. Nevertheless, Alan Greenspan stuck to this view pretty consistently, even during the dot.com bubble, when companies with no declared profits or dividends were being valued at billions of dollars. Who was he to second guess the views of millions of investors, as reflected in market prices? Even if he could identify a bubble, popping it would require significantly higher interest rates. That would force the economy into a recession, the very thing central banks were trying to avoid.

But to his critics, Mr Greenspan's actions after 'Black Monday' had given investors a one-way bet: he would intervene if the market fell sharply, but not if it rose quickly. Charles Dumas, an economist at Lombard Street Research, quipped that Greenspan displayed 'asymmetric ignorance'; he knew when markets were too low but not when they were too high. However, for much of his nineteen-year career in charge of the Fed, Alan Greenspan was fêted as a sage. Bob Woodward, one of the investigative reporters who helped bring down President Nixon, published a book giving Greenspan the title of Maestro in 2001.[19] In retrospect, the publication of that book marked the point when the reputation of central bankers reached its zenith. They had been charged with keeping inflation low; by and large, it did stay low. They had been charged with heading off recessions; a brief downturn in 1990–91 was followed by a prolonged boom. Central banks were the active players in economic policy, cutting and raising interest rates on a monthly basis. Finance ministers, by contrast, used annual budgets as a means of tinkering with social policy and incentives, rather than trying to control overall demand.

In the bad old days of the 1960s and 1970s, central bankers had been perceived as being under the thumb of politicians. It is only natural for politicians to want lower interest rates and higher fiscal deficits. That helps to buy votes. But central banks failed to stop their excesses. Gradually, however, central banks were given the right to set interest rates without political interference. New Zealand set the tone in 1989, giving its bank independence along with an inflation target. In Britain, the Labour government handed over the responsibility for setting interest rates to the Bank of England in 1997. The

Federal Reserve has had the right to set US rates from its foundation in 1913 and the European Central Bank has had the same ability since 1999.

This freedom is not absolute. What governments have given, they can take away. They also have the right to appoint central-bank heads, which allows them to pick a sympathetic soul if they wish. They can also change the bank's mandate to aim for, say, more inflation and growth if they choose.[20]

Such changes may well occur in future, if the economic situation gets desperate enough. To date, politicians have decided that independent central banks are a price worth paying. By making monetary policy more credible, central banks may have ensured that interest rates have been lower than they might have been had the politicians still been in charge. In turn, growth may have been higher than would otherwise have been the case and voters, accordingly, happier.

Was this era of central-bank success down to skill, or luck? The 1980s and 1990s saw another enormous change in the macro-economic picture – the arrival of China, and then the former Soviet Union and its satellites, into the capitalist world. At a stroke, this added hundreds of millions of workers to the available labour force. This ensured that wages in the Western world were under steady downward pressure; business had the option of seeking lower-cost suppliers in Eastern Europe and Asia.

This huge addition to the labour force was like a deflationary shock to the global economy. Given full rein, it might have caused wages to fall in the West, but given that prices would have fallen as well, real (after inflation) incomes might have risen. (Something similar happened in the late nineteenth century as steamships opened up the vast farmlands of the US and Argentina to European consumers; food prices fell, as did the price of farmland and the number of European agricultural workers, but the result was a boost to the real incomes of factory workers.) By repeatedly cutting interest rates, the central banks prevented deflation from taking hold. Viewed in this light, the remarkable thing in the 1990s was not the low level of inflation; it was that there was any inflation at all.

The central banks were frightened of creating deflation because of the high level of debt. They had seen what had happened in the

1930s when prices fell sharply. The nominal level of debts stayed the same but the incomes of debtors dropped, making it impossible for them to service their debts. Central banks were very reluctant to allow even mild recessions because of this debt problem. Perhaps, however, recessions are necessary to clean out the system. The economy needs to ditch the old industries and start developing new ones. Preventing recessions may be a little like the old practice of preventing even small fires in national forests; the effect is to allow a lot of brushwood to build up so that when a fire does happen, it is catastrophically big.

None of this would have happened under the gold standard or the Bretton Woods system. Under the former, the US reserves would have run out long before China had built up such huge surpluses; under the latter, trade deficits could not last for ever (indeed that is why the system broke down).

REGULATION

This 'markets are right' philosophy was also reflected in light-touch regulation. It was assumed that the private sector would act to regulate itself. It would not lend money to those who might not pay it back; it would not take risks that might destroy its balance sheet. After all, the executives of banks were also shareholders. Why should they risk the loss of their fortunes?

This assumption was proved spectacularly wrong in 2007 and 2008. Why did the bankers get it so wrong? One possibility is that executives may not have realized how much risk was being taken. The operations of banks had grown so complex, and the minutiae of financial products so hard to grasp, that the boards of directors simply could not keep pace with what their employees were doing.

Another problem was peer pressure. Bank executives were judged on their ability to generate profits for their shareholders and to push the share price higher. If a rival bank appeared to be making lots of money in one area (such as sub-prime lending), the executives would feel obliged to follow suit. Chuck Price, the former head of Citigroup, once said that 'When the music stops, in terms of liquidity, things will be complicated. But as long as the music is playing, you've got to get up and dance. We're still dancing.'[21] For Price and his ilk, failure to generate enough profit in the short term would simply lead to the sack.

The likes of Dick Fuld at Lehman Brothers and Jimmy Cayne at Bear Stearns lost hundreds of millions of their own money when their banks collapsed. So why weren't they more cautious, as Greenspan's theories suggested they should be? Part of the reason is psychological – the type of people who rise to the top of investment banks will inevitably be those who are used to taking risks. They will perceive themselves as smarter and savvier than average, and thus unlikely to fail. After all, most of their big bets will have come off in the past.

Similarly, each banker sees himself in competition with rivals at other firms. The money is just a way of keeping score; they will always want more than the next guy. That means taking more risks. Their long-term prosperity is assured because they have already cashed in vast numbers of shares in previous years.

From time to time during the 'great moderation', the risks involved in banking were revealed as banks went bust. The collapses of Johnson Matthey in 1984 and BCCI in 1991 showed that banks could go bust the old-fashioned way: by lending money to people who could not pay it back. The failure of Barings in 1995 was a more modern story, linked to the derivatives market. It revealed an astonishing naivety and lack of controls on the part of the Barings management.

Nick Leeson was a relatively junior banker operating out of Barings' Singapore office. His early career did not suggest he was destined to become a star. What he was supposed to be doing was indulging in arbitrage between the Singapore and Japanese markets, buying low on one exchange and selling high on the other. It was the equivalent of combing the streets looking for dropped £20 notes. One might expect the odd gain, but not a bonanza. So when Leeson started to report bumper profits, what did Barings' management (back in London) think? That the Singapore and Japanese markets were highly inefficient? That Asians were too stupid to exploit the same opportunities as Leeson did?

The more obvious answer was staring them in the face. Not only was Leeson making the trades, he was handling the back office duties as well; reporting and settling the deals. It was like allowing a schoolboy to mark his own homework. It turned out that Leeson was not so smart. He was losing money, not making it, and hiding the losses in an 'error account'. The bumper profits were an illusion. As the losses mounted, he took bigger and bigger risks to try to repair the situation, and when a Japanese earthquake caused the Tokyo stock market to slump, he was wiped out.

Barings' head office did not ask for proof of Leeson's profits, in the form of hard cash. In fact they were more than willing to send him money to finance his successful operation. 'It was not actually terribly difficult to make money in the securities markets,' said Peter Baring, the firm's chairman, just two years before the company's collapse.[22]

The Barings failure revealed the dark secrets at the heart of the financial boom. First, high returns are nearly always accompanied by high risk. Secondly, traders have every incentive to take risks with 'other people's money' to inflate their own bonuses, and few incentives to admit their mistakes. However, the bank's failure was dismissed as a one-off. The title of Nick Leeson's autobiography, *Rogue Trader*, tells the tale. He was operating outside the system, not within it.

It was assumed by regulators that private businesses would have every incentive to control their risks, particularly as other banks would be trading with them every day, and thus be watching for signs of weakness. The ever-efficient market would supply the discipline. Indeed in 2004, the Securities and Exchange Commission, the leading US regulator, removed the caps on the amount of leverage that the leading broker-dealers (a category that included Bear Stearns and Lehman Brothers) could use. There were thus no constraints on the ability of the investment banks to bet the franchise.

The system was not just huge, it was complex. The big banks were each conducting millions of transactions with each other every day, some that involved loans, some that involved trades of shares or bonds, some that involved derivative instruments such as options and swaps. At the same time, they were dealing with outside entities – hedge funds, insurance companies, pension funds – each of which had links with several different banks.

In many cases, the banks demanded collateral from those they dealt with – counterparties had to pledge government bonds or other securities against the value of the deal. Thus if the counterparty went bust, the banks could seize the collateral. This protected the banks against the failure of an isolated counterparty. The far trickier problem was how the system could be insured against widespread failure. On this point, the regulators had received a warning back in 1987.

The fall of share prices on Black Monday was not the result of a fundamental reappraisal of the economic outlook. Share prices had risen very fast in the first half of 1987 and it was natural for investors to take some profits. The speed of the decline was the result of a technical change in market practice, called portfolio insurance.

Portfolio insurance had been developed as a way for investors, in particular the giant pension funds and insurance companies, to protect themselves against market declines. These funds were the biggest investors in the stock market. They had diversified their risk by owning shares in many individual companies, but this still exposed them to the danger that the stock market as a whole might go down.

The answer was to use the financial futures market. As we have seen, financial futures were an adaptation of the commodity futures that had been used by farmers (and producers using raw materials) since the mid-nineteenth century. In the 1970s, they were used to cover currency movements and the same structure was adapted for the stock market. A stock-market future allowed the investor to buy or sell a contract on a particular index; in the case of the US, the most popular version was the S&P 500, a much broader market measure than the Dow Jones Industrial Average.

Say it is June and you are a big investor who is worried about a market fall before September. The S&P 500 is trading at 1,000 and you are worried it might fall to 900 over the summer months. The futures contract on the index is trading at 990. You sell enough futures contracts to cover your risk. If the market does fall as you fear, then so will the price of the future; you can buy it back at 900 and make a profit. That profit will offset the loss you have suffered on your underlying stock market position. You have insured yourself.

That is how the system worked in theory. As so often in the world of finance and economics, what happened in practice was quite different. As the stock market fell, more people wanted insurance; so they sold the S&P future. But the decline in the future sent a signal to the stock market that investors were worried. So share prices fell, necessitating more insurance, and so on.

Economic theory often suggests that an individual actor has little impact on the fundamentals; that we can buy or sell without moving the price against us. But big investors do have to worry about such factors, since they comprise the bulk of the market. In short, the system could not insure itself; there was no one to take the other side of the trade.

However, central bankers focused less on what had caused the 1987 crash than on how their actions in cutting interest rates had prevented a repeat of the depression. They regarded 1987 as an example of successful policy.

THE BIGGER, THE BETTER

Back in 1987, the line between commercial and investment banking, established by the Glass–Steagall Act of 1934, was still fairly distinct. There was no sign of any panic about the health of the deposit-taking banks. But as the banks became all-singing, all-dancing conglomerates, and as they consolidated into larger groups, systemic risk increased. Regulators, however, continued to assume that the market could handle the risks itself. After all, weren't the banks hiring the best and the brightest, the mathematicians and 'rocket scientists' who could model the markets?

These whiz-kids were needed to deal with the complex derivative products that had developed since the 1970s and were to play such a big role in the sub-prime crisis. Derivatives were a classic double-edged sword – they allowed some people to buy insurance against risks (such as a sudden surge in oil prices) but they allowed (indeed required) others to speculate that such risks would occur. In the benign view of Alan Greenspan, derivatives spread risk around the system and made it safer. Alas, this view broke the rule that the system could not insure itself.

Banks may have had an ulterior motive for the growth of derivatives. The more complex the product, the harder it was for investors to see the price. The result was fat fees for the banking sector. But perhaps the banks deceived themselves in the long run. One particular risk measure, called value-at-risk (VAR), got built into the system in the wake of Black Monday. Dennis Weatherstone, the chief executive of J P Morgan, was disturbed by the events of 1987. He asked his team to provide a measure of how much the bank was exposed to sudden market movements. VAR was developed to provide that information; it aimed to measure the maximum loss the bank could suffer on 95 per cent (in some cases 99 per cent) of all trading days.

Some see the use of VAR as contributing to the crisis by providing false comfort to bank executives. Author Pablo Triana compared the method to a passenger airbag that works 95 per cent of the time, but not during the vital 5 per cent of occasions when your car has a crash.[23] Nassim Nicholas Taleb writes of the 'ludic fallacy', the belief that the odds of market movements can be rigorously computed, like the odds of winning a poker hand.[24] The problem, as Taleb points out, is that the range of probabilities is not known in advance. In poker, there are only fifty-two cards (or fifty-four with the jokers) in the deck. With the markets, we are in the realm of 'Knightian uncertainty' or, as the former US Defense Secretary Donald Rumsfeld put it in another context, 'We don't know what we don't know.'

In mathematical terms, the easiest way of modelling markets is to use what is known as a 'normal distribution' or bell curve, in which most data points lie in the middle of the range. In nature, this works very well; most people are between five feet and seven feet tall. Extreme outliers (below 1 foot or over 10 feet) are unknown. In markets, we get 'fat tails' of the bell curve, or more extreme examples than one might expect. David Viniar, chief financial officer of Goldman Sachs, said in August 2007, 'We were seeing things that were 25-standard deviation moves, several days in a row.'[25] Since, under a bell curve, 25-standard deviations have an infinitesimal chance of occurring, this shows that the VAR model was simply wrong.

Of course, modellers can allow for different probability distributions than the bell curve. But they still don't know *which* distribution will occur. Take too cautious a view and you will take little risk, and some other investment bank will take all the profits. To the aggressive heads of investment banks like Dick Fuld and Jimmy Cayne, this was the clinching argument. Those who advocated caution were not being team players.

The Bank of England's Andrew Haldane gave an insight into the bankers' motivations in a speech in early 2009.[26] The bank, along with the Financial Services Authority, had conducted a series of seminars with banks on the subject of stress-testing the institutions' portfolios. The regulators noticed that the stresses being calculated were quite mild in their impact. What was the explanation? One banker came clean:

There was absolutely no incentive for individuals to run severe stress tests and show these to management. First, because if there were such a severe shock, they would very likely lose their bonus and possibly their jobs. Second, because in that event the authorities would have to step in anyway to save a bank and others suffering a similar plight.

Another issue was that the figures in the VAR models also tended to be heavily influenced by recent observations. So a long period of low volatility tended to reduce the potential loss generated by the model, thereby persuading banks to take more risk (just as Hyman Minsky predicted).

As Taleb points out, this creates a very dangerous mindset. His 'black swan' example dates back to the philosopher David Hume; just because you see a thousand white swans does not mean there cannot be a black swan (as there are in Australia). But another example of his reasoning is even more illuminating. Turkeys are fed by the farmer for 364 days, and must presume the farmer to be a benign caregiver; they have no way of anticipating that, on the 365th day, the same farmer will slaughter them for our Thanksgiving or Christmas meal.

In the case of the markets, an analysis of the data may lead investors to take very similar positions, for example, to take bets on the direction of the housing market. The same reasoning can lead them to assume that these bets are very liquid, since they have had no problem in taking on these positions. But once again, they are taking false comfort. If the banks pile into the asset class, its price will go up, and they will look smart. But if they try to sell, not only will the price start to fall, but they may find it impossible to find any buyers. These are what are known as 'crowded trades'.

This was a more general problem for the finance sector in 2007–08.

In many ways, the new types of financial institution that had grown up post-1980 – such as private equity firms and hedge funds – were ways of making bets on liquidity. In theory, illiquid assets should pay higher returns, since investors need compensation for being unable to sell their holdings immediately. Private equity and hedge fund firms bought such assets to take advantage of these higher returns. This was fine, as long as they themselves were not reliant on short-term funding. But when they were (when, for example, hedge fund clients wanted their money back or brokers withdrew their lending facilities), they found themselves with the historical problem of the banking sector: they had borrowed short and lent long.

The key error was assuming that a large group of investors could hedge, buy insurance in other words, against market falls. Someone must take the other side of that contract. Such insurance can be easy to purchase in good times, but in bad times, no one will be willing to provide it. The system cannot insure itself. Making a huge bet, particularly on illiquid assets, is thus a very perilous pastime.

The collapse of Long-Term Capital Management in 1998 was a classic example of this. LTCM was a hedge fund led by a bond trader called John Meriwether who had worked at Salomon Brothers, then one of Wall Street's leading firms. He hired a stellar team, including two Nobel prize-winning economists, Robert Merton and Myron Scholes.

LTCM pursued a strategy called arbitrage, buying assets that looked artificially cheap and selling short (betting on a falling price) similar assets that looked expensive. A classic example was in the US Treasury bond market. Investors were keen to own the latest issue of the thirty-year bond because of its liquidity. They were less keen to own last year's issue, that is, a bond expected to mature in twenty-nine years. But both were obligations of the Federal government. So buying the twenty-nine-year issue and shorting the thirty-year one made sense.

However, the price discrepancies were quite small so making a decent return required a lot of leverage. At the peak LTCM was borrowing $30 for every $1 of capital. And nearly all its bets involved, in essence, the buying of illiquid assets and the shorting of more liquid ones. The big banks were making similar bets. So when sentiment turned risk-averse in 1998, it was rather like a game of musical chairs;

everyone piled into the liquid assets and the illiquid assets plunged in price. LTCM's capital started to shrink and it could not get out of its positions; there were no chairs left. Leverage and illiquidity had brought it down.

The LTCM story stands as a metaphor for the whole era. Smart people decided they could beat the system, and persuaded others to give them the resources to do so. In a sense, they were like a poker player who persuades his friends to back his system for making money at Las Vegas. If he has some skill and the luck is on his side, he will make money for a while. But if his luck changes, his friends will bear the losses. It's a good deal for the poker player, but not for his friends.

A CHANGE OF ATTITUDE

The bank manager of old – the stuffy Captain Mainwaring of *Dad's Army* – disappeared in the 1980s and 1990s. Banks became more willing to take on risk. But if one accepts the Taleb argument – that the future is inherently unknowable – this was a big mistake. Having a lot of debt, in Taleb's view, makes the borrower very dependent on accurate forecasts. The right response to uncertainty is to borrow as little as possible.[27]

This change in attitude may also explain why bankers are no longer in the sound-money camp. Modern bankers have no interest in deflation; they have every interest in ensuring that the gravy train of higher debt and rising asset prices keeps rolling. Unlike 1929–31, when the City was urging caution on the British government, there was no real financial lobby for balanced budgets or higher interest rates. The developed economies went into the crisis of 2007–08 with the banks cheering them on.

9

The Crisis Begins

'When you borrow a lot of money to create a false prosperity, you import the future into the present. It isn't the actual future so much as some grotesque silicone version of it. Leverage buys you a glimpse of a prosperity you haven't really earned.'

Michael Lewis, *Boomerang*

For a period in the autumn of 2008, financial regulators really feared that the banking system might collapse. Automated teller machines would not deliver cash; companies would be unable to meet their payrolls; suppliers would not be paid for goods. The prospect was of a complete economic meltdown.

All this was because the post-1971 bubbles, described in Chapter 7, had burst. As was discussed in the previous chapter, banks had over-expanded their balance sheets and had become overexposed to property risk. The owners of residential (and commercial) property proved unwilling or unable to service their debts. As a result, the banks' capital reserves were in danger of being wiped out.

The massive government and central bank intervention that followed completely changed the tone of the political debate. A free-market Republican administration in the US, with a Treasury Secretary from Goldman Sachs, took equity stakes in the banks – a step that would have been condemned as 'socialism' had it been taken by the Democrats. Short-term interest rates were lowered almost to zero – in the Bank of England's case to levels unprecedented in its 300-plus-year history. Budget deficits were allowed to rise to levels unseen outside major wars, and to aid the recovery process, central banks decided to buy government debt with newly created money as a way of holding down bond yields. Many of these steps would have been seen as heresy by central bankers of past generations. The school of 'sound money' and 'balanced budgets' had been roundly defeated.

Many books have been written about the collapse of Bear Stearns and Lehman Brothers, and this is not another one. A lot of the focus has been on the folly of individuals: the investment bankers who presided over the collapse of their firms, the central bankers who kept interest rates too low, the individuals who borrowed too much to buy houses they could not afford, and the strange new derivative instruments that fuelled the speculation.

But let us try and look at the crisis in the light of this book's thesis. Money (debt) expanded to gratify the desire of consumers and businesses for greater economic activity (more trade). But some of that money was used to buy assets, in the form of shares and houses, which rose rapidly in price. Banks did what they always do: borrow short term to lend long term against the security of property. And as has happened regularly through history, they went too far. The 'Minsky moment' then happened and the spiral went into reverse. Or to put it another way, the pyramid scheme ran out of new clients.

Given that the crisis took forty years to build, it is not surprising that forecasters were taken aback by the timing. The economist Tim Congdon wrote a book called *The Debt Threat*[1] at the end of the 1980s; another economist, Peter Warburton, wrote *Debt and Delusion* at the end of the 1990s.[2] The failure of the crisis to arrive at those points made it possible for optimists to argue that higher debt levels were just a sign of a more sophisticated economy and financial system. Higher debts were not an economic risk since they were backed by higher asset prices, and because the debts ultimately cancelled each other out.

It was hard to gainsay these arguments with any statistical precision. Just as there is no iron rule that says when there is too much money in an economy, there is no ratio of debt-to-GDP that is 'too much'. For a start, GDP is a measure of annual activity, not of total wealth (the land, factories, oil, etc.). Financial analysts would not compare the size of a company's debts with its annual revenues but that's what a debt-to-GDP ratio effectively does.

Nevertheless, we have some idea that a limit exists. In the cases of

Iceland and Ireland, total debt ratios of eight to ten times GDP promoted financial crises. Eventually, at some extreme level, the borrowers will be unable to service their debts – a development that will come as a nasty surprise for the creditors. So we can be fairly certain that if debt (credit) grows much faster than the economy for a prolonged period, then a crisis will occur. If we drive on a motorway at a steady speed of 100 miles per hour, we may not crash immediately but we will crash eventually.

When the crisis came, the authorities reacted as they often do. They acted to safeguard the interests of borrowers rather than creditors, and the cost of mortgage borrowing was sharply reduced. They sought to drive down their exchange rates in order to prevent a deflationary spiral. The return on savings was driven down to zero. When there was a conflict between the central bankers' twin duties of safeguarding the currency and protecting the financial system, they chose the latter.

AS UNSAFE AS HOUSES

The debt crisis broke in 2007. It started with the most egregious bubble, that in American sub-prime mortgage lending. Like the many previous bubbles described in Chapter 7, it involved a boom in lending that pushed asset prices up to unprecedented highs. What made the crisis so pervasive was the way that mortgage loans had been repackaged and distributed. No one was quite sure where the risks had ended up and who was most exposed. The combination of that uncertainty and the highly geared nature of the financial sector proved calamitous.

The boom had required lending standards to be relaxed so more buyers could be enticed into the market. The Ponzi scheme needed a new set of suckers. Since house prices had risen so far, they were out of reach of people on low incomes. So it became standard for the borrower to claim a fictitiously high level of income to qualify for the loan. Even then, they could not afford to pay the full rate of interest. They were thus given 'teaser' loans in which low initial payments would be followed by much higher ones after a couple of years. By that stage, the buyers were assured, house prices would have risen and it would be possible to refinance the loan.

Why didn't self-interest operate to stop this scam from happening? Unfortunately, most participants had an interest in the boom continuing. The house buyers usually did not have to put down a deposit and were unlikely to face any penalties if they walked away from the loan. So the mortgage deals gave them the ability to live in a nice house with the possibility of a gain if the bubble kept inflating. It was like renting, with an option on house prices.

The real estate agent who sold the house and the mortgage broker who arranged the loan were motivated by commission. For them, doing a bad deal was better than doing no deal at all. The mortgage lenders should have been concerned, but they too had short-term goals. The loans were quickly sold on to outside investors. And the investors? They were motivated by a search for high yields and were too lazy to think carefully about what they were buying.

For the whole system to keep working, house prices needed to keep rising rapidly so the loans on the houses could be 'flipped' – refinanced with the benefit of higher capital values. Once house prices started to falter, defaults rose rapidly; the homeowners were unable to meet the interest payments and had no interest in maintaining a link to the property without the prospect of a quick gain.

All these loans had been bundled into mortgage-backed securities; in essence, bonds which were secured on the housing loans. The mortgage payments on the loans were used to pay the interest on the bonds. As defaults rose, the sub-prime lenders found it more difficult to get finance. Their business model was built on getting rid of the mortgages as quickly as they created them; in the absence of the cashflow from sales, they were unable to meet their debts.

The problem then rippled through the chain. The mortgage-backed securities had been bundled into other securities called 'collateralized debt obligations' (CDOs). These were designed to give investors a diversified pool of high-yield assets. Such assets were attractive as an ironic consequence of the great moderation; yields on cash and government bonds were low so investors were happy to chase higher returns.

These CDOs had been organized in tranches, like a kind of trifle. Each layer had different rights and expected returns. The so-called equity layer was the riskiest; it paid the highest yield but suffered the first losses when the bonds in the portfolio defaulted. Below that were tranches with lower yields, which bore the burden of the next defaults. The underlying assumption was that very few mortgage-linked bonds would default. After all, that is what an era of rising house prices had suggested. The portfolios were diversified by region and by mortgage lender to add further protection. As a result, the largest tranche in the portfolio was regarded as very low-risk, and was rated AAA, the highest-possible level, by ratings agencies such as Moody's and Standard & Poor's. That made the bonds all the more attractive to investors who needed secure assets for accounting or regulatory reasons; bizarrely enough, this included the banks.

One further wrinkle is needed to explain the disaster. The banks often set up the CDOs; this involved them buying the underlying mortgage bonds before selling them in the market. They also lent the money to investors who bought the CDOs, often via off-balance sheet vehicles, known as conduits. This was the most telling flaw. If all this financial shenanigans had any justification, it was that risk was being dispersed from the banks. The CDO industry ensured the banks were still involved. Worse still, they still had exposure to the risks but were no longer monitoring the quality of the borrowers as closely as they used to.

When the 2006–07 loans started to default, the whole system froze. The mortgage lenders most exposed to the sub-prime area, such as New Century, went bust when they could not offload the duff loans. When the mortgage-backed bonds went wrong, banks were caught with lots of them on their books. Sometimes this was because they had bought bonds with the aim of putting them into CDOs; as the bad news leaked out, new CDO issuance became impossible. In other cases, banks ended up owning the bonds because the conduits (the vehicles that had bought CDO tranches with borrowed money) went bust.

The prices of CDO tranches plunged. There were no buyers so they were impossible to sell. No one knew who owned what or how much each bank was exposed. It was tempting to assume the worst. Bear Stearns, a US investment bank, had run two high-profile funds that invested in the sub-prime mortgage market (one had the amazing name of the High-Grade Structured Credit Enhanced Leverage Fund); when they got into trouble, Bear Stearns propped up the funds to avoid the embarrassment of client losses. Lehman Brothers, another investment bank, had been aggressively expanding into property lending.

Such banks were dependent on funding from the wholesale market; in other words, from other banks and institutions. As mortgage-related losses spread, each bank was determined to secure its own funding and equally determined not to be exposed to firms in trouble. Rumour fed upon rumour; the weak banks saw their share prices plunge and the cost of insuring their debt surge.

That insurance was in the form of another derivative, called a 'credit default swap' (CDS). The name was more complicated than the concept: Party A worries that a bond issuer might default on its interest payments, so it pays Party B a regular payment, like an insurance premium, as protection against this eventuality. If the bond issuer does default, Party B will compensate Party A for its losses, just as an insurer will cover fire damage.

What made CDSs controversial is that investors did not need to own the bond to insure against its default. A speculator could buy insurance in the belief that a company was in trouble, hoping to benefit from the disaster. As more people bought insurance, the price would go up. The speculator could then sell the CDS contract at a profit. Critics argued that this encouraged chicanery. The unscrupulous could buy default insurance on a company, spread damaging rumours about it and profit from the result. Worse still, the rest of the market would see the rising cost of default insurance as a sign that the company really was in trouble. Some investors would sell the shares while others would use a tactic called 'selling short' to bet on a falling share price. (Short-sellers borrow the shares from another investor and sell them in the market. When the time comes to return the borrowed shares, the short-seller buys the shares again. If the price has fallen, the short-seller makes a profit.)

If there are enough short-sellers, the share price will indeed decline under the weight of sell orders. In turn, this will cause genuine bond investors to have worries about the company's health, and to buy default insurance as a result. The cost of CDSs would rise, with a further dent to sentiment. A corporate death spiral could ensue.

In the case of an industrial company, it might be able to stop the rumours by announcing higher profits; the financial rumours would not have reflected the underlying health of the business. But in the case of a bank, negative sentiment causes customers to withdraw their deposits or lenders to charge more than their funding. Bad news in the market does impact on their business.

That is what happened in an astonishing six months during 2008. Bear Stearns and Lehman Brothers were the smallest of the big investment banks and the most heavily exposed to the housing market. So other banks became reluctant to provide the short-term funding that the duo needed. And other investors began to speculate that the investment banks might go bust. The share prices of Bear and Lehman fell sharply, and the cost of insuring their bonds rose dramatically.

The heads of Bear and Lehman reacted with bewilderment and fury. They became convinced that they were the victims of a conspiracy. After spending years touting the benefits of free markets and decrying government intervention, the Wall Street barons now called on the authorities to prevent people speculating in CDSs and from selling their shares short. In many cases, it was the Wall Street firms who had financed these activities. A ban would cost their clients money.

Credit default swaps also created a further problem. Someone had to bear the losses when bonds actually did default. Even a rise in the cost of insurance was a problem for those who had already written insurance, since it increased the potential size of their losses. That was because of a technicality in the way the swaps were designed; the insurer had to put up collateral to show they were good for the money if default occurred.

The problem showed up at one of the world's largest insurance companies, AIG. Its financial products unit had agreed to insure the AAA portions of sub-prime mortgage CDOs. The unit's head, Joseph Cassano, thought this was essentially 'free money' since it was highly unlikely the bonds would ever default. Accordingly AIG insured $62 billion worth. But as the crisis accelerated in the autumn of 2008, AIG's position went heavily into the red; its counterparties, including Goldman Sachs, demanded more collateral. The financial strain proved too much and the whole group had to be rescued by the US government, which had to inject $182 billion of capital.

The details may seem forbiddingly complex, but what toppled so many banks and a giant insurance company was, at heart, a simple problem. The financial system had accumulated a series of claims on America's housing stock. These claims were collectively worth far more than the houses themselves. Once that became clear, the value of some of these claims had to be wiped out. The crisis of 2007–08 was simply a mad scramble as investors tried to offload the claims. But, by definition, not everyone could do so. Like a game of Old Maid, the losers were the ones left holding the wrong card.

The autumn of 2008 was a classic example of market panic. Investors ceased to care about the return *on* their capital and started to worry about the return *of* their capital. The only way to halt the crisis was for governments to step in and guarantee the banking sector. The result, however, was a phenomenal rise in the level of sovereign (government) debt. In time, this eventually led to the second stage of the debt crisis, which began in early 2010 with concerns about the finances of Greece.

Shifting the debts from the private to the public sector still leaves the system with an awful lot of debt on its books. A McKinsey study in 2010[3] found that the total debt levels (i.e. totalling those of governments, companies and individuals) was 466% of GDP in Britain, 366% in Spain, 322% in France, 315% in Italy and 296% in the US. These figures are the culmination of the long historical processes that have been described in this book. On average, in the ten economies studied by McKinsey, total debt had risen from about 200 per cent of GDP in 1995 to more than 300% by 2008. In percentage point terms, the biggest increases were in the UK and Spain, with 157 and 150% respectively. But before we turn to the sovereign debt crisis that has gripped the world, let us look at the other building blocks of the debt mountain.

CONSUMER DEBT

Although consumers have always borrowed, the generation that lived through the 1930s tended to be highly suspicious of personal debt. My father refused to have a credit card, cutting up an unsolicited version that arrived in the mail and returning it with a stern lecture on inflation. My favourite (possibly apocryphal) story of the 1930s was of the lady who bought a washing machine on hire purchase and refused to use it until all the instalments had been paid.

Economists generally agree that consumer credit is very useful for the economy. Some countries have too little consumer debt. In Russia, for example, mortgage debt is just 3 per cent of GDP. The ability to borrow allows people to smooth consumption over their lifetime; families can borrow money when the children are young, and pay off the debt when they leave home. This should mean that consumption is less prone to sudden swings, and thus recessions less severe.

The big change in the modern era has been for consumer credit to be supplied through the banking system. Before the Second World War, you had to be a very respectable person indeed for the bank to extend you an overdraft; they would naturally demand security in the form of property. A local dignitary might be required to vouch for your character as well. In Britain, the building society movement was created to channel the funds of small savers into the hands of those who wanted to buy houses. But the societies had fairly strict credit standards. A sizeable deposit was needed and a low multiple of salary was allowed. Up until the 1980s, potential homeowners approached the building society in a spirit of supplication, hoping to be approved.

As the financial sector was liberalized in that decade, the tone changed. Banks and other financial institutions began to compete hard for mortgage business, which appeared to offer excellent returns. Falling interest rates made it easier for homeowners to service their loans and rising house prices improved the value of the lenders' collateral. Lending standards were steadily reduced, with the size of the deposit required falling from 25 per cent to 10, 5 and then zero. Incredibly, products like option adjustable rate mortgages (ARMs) effectively allowed US homebuyers to borrow more than the value of the house; borrowers were allowed to pick their own interest rate, with any shortfall being added to the size of the loan. Potential homebuyers were allowed to borrow greater multiples of their income and, in some cases, not required to provide any proof of their income at all (so-called 'liar loans').

There was a rapid rise in mortgage debt after the 1980s; in both the UK and the US, mortgage debt rose from a little over 30 per cent of GDP in 1983 to around 80 per cent by 2006. Surprisingly, mortgage debt-to-GDP ratios were even higher, at nearly 100 per cent of GDP, in Denmark and the Netherlands.

Meanwhile, the world of unsecured credit changed irrevocably with the advent of the credit card. As we have already seen, consumer credit developed steadily through the nineteenth and early twentieth centuries. It was not until the late 1950s that credit cards emerged, giving consumers the ability to pay for a wide range of goods and services. (Initially, the cards were aimed at the better-off; often they were charge cards and had to be paid off each month, reducing the lenders' risk.) None of this would have been possible, of course, in a world of usury laws. Campaigns against excessive credit-card rates have been launched at various times over the last fifty years. But consumers have generally welcomed the extra flexibility and convenience that the cards bring.

The idea of sending consumers an unsolicited offer to take out credit would have seemed like madness to bankers in the Victorian era. In fact, it has turned out to be a very profitable business. First, the ease of usage meant card users were for a long time relatively indifferent to the interest rate charged, allowing issuers to impose a rate that more than compensated them for losses. Second, the issuers were also able to charge merchants a fee for servicing card transactions. Although some stores held out against the trend (Marks & Spencer in Britain was a notable example), card use became so common that stores had to accept them. Cards became ubiquitous once shops stopped accepting personal cheques because of fraud problems.

In all this, money illusion played a key part. Back in 2006, the BBC ran a programme on consumer debt. One middle-aged man recalled the first day he used a credit card: 'I felt instantly richer', he said. But of course, he wasn't. Either he paid his credit-card bill in full every month – in which case he didn't really need the card and was no better off. Or he failed to pay off the bill, in which case he was poorer, as he now had to repay the cost of his purchases, plus the interest payments. However, people have an innate inability to defer their pleasures; if they see, say, a 50-inch TV screen, they want it now. They do not want to spend two years saving up to buy the product, so they are happy to pay (in the form of interest payments) over the odds for it.

But there is an element of rationality about credit-card use. Academics point out that, although shopkeepers pay a fee to credit-card issuers, they do not charge differential rates for cash buyers. Instead, merchants increase the prices they charge to reflect the fees they pay credit-card issuers. The effect is that cash buyers are subsidizing the card users. One study found that each American cash-using house-holder pays $149 a year to each card-using household.[4] Since card use tends to be related to household income, this is a transfer of wealth from poor to rich; low-income households (those earning less than $20,000 a year) pay $21 a year each while those earning more than $150,000 a year get nearly $750 a year of subsidy.

Failing to cope with one's debts is not the badge of shame it was in the nineteenth century. In Britain, those who are overwhelmed by their debts can enter an individual voluntary arrangement (IVA). Under an IVA, a court can assess the borrower's income and expenditure and decide what it is reasonable for the borrower to pay, given the need to spend money on essentials. These 'essentials' can include mobile phone contracts and satellite TV subscriptions. In the US, personal bankruptcy laws were favourable to debtors until a tighter system was introduced in 2005.

Consumer credit has grown at an exponential rate since the Second World War. In 1945, US consumer credit totalled just $5.7 billion; within ten years, it had risen nearly eightfold to $43 billion. From that point on, the records tumbled: $100 billion was reached in 1966, $500 billion in 1984 and $1 trillion in 1994. By July 2008, just before Wall Street's collapse, the total reached $2.6 trillion, or over $8,000 for every man, woman and child in the country. In the McKinsey study mentioned above, consumer debt in mature countries (defined as Canada, France, Germany, Italy, Japan, South Korea, Spain, Switzer-land, the US and the UK) rose by $10.8 trillion or 66 per cent between 2000 and 2008.[5] That was the largest single component in the near $40 trillion increase in total debt over that same period.

When J. K. Galbraith updated his book *The Affluent Society* in 1984[6] he noted that increased demand and increased consumer debt were inexorably tied together. He predicted that ways would be found to extend the process, by lengthening the period of repayment, reduc-ing the size of the deposit, and lowering the standards for creditwor-thiness. In every respect, he proved to be correct. Eventually, however, Galbraith warned that the process would have to come to an end. And what would happen then, he wondered, given that 'an interruption in the increase in debt means an actual reduction in demand for goods'.

The debt crisis provides some clues. After the collapse of Lehman Brothers, credit-card companies started to restrict the amount of credit they offered and consumers started to use their cards less often. The total amount of US credit-card debt fell in every month for the next two years and, by November 2010, was 15 per cent below its peak. 'Although our economy has experienced other long episodes in which revolving credit growth has slowed, we have never seen such a prolonged period of outright decline,' said Elizabeth Duke of the Federal Reserve Bank of Philadelphia.[7] In part, this was because the default rate on credit cards rose from 4 per cent in 2007 to more than 9 per cent in 2009. Ms Duke concluded that consumers were switching from credit to debit cards, first to avoid charges and secondly, to keep a tighter rein on their spending. Buying on the never-never became less fashionable.

CORPORATE DEBT

The corporate sector has had a more mixed attitude to debt. As recounted in the last chapter, the banks have been enthusiastic borrowers. However, indebtedness in the rest of the corporate sector did not reach the same heights. Nevertheless, it rose from 58 per cent of GDP in 1985 to 76 per cent in 2009, according to the consultancy firm Smithers & Co. This was not just an American phenomenon. The McKinsey study found that non-financial corporate debt in mature economies grew by \$9 trillion, or 44 per cent, between 2000 and 2008.[8]

The result was a decline in corporate credit quality. Ratings agencies grade all corporate debt on a scale of AAA (the best quality) to D (in default). More indebted companies tend to have lower ratings. According to Standard & Poor's, the rating of the average corporate bond declined from A in 1981 to BBB- by 2010. That shift is quite remarkable. The ranking of BBB- is the absolute minimum required to qualify for investment grade status – the kind of bonds suitable for conservative investment institutions. If the rating slips any further, the average company will be classed as a 'junk bond', a category that, before 1980, was only deemed suitable for the wildest speculators.

The riskiness of corporate debt illustrates that the nature of creditors as well as that of borrowers has changed. Corporate bonds were once tucked away in pension funds and charity endowments, institutions that were interested in safety of capital. They only wanted the best-rated bonds. But in the 1980s and 1990s, a whole new breed of specialist investors emerged, in particular hedge funds, which were happy to take on higher risk in the hope of higher reward. The low level of short-term interest rates and of government bond yields encouraged this tendency – hedge funds needed to buy higher-yielding assets if they were going to offset their fees.

For the borrowers, keeping a cash hoard was no longer in fashion. Indeed companies were criticized for holding 'idle' cash. Academics argued that companies should put the money to work, by making acquisitions or investing in new factories, or they should return it to shareholders who could then invest the money in a company with more attractive growth potential. Activist shareholders often demanded that executives should adopt such policies.

In theory, companies could finance themselves entirely with equity (cash raised from shareholders who would never be repaid), with debt, or with some combination of the two. The academics suggested that, other things being equal, the exact mix was irrelevant to the value of a company. That value is determined by the cashflows generated. The company can use those cashflows to pay dividends to shareholders, or interest to creditors. Adjusting the mix changes the value of the equity and bond proportions, but not the total.

However, other things were not equal. In most countries, companies can deduct the cost of interest payments from their tax bill, but not their dividend payments. This led many commentators to assert that a balance sheet with more debt was more 'efficient'. Of course, such balance sheets were also more risky but, as we have seen, the 'great moderation' of the period from 1982 to 2006 meant that recessions were rare and mild, so companies were rarely punished for piling up the debt.

American companies may have been more inclined to take risks because of their country's favourable bankruptcy laws. These laws arose out of the country's debtor-friendly culture. In particular, they were influenced by the railroad boom and bust of the mid-nineteenth century. Lenders realized that the value of a railroad was much reduced if it ceased operating; the metal rails and wooden sleepers were not worth much. It was better to keep the business intact and hope that a rival operator would buy it as a going concern. In the twentieth century, that system evolved into 'Chapter 11', a structure that allows companies to keep operating and prevents creditors from foreclosing on the business. Instead, a court takes charge, gives the company in trouble breathing space and, if necessary, ensures that the creditors are paid in order of seniority. The process has allowed many companies to survive recessions. The potential cost is that 'zombie' businesses are allowed to keep going (as has happened particularly in the airline sector) with the result that efficient companies can never earn a decent return. Many commentators think that the risk-taking attitude of American entrepreneurs has been encouraged by the relaxed attitude to bankruptcy.

With their fear of failure reduced, executives had plenty of incentives to load their companies with debt. For a start, after the mid-1980s, much of their remuneration came in the form of share options; these gave the managers the right to buy shares at a set price. By borrowing money to invest, or make an acquisition, the executives took a chance on growth. If the gamble worked, profits would soar and they would make millions from their share options. If the gamble didn't come off, the options would expire, worthless, but the executives would be no worse off than when they started. For them, it was a one-way bet. In contrast, the shareholders would pay part of the profits from a successful gamble to the managers, and would bear all the costs of a failed gamble.

The rise in takeover activity, and the increasing tendency of boards to fire underperforming chief executives, also encouraged greater risk-taking. Both encouraged managers to think short term rather than long term, when someone else would probably be in charge. And it also meant that companies tended to be classed either as predators or prey; if they were not taking over their competitors, they risked being taken over themselves. A successful acquisition meant that the chief executive could justify a higher salary; being taken over meant the chief executive would lose his job.

Executives were also surrounded by people who had a tendency to recommend the greater use of debt. Investment banking advisers earn their money from arranging bond issues and takeovers; they earn nothing if companies keep money in the bank. Analysts are usually looking for the hot new stock to recommend to their clients. They are likely to favour businesses which are pulling out all the stops in a dash for growth, rather than those that are husbanding resources in case of recession.

And then there is the private equity industry. This sector exists to buy publicly quoted companies and then refinance them, a process that usually involves taking on more debt (before selling the company back to the market at a higher price). The term 'private equity' itself is something of a marketing triumph: the sector used to be known as leveraged buyout funds, which gives more of a sense of the risks involved.[9]

How does private equity work? The first step is for those who run the funds, known as general partners, to raise money from investors, known as limited partners. The most successful private equity managers, such as Blackstone or Kohlberg Kravis Roberts, have long-established relationships with the kind of investors (pension funds, university endowments) that can afford to support their deals. The limited partners will agree to invest in a fund for an extended period, often ten years.

Armed with these commitments to invest, the private equity managers will go looking for target companies. Often these will be struggling companies which are out of favour with the stock market; this makes it possible for the private equity groups to buy them at a decent price. The ideal target will have plenty of assets and a strong cashflow, for reasons that will become apparent. The general partners will use the money of the limited partners to finance part of the acquisition price. But the bulk of the deal will be funded in the form of debt, initially borrowed from banks but eventually in the form of 'leveraged' loans that will be bought by outside investors. This debt will of course be tax-deductible.

If the acquisition is successful, the private equity group may bring in outside managers, but just as often it will work with the company's existing managers. These managers will be incentivized with share options, or bonuses, that will pay off if the company is sold at a higher price, and they will look to pay off the debt bill, either by cutting costs or by selling surplus assets. If the process is successful, the equity (the bit owned by the limited partners and the managers) will become worth a lot more. If the process is unsuccessful, the equity will prove worthless and some of the lenders may take a hit.

The general partners (those who run the fund) will earn their cut in two ways. First, they will take an annual management fee, which may be as much as 2 per cent of the funds invested. This fee is designed to cover the managers' running costs. Secondly, they will take a performance fee, known as 'carried interest', when the assets are sold, often 20 per cent of all profits after an agreed hurdle return has been reached. It is this carried interest that has made private equity fund managers rich. And it has also aroused plenty of controversy, given that it is taxed in many jurisdictions as a capital gain, rather than as income. Since capital gains usually bear a lower tax rate, this results in the anomalous situation where private equity managers are taxed at a lower rate than their office cleaners, as one financier memorably described it.

That is not the only complaint about private equity. In the view of their critics, the managers are asset-strippers, storming into companies, firing staff, managing for the short term and all on the back of tax-deductible debt. The question of whether they actually deliver enhanced returns to investors is another subject of debate, with some arguing that the returns are minimal, once the use of leverage and the overall rise of the stock market are accounted for.[10]

Private equity managers naturally dispute these findings. They argue that their system aligns the interests of managers and investors; that they only prosper when their clients do well. They also argue that they improve the companies they manage and have an interest not just in slashing costs, but in growing the companies so they can be sold at a higher valuation.

What can hardly be in dispute is that the climate for private equity over the last twenty-five years has been extremely favourable. Investors have sought out their services, believing that they needed to diversify away from the stock market into 'alternative assets', a category deemed to include private equity along with hedge funds and commodities. The Yale endowment fund pioneered this approach with some success.

(It has some odd consequences. A pension fund could own a stake in a public company, sell the stake to a private equity group which will manage it on the fund's behalf for a higher fee, and then buy a stake in the same company at a higher price when it is refloated on the stock market.)

Private equity managers have benefited from the combination of cheap debt, rising asset markets and infrequent recessions. The loss of any one of those components might have restricted their growth: the lack of cheap debt would have made it difficult to finance deals; flat or falling asset markets would have made it harder to sell at a profit; and frequent recessions might have crippled companies burdened by high debts. Conceivably, all three components might not operate in the managers' favour over the next twenty years. There is also a feast-and-famine tendency to private equity. Investors are most likely to favour the sector when past returns have been high. Past returns are most likely to be high when asset prices have risen. Thus private equity managers are most likely to have money to invest when indices are high. They will bid against each other, forcing prices even higher and requiring the use of more debt. The result is that returns on such deals are likely to be lower-than-average.

Private equity may no longer be the dominant force it was in the 1990s and 2000s. And non-financial companies in general may also decide to take a more cautious attitude towards their balance sheets in the wake of the credit crunch. That change may last for a long time. In Japan, companies have spent much of the last twenty years reducing their debts and hoarding cash.

However, a cautious corporate sector will only make it more difficult for economies to generate growth. In turn, that will make life more difficult for governments, the subjects of the next chapter.

10
Not So Risk-free

'The path pursued by fiscal authorities in a number of indus-
trial countries is unsustainable. Drastic measures are neces-
sary to check the rapid growth of current and future
liabilities of governments and reduce their adverse conse-
quences for long-term growth and monetary stability.'
'The Future of Public Debt: Prospects and Implications',
Bank for International Settlements Working Papers, 300

Once upon a time, politicians believed in balanced budgets. The exem-
plar was William Gladstone, the nineteenth-century British Liberal
Prime Minister. Gladstone, who was also a devout Christian, was no
great enthusiast for military adventures and believed that wars should
be financed from current taxation. Once they realized the cost, he
thought, voters might be less enthusiastic about sending troops into
battle. Many a war might have been avoided had his precept been
followed.

In the twentieth century, the attachment to balanced budgets disappeared. In part, as we shall see, this was down to the influence of
Keynes and the use of deficit spending to support the economy. But it
was also because of the way that politicians behaved towards their
voters.

Public choice theory states that governments do not act in response
to some higher notion of the public good but in response to their own
self-interest. Bureaucrats want to expand their empires to increase
their power. Politicians favour the special interests that finance their
campaigns. The interests of the typical voter will be overwhelmed by

the power of lobby groups, which can devote time and money to advancing their cause. Each policy decision might represent a big gain to the lobby group, but only a small cost to the typical taxpayer. Over time, however, these costs add up and government gets larger and larger.

Another term for the problem is 'clientelism'. When political parties get into office, they need to reward their supporters with jobs, tax breaks and subsidies. Once added, these boondoggles are rarely abolished; all that happens when a different party gains office is that the goodies are handed out to different clients. This process can go on for a long time because governments appear to have little in the way of a credit limit. Their debt is usually regarded as risk-free by investors since they can pay it back by raising taxes or printing money. Governments usually borrow at the lowest interest rates in their domestic market.

POST-WAR DEBT CRISES

Walter Wriston, a Citibank chief executive, summed up this attitude to government funding as 'Countries don't go bust'. But of course, nations do default on their debts, as our history tour in Chapter 2 demonstrated. And several countries may be about to let creditors down again, as the aftermath of the 2007–08 credit crunch overwhelms the weakest developed nations.

Creditors have always had great difficulty in dealing with sovereign debtors. Lend to your own government or monarch and you run the risk that the authorities will use their power to change the laws, and deny you repayment. Lend to another country and your rights are even less likely to be enforced. Even if sovereign debtors agree to pay their creditors back, they may cheat in the way that they do so. They may pay back the money in debased coinage, or a devalued currency. So exchange-rate systems evolved as a way of keeping debtors honest. And they had advantages for both sides. If creditors could be reassured about their rights, they would lend more money and at lower rates. Good debtors, like Britain and the Netherlands, had financial advantages over bad debtors, like eighteenth-century France. Britain's financial success encouraged other countries to follow its example.

But the willingness of countries to follow prudent financial policies proved no more permanent than the willingness of most January revellers to follow their New Year's resolutions. Carmen Reinhart and Kenneth Rogoff recount that sovereign default has occurred in a number of waves, starting with the Napoleonic Wars.[1] In the 1840s cycle, nearly half the countries in the developed world were in default. There was a 1870s to 1890s wave, associated with falling commodity prices, and a 1930s to 1950s phase, linked to the Great Depression and the war.

Since the Second World War, the issue of sovereign default has been associated with developing countries. The 'third-world debt crisis' of the 1980s was the biggest. Banks had expanded in the 1970s, in part by recycling the surpluses generated by the oil-exporting nations. These had been lent to governments round the world, helping them to pay for higher oil prices. However, the American recession of the early 1980s had an adverse impact on the US's southern neighbour. In 1982, Mexico announced that it would be unable to meet its debt repayments and the crisis quickly spread to the rest of Latin America. US banks (including Wriston's Citibank) were exposed to heavy losses, and only some generous accounting treatment allowed them to survive. The so-called Brady plan, named after US Treasury Secretary Nicholas Brady, allowed banks to exchange their illiquid holdings of Latin American debt into more liquid instruments, backed by US Treasury bonds.

Just as investors were recovering from those losses, Mexico suffered a further debt crisis in 1994, when it devalued the peso and required emergency aid from the US government. But the big surprise of the 1990s was that debt problems spread to Asia. The continent had a much better reputation than Latin America and was noted for its 'tiger' economies, characterized by low labour costs and heavy investment in manufacturing. The success of South Korea, Thailand and Taiwan sparked talk of an 'Asian miracle'.

While these economies did achieve rapid growth rates, and captured market share in many world industries, their growth model also had a flaw. Many Asian countries pegged their currencies to the dollar to maintain export competitiveness, just as China does today. However, US interest rates were lower than those in most Asian countries. That encouraged Asian companies to borrow in dollars rather than in their own currencies. The stage was set for another speculative bubble, in which Asian companies borrowed from local banks to invest in commercial property. When the property bubble burst, and the banks collapsed, Asian countries had to turn to the outside world for help.

In the 1980s and 1990s, sovereign debt crises forced governments to turn to the International Monetary Fund. The demise of the Bretton Woods system had caused the fund to remake itself as an emergency provider of finance to the developing world. These loans often carried strict conditions that reflected what was known as the 'Washington consensus', in favour of free markets and reduced public spending. The negotiations between governments and the fund carried an echo of the 'bankers' ramp' that Britain faced in 1931. Governments that followed the IMF prescriptions faced street protests and were often accused of selling out to Western creditors.

The accusation of financial colonialism carried greatest weight in Africa. That continent suffered from continued crises in the 1980s and 1990s. A host of problems, including falling commodity prices, famine-inducing droughts, corruption and civil wars linked to superpower rivalry, caused Africa to lag far behind the growth performance of Asia. Many countries were saddled with debts that they had little hope of repaying.

Africa's plight inspired campaigners to revive the moral case for debt relief that would have been familiar to medieval Christians. The Jubilee Debt Campaign takes its name from the idea of an occasional festival of debt forgiveness – the original meaning of the word jubilee. Campaigners argue that it is unjust that poor countries should be forced to devote money to debt repayment when their populations are short of food, and the money would be better deployed paying for healthcare and education. They also use the concept of 'odious debt', developed by the lawyer Alexander Sack, to deal with the problem of deficits incurred by tyrants and kleptocrats.

Sack argued that debt was odious if there was: an absence of bene-fit for the population of the debtor nation; an absence of consent by the citizens of the country concerned; and an awareness by creditors of how the funds were being used.[2] His ideas reflected the realities of history. The Bolshevik regime repudiated Tsarist debts when it took power in 1917 and the Chinese communists did the same in 1949. The people should not pay for debts incurred by the capitalist oppressors, the new governments proclaimed.

In the modern world, the odious debt argument does seem to apply to Africa. Why should the people of the Democratic Republic of Congo be responsible for debts run up by the former dictator Joseph Mobutu, who enriched himself and his cronies from the proceeds? Even when the borrowed money is not stolen by rulers, governments may have spent it on arms deals, or prestige projects that did not benefit the citizens concerned.

The counter-arguments to the debt campaign generally rest on two premises. The first is the problem of moral hazard; if some countries are allowed to repudiate their debts, what message does that send to those countries that are still trying to pay up? The second is practical. Creditors may have to put up with defaults on existing debts. But they will not extend any new loans once the principle of default has been established.

Nevertheless, the debt relief campaign gained traction. A mechanism for debt forgiveness already existed in the form of the Paris club, a gathering of finance officials from nineteen developed nations. But a more formal system, known as the Heavily Indebted Poor Country Initiative (HIPC) was launched in 1996 and then remodelled in 1999, after a mass demonstration at the G8 summit in Birmingham the previous year. Eligibility for the HIPC is based on criteria such as debt sustainability, the ratio of debts to export earnings. It is also an intensely political process. Debt relief was granted very quickly to Iraq after removal of Saddam Hussein's regime, for example, since the rich world wished to see a stable government in Iraq. But political involvement was inevitable given the roles of the International Monetary Fund and World Bank in the debt forgiveness process.

A further round of campaigning, associated with the G8 summit in Gleneagles in 2005, led to another acronym, the Multilateral Debt Relief Initiative (MDRI). This promised that some $50 billion of debt owed to the World Bank and IMF should be cancelled. By 2010, the IMF reckoned that some thirty countries, from Afghanistan to Zambia, had benefited from the scheme.[3]

Has the process done any good? Some critics say that it allows Western politicians to look caring and inflate their aid budgets by replacing cash aid with debt relief. Figures from the OECD[4] suggest the issue of hypocrisy should not be overstated; in 2008, total development aid from the major developed economies was $121.5 billion, of which debt relief counted for just $8.8 billion. The OECD reckons that, in 2009, development aid rose by 6.8 per cent, excluding debt relief, despite the pressures on government finances.

Nevertheless, the West is still giving with one hand and taking away with the other. In 2005, for example, the Jubilee Campaign calculated that the very poorest countries received $40.4 billion of aid from the West, but had to pay out $43.2 billion in debt service. And some countries are running up debts faster than they are being forgiven.[5] However, where debt relief has occurred, campaigners argue that governments have been able to improve their healthcare systems and devote more money to education. Whether Western politicians will be so keen to forgive developing world debts now their own countries are following austerity programmes is an interesting question.

THE CURRENT CRISIS

Many poor countries are still struggling to deal with their debts. But the striking thing about the latest crisis is the shift of focus from the developing world to the developed. The IMF reckons the average developed country will have government debt of more than 100 per cent of GDP in 2015, compared with just 30 per cent in emerging markets. To put that in cash terms, Eswar Prasad, an economist at Cornell University, reckons that the average debt burden per worker in rich countries will rise from $31,700 in 2007 to $68,500 in 2015.[6]

The problem has grown significantly since 2007. The table below, taken from the BIS paper cited at the start of the chapter, shows that the debt-to-GDP ratio has risen by more than twenty percentage points in many countries. In Britain, it will have doubled between 1997 and 2011. The annual budget deficit has grown by ten percentage points or more in some cases. This is pretty much what might have been predicted; Reinhart and Rogoff found that past banking crises caused the absolute level of public debt to rise by 86 per cent.[7]

Table 1. Fiscal situation and prospects

	fiscal balance			structural balance[1]			general government debt		
	as a percentage of GDP								
	2007	2010	2011	2007	2010	2011	2007	2010	2011
Austria	-1.0	-4.6	-3.5	-2.3	-3.6	-3.2	60.7	72.2	72.3
France	-2.8	-7.1	-5.9	-3.0	-4.6	-3.8	64.2	82.3	86.8
Germany	0.3	-3.3	-1.7	-1.1	-2.3	-1.4	65.0	84.0	82.6
Greece	-6.7	-10.4	-8.0	-10.4	-11.4	-6.9	105.4	142.8	165.6
Ireland	0.1	-32.0	-10.3	-8.4	-8.9	-6.8	24.9	94.9	109.3
Italy	-1.5	-4.5	-4.0	-2.5	-3.1	-2.6	103.6	119.0	121.1
Japan	-2.4	-9.2	-10.3	-2.6	-7.4	-8.1	187.7	220.0	233.1
Netherlands	0.3	-5.3	-3.8	-1.3	-4.5	-3.4	45.3	63.7	65.5
Portugal	-3.2	-9.1	-5.9	-3.3	-9.4	-4.0	68.3	92.9	106.0
Spain	1.9	-9.2	-6.1	-1.1	-7.2	-4.4	36.1	60.1	67.4
United Kingdom	-2.7	-10.2	-8.5	-3.4	-8.0	-6.3	43.9	75.5	80.8
United States	-2.7	-10.3	-9.6	-2.2	-7.0	-6.4	62.3	94.4	100.0

Note: 1. Cyclically adjusted balance.

Sources: IMF World Economic Outlook

More than in most countries, US public opinion has been exercised by the national debt. The independent presidential campaigns of Ross Perot in 1992 and 1996 were driven, in part, by his warnings on the issue. The subject was neutered by the 1990s boom, during which the Clinton administration managed to run a fairly conservative fiscal policy. Budget surpluses during that period were so common that Alan Greenspan, the chairman of the Federal Reserve, started to wonder aloud about what would happen to the bond market if the trend continued; the Fed ceased to issue the thirty-year Treasury bond, previously the benchmark for the market.

In the 2000s, a combination of President George W. Bush's tax cuts, the military campaigns in Iraq and Afghanistan and a sluggish economy sent the deficits, and the debt total, up again. A sharp drop in tax revenues during the credit crunch, particularly from the corporate sector, exacerbated the problem. As noted in the Introduction, by 2008, the national debt total passed $10 trillion, requiring an extra digit on the Times Square debt clock.

The cost of bailing out the banks, and the apparent willingness of government to reward the sector's bad behaviour, caused a renewed surge of public anger. So when the newly elected Obama administration reacted to the crisis in classic Keynesian fashion, unveiling a near $800 billion stimulus plan, it faced a wave of public opposition.

The 'tea party' campaign took its name from the revolutionary movement that protested against British taxes by dumping tea in Boston harbour. It seems to have started with a rant by Rick Santelli, a correspondent for the CNBC financial channel, about a US government plan to help those with mortgage debts. The movement channelled a number of areas of public discontent. Apart from the unpopularity of the bank bailout, there was a general feeling that it was 'un-American' to use public money to bail out businesses, even the auto companies with their hundreds of thousands of employees, on the grounds that people should stand on their own two feet. In addition, the tea party members saw the bailout as a further sign of government intrusion into the economy – a trend that was exemplified by the Obama healthcare plan. The tea party also argued that the current generation was being irresponsible in passing debts on to its children and grandchildren. And it tapped into the age-old cultural divide that pitted the heartland states (many of which had supported William Jennings Bryan 100 years ago) against the coastal elites, as represented by the 'blue states' that voted for Barack Obama.

One could argue that the positions of the tea party are not very coherent. They want the deficit to be cut but without raising taxes. They want spending to be cut but not the expensive Medicare and social security programmes on which many elderly tea party supporters rely. One could also argue that balancing the budget would involve a recession that would hit tea party members hard, so they should be careful what they wish for. But the rise of the tea party shows that there may be political limits to the ability of economies to take on more debt. The irony is that the US has not faced any creditor pressure to tighten its belt. Even as the debt burden soared, and after the country's credit rating was downgraded for the first time in its history, yields on Treasury bonds fell. By September 2011, the yield on ten-year Treasury bonds fell below 2%.

Why were creditors so forgiving? The US debt burden may look bad, but it is the one-eyed man in a sightless world, relatively speaking. It remains the world's largest economy, with the most liquid markets, a history of reliable debt service, and the ability to borrow in its own currency. Moreover, it is a relatively closed economy, with only a small proportion of activity made up by foreign trade. As a result, while a fall in the pound might push up UK prices quite quickly, a fall in the dollar is less likely to lead to a rise in American inflation. However, as Martin Wolf has remarked, 'The very factor that makes borrowing large sums relatively safe for Americans – that they are borrowing in a currency they can create at will – also makes borrowing riskier for their creditors.'[8] As we shall discuss later, the US faced huge long-term fiscal challenges.

THE EURO-ZONE CRISIS

Europe, not the US, has been at the centre of the sovereign debt crisis. As outlined in Chapter 6, the euro had a number of design flaws, including a failure to impose fiscal or current-account discipline on member countries. This was a failure at both the public- and the private-sector level; for many years, investors were willing to buy the sovereign debt of peripheral euro-zone members on similar yields to those prevailing in Germany or the Netherlands regardless of the risk.

The initial focus of market concern were the countries known by the acronym PIGS – Portugal, Ireland, Greece and Spain. These countries suffered in various combinations from the problems of an over-large banking sector that had become exposed to a housing boom and bust; an uncompetitive economy signalled by repeated current-account deficits; and a bloated state sector, with high private-sector unemployment. The different causes all had the same effect: a sharp rise in the level of government debt relative to GDP.

In the 1990s, these European countries would have dealt with the issue by devaluing their currencies and regaining competitiveness. But that option is ruled out by euro membership. Instead, the only option is to get their costs in line with those prevailing in Germany. That can happen in one of two ways. German costs could rise, via a policy of keeping German inflation above the euro-zone average for several years. But the Germans, given their history, are unwilling to follow such a plan. In any case, the German economic model is built on a competitive export industry. Germany went through the pain of re-absorbing the communist east of the country in the early 1990s and joining the euro at too high a rate in 1999. Allowing its costs to rise would destroy all that hard work.

In the absence of German inflation, or a currency devaluation, an improvement in the competitiveness of the PIGS can only come through lower domestic costs via a painful period of austerity and devaluation. In a sense, the euro represents a modern version of the gold standard in which countries must make sacrifices to retain their exchange rate. And those sacrifices are hard to make in a democratic country.

Greece was the first country to get into trouble. It had joined the euro in 2001, slightly after the other PIGS countries, thanks to its long history of higher-than-average inflation rates and large budget deficits. And although it appeared to qualify under the deficit rules, it has subsequently admitted that creative accounting had been used to massage the figures.

The country may have hoped that joining the single currency would impose an external discipline. But it failed to knuckle down to the task of being competitive; by 2010, its costs had risen 25 per cent relative to the rest of the euro-zone.[9] This had resulted in current-account deficits of more than 10 per cent of GDP in each of 2006, 2007 and 2008. In October 2009, the newly elected Prime Minister, George Papandreou, admitted that the fiscal deficit for the year would be 12.5 per cent of GDP, and not the 6 per cent it had earlier reported. Market confidence was shattered and Greek bond yields started a seemingly inexorable rise.

Greece showed signs of descending into a debt trap, in which financing the deficit gets harder and harder. One of the preconditions for a debt trap is that the interest rate on the debt is higher than the likely growth rate of the economy. When that happens, the country can be paying out more in interest than its income is growing. A high interest bill won't matter if the debt level is small. But, of course, a country is most likely to face high interest payments when its debts are large and creditors are worried about repayment. For any debt level around 100 per cent of GDP, the debt trap bites very sharply. And a debt trap can turn into an imminent crisis if a lot of the country's debt is short term. That is because interest costs increase when the debt is rolled over, and the average debt cost rises very quickly.

The best way of escaping from a debt trap is not to add to the problem. So a country needs to run what is called a primary budget surplus; that is, its revenues need to exceed its expenditure before interest costs. Run a primary surplus for long enough and eventually the debt-to-GDP ratio will decline. But it needs years of austerity to achieve this goal. Greece started to embark on this process in late 2009, in the face of street protests and strikes. The crisis revealed lots of wasteful public spending and a tax system that had allowed the wealthy to get away with non-payment. The Greek economy was revealed to be dysfunctional.

Ireland entered the crisis in a good degree of fiscal health; its debt-to-GDP ratio in 2007 was just 25 per cent. Three years later, it was 98 per cent, thanks to the government's commitment to guarantee the deposits (and senior bonds) of the banking sector. The bank sector was recovering from a lending spree, fuelled by the success of what was known in the 1990s as the 'Celtic tiger' economy.

Ireland's credit boom was in part caused by euro-zone membership. The European Central Bank sets interest rates for the region on the basis of average conditions. Inevitably, rates will be too low for some countries and too high for others. Irish GDP grew, in real terms, by 6.2% in 2005, 5.4% in 2006 and 6% in 2007; over the same three years, German GDP grew by 0.8%, 3.2% and 2.5% respectively. Short-term interest rates for both economies ranged between 2% and 4% over the same period.

That level of interest rate may have been right for Germany, but for Irish borrowers, taking on debt at 2–4 per cent seemed like a no-brainer in an economy growing at two or three times that rate. Debt as a proportion of household income roughly doubled, from 100 to 200 per cent, between 2002 and 2007. A lot of that borrowed money was used to buy houses. German house prices rose 2.6 per cent over the 2005–07 period; Irish house prices rose 48 per cent.

When Irish property prices started to fall in 2008, the ramifications were extremely serious. Around one in eight Irish workers were employed in construction at the height of the boom. If one allows for related businesses like estate agencies, it may have been one in five.[10] The resulting blow to employment from the housing crash sent tax revenues down from €47 billion in 2007 to €33 billion in 2009, causing the deficit to surge.

It quickly became clear that many of those who had borrowed to build, or buy, houses could not repay their debts. That naturally created doubts about the financial health of the Irish banking system, which had grown like Topsy over the previous decade. Figures from the European Commission show that Irish financial institutions expanded by the equivalent of 750 per cent of GDP between 1999 and 2009.[11]

As with Bear Stearns and Lehman Brothers, the Irish banks faced the danger of a run by wholesale lenders, who provided the short-term finance that allowed the banks to operate. To head off a catastrophe, the Irish government stepped in to guarantee, not only all bank deposits, but also all bank debt. In the short term this proved a success, with the Irish banks attracting deposits from British citizens worried about the health of the UK banks.[12] In the long term, this was disastrous, since the Irish banks were too large for the state to support without inflicting huge costs on its taxpayers. In 2010, the cost of injecting capital into Anglo Irish Bank and the Irish Nationwide Building Society pushed the annual budget deficit up to an astonishing 32 per cent of GDP. Standard & Poor's, the ratings agency, estimated that the bank guarantee might eventually cost Ireland 50–58 per cent of GDP.

Ireland reacted quickly to the resulting fiscal mess. It unveiled a series of austerity programmes, including tax increases and cuts in public-sector wages, in an attempt to keep the lid on its deficit. It did its best to reassure the financial markets. But the housing bust so weakened the economy that GDP fell in nominal terms by almost a fifth. With a shrinking economy, the debt-to-GDP ratio deteriorated despite the budget-cutting measures.

The weak condition of its banks acted as a continuous drain on the Irish government's credibility. In September 2010, the Irish banks had to roll over some €25 billion of government-guaranteed debt. That seemed to reawaken the market's doubts. In the following month, Ireland accepted an €85 billion bailout from the EU, including a contribution from Britain, to prevent it from paying the high rates demanded by the markets. In the subsequent political backlash, the Irish Prime Minister, Brian Cowen, was swept from office.

Spain had looked better, in terms of its government debt-to-GDP ratio, than the other three countries in the markets' sights. But it had a huge private-sector debt ratio of around 180 per cent of GDP and the crisis has shown that private debt can easily become public debt. The annual compound-growth rate of total Spanish debt between 2000 and 2008 was a remarkable 7.4 per cent, more than twice the increase in US debt over the same period.[13]

The debt mountain was a result of a building boom, in which the stock of Spanish housing went up 35 per cent in a decade while prices tripled. Dhaval Joshi, an analyst at the research group BCA, reckons that around a third of this private-sector debt, some €600 billion worth, could default because of the collapse in the Spanish property market.[14] Such write-offs would be the equivalent of 55 per cent of GDP. Barclays Capital summed up the problem by lumping together government and senior bank debt (where bondholders have a strong

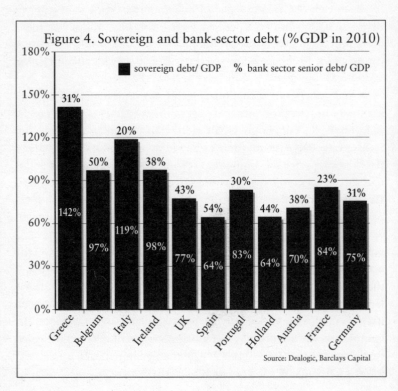

Figure 4. Sovereign and bank-sector debt (%GDP in 2010)

Source: Dealogic, Barclays Capital

claim on the bank's balance sheets).[15] As you can see from the chart opposite, Spain's bank debt is almost as large as that of the government. Add the two components together and all the countries featured have a combined debt ratio of more than 100 per cent of GDP.

Spain's socialist government, somewhat reluctantly, started to take action once it was clear that the markets were concerned about the budget deficit, which hit 11 per cent of GDP in 2009. Civil service pay was cut and VAT increased, despite street protests and a general strike. But unlike Ireland, Spain has an inflexible labour market. Labour laws make it difficult to fire workers, dividing the economy into insiders with protected jobs and outsiders without them. In mid-2011, unemployment was 21 per cent. Attempts to reform the labour market have been made but face considerable union opposition.

Portugal did not enjoy the housing booms experienced by Ireland or Spain, nor is its banking system excessively large (senior bank debt is 30 per cent of GDP, on a par with Germany's). But its government debt-to-GDP ratio of 83 per cent is still too high and it has run a current-account deficit in every single year of euro membership, indicating a lack of competitiveness. Those deficits were 9.5% of GDP in 2005, 10% in 2006, 9.4% in 2007 and 12.1% in 2008.

Prolonged current-account deficits imply that foreigners are building up claims on the Portuguese economy every year. That puts the onus on the Portuguese government to retain investor confidence. But it was slow to act, not unveiling an austerity programme until September 2010. By that time, doubts over the health of the country's banks had forced them to depend on financing from the European Central Bank. Capital inflows from official sources replaced inflows from private sources.

The crisis affecting the weaker economies in the euro-zone bears a remarkable similarity with the case of Argentina which, as already noted, imposed a currency board in 1991, under which all its currency, the peso, was backed one-for-one by US dollars. Just as Greece shackled itself to Germany to import monetary credibility, Argentina tied itself to the US in a desperate effort to eliminate hyperinflation. The strategy worked for a while, just as membership of the euro delivered early benefits for Greece. But it was not accompanied by sufficient reform, particularly at the provincial level, where public spending grew unchecked. The strains told after ten years as the markets began to doubt that Argentina would incur the pain required to maintain the peg. As one historian of the Greek crisis sagely remarked, 'A currency arrangement can bolster a strong economy, but it cannot create one.'[16]

BAILOUT TIME

The European authorities followed the classic pattern of denial, anger and acceptance in dealing with these issues. Their initial response was to deny that there was any chance of a sovereign-debt crisis in the euro-zone, followed by an attack on the 'speculators' who were causing a problem where none existed.

The Greek crisis precipitated a change in attitude. As Greek bond yields rose to double-digit levels in the spring of 2010, it became clear that help would be needed. But Germany's Chancellor, Angela Merkel, was reluctant to approve a deal in the run-up to a crucial regional election in North Rhine Westphalia. The delay added to the sense of panic, and Merkel's CDU party lost the election anyway.

A €110 billion bailout package for Greece was agreed in May 2010, involving three-year loans from euro-zone countries and the IMF. In return, Greece was forced to pledge further austerity measures. That was swiftly followed by the establishment of a €750 billion scheme, dubbed the European Financial Stabilization Facility (EFSF), which would provide back-up financing for other countries in difficulties. The EFSF would raise funds, with the backing of EU governments, and then lend them to nations in trouble.

The aim was to overpower the markets with 'shock and awe', convincing investors that governments would always be able to get cheap financing. The hope was that the facility might never need to be used. If investors were reassured, yields would fall and countries could finance themselves at reasonable rates.

But only six months later, Ireland had to be rescued with an €85 billion package to allow the country to bolster the capital of its struggling banks. Britain, while not a member of the euro-zone, contributed to the deal because of its close trading links with Ireland (and because it made a profit on the loan, charging the Irish more than Britain paid to borrow). Portugal in its turn was rescued in a €78 billion deal in May 2011.

The European Central Bank was also wheeled into action. It had already been supporting the banks of the troubled countries by providing financing at a time when it was difficult to raise money from the markets. In May 2010, it agreed to buy the bonds of distressed countries in a bid to keep yields down. Technically speaking, this was not Quantitative Easing (QE) since the ECB was not expanding the money supply; it sold an equal amount of assets in order to avoid injecting cash into the markets.

Nevertheless, given the way the ECB was set up as the guardian of European monetary stability, this was a bold move, and one that went against the tone of its pre-crisis statements. Its initial interventions were fairly small scale by the standards of other central banks. By June 2011, the ECB had bought €74 billion of bonds. According to Capital Economics, had the ECB wanted to match the Bank of England's buying spree, which amounted to 25 per cent of the gilt market, it would have had to buy €493 billion worth of bonds.[17]

However, these bailout plans showed little sign of working. For a start, the rates paid on the emergency loans were higher than the recipient countries could afford. Secondly, loans did not deal with the real issue. In a paper for the Legatum Institute, former IMF official Desmond Lachman argued that a bailout can help with a liquidity problem, not a solvency problem.[18] And peripheral euro-zone countries have a solvency problem 'in the sense that, absent a debt restructuring and an exit from the euro, the correction of the periphery's finances cannot be achieved without provoking the deepest and most prolonged of domestic economic recessions'. Bailouts just postpone this outcome. If the economies are still uncompetitive, they will keep running up current-account deficits that will add to the debt. If they pursue savage austerity measures, their economies will probably shrink, in which case their debt-to-GDP ratios will rise.

Indeed, by the summer of 2011, one year after the initial Greek bailout, that was exactly what seemed to have happened in that country. The Greeks needed more money from the EU and IMF, which demanded further austerity measures in return. These austerity measures were passed by the Greek parliament in late June in the teeth of strikes and violent protests. For the Greeks, these 'rescue packages' simply mean further debt that still has to be paid back, and an abrupt decline in their standard of living.

Other EU nations were desperate to avoid a formal Greek default. First, much Greek debt was in the hands of the wider international banking system; a default might thus precipitate a further banking crisis. Secondly, the EU feared that the failure of Greece would simply prompt the markets to switch their attentions to Portugal, Ireland, or (far worse) the much-larger Spain and Italy. Once the principle of default was applied in one nation, why not the others? By delaying any Greek default, the EU hoped to give the banks (and governments in other countries) the chance to repair their finances. This policy of 'fudge and nudge' actually had the opposite effect. In the summer of 2011, the yields of Italian and Spanish bonds started to rise sharply. The result was yet another crisis summit, at which the European Central Bank agreed to buy the bonds of the two countries and push yields down. It looked like another 'sticking plaster' solution.

The best way out of a debt crisis is growth, and there seems little prospect of rapid growth in the GDPs of Greece, Portugal or Spain. (Ireland may be another matter because of its success in attracting international companies.) The first two have probably been living beyond their means for years, too dependent on subsidies from the EU and government spending. Spain enjoyed a construction boom and it may be hard to shift those workers to new, more productive industries. Because of this, the German and French governments agreed that the EFSF (scheduled to expire in 2013) would be replaced by a longer-term mechanism which could involve extending debt maturities and forcing creditors to accept they will not be repaid the face value of their assets.

But if one accepts that the Greeks will simply be unable to afford to pay back their debts, there is only one alternative to default: other nations will have to pay their debts for them. This implies a form of fiscal union; in the US, the Federal government is willing to send aid to individual states in times of crisis. But such an option will not be popular in the rest of the EU; this is true of Germany, which will have to foot a large part of the bill, but also in places like Finland, where the True Finn party saw its vote soar when it opposed bailouts for other countries. Even if the rich countries, like Germany, could be persuaded

to guarantee Greek (or Italian) debts, they would demand a high political price: an effective veto over the budgetary policies of such countries.
That might be anathema to voters in Greece and Italy. The euro-zone
could still break apart in the face of these political divisions.

The European bailout packages represent the end of a long process
in which bad debts have been passed up the chain – from private-sector
borrowers to banks, from banks to governments and from weak
governments to strong ones. The next test is how much debt those
strong governments are willing or able to absorb.

THE HIDDEN DEBTS

Official debt figures measure, by and large, only what the state has
actually borrowed from the markets. But on top of these explicit debts,
governments have usually made a number of unfunded promises. These
largely consist of benefits promised to potential retirees, in the form
of pensions and health spending. These promises are tempting to make
in the short term, since the full cost is often unrecognized. The full
burden will only come due on some other leader's watch. As will be
explained in the next chapter, ageing populations are a huge problem
for developed economies, acting as a drag on growth as well as pushing up public spending. If these promises are kept, then the effective
debt burden of western nations may be substantially higher.

A paper by Jagadeesh Gokhale for the free-market Cato Institute
in the US calculated that these total European liabilities were the
equivalent of multiples of GDP, with figures ranging from two-and-a-
half times in Spain to more than fifteen times in Poland.[19] The EU
average was 434 per cent of GDP. (In Britain's case, the number was
more than four times GDP.) If nothing is done, the BIS economists
project that gross debt-to-GDP ratios will reach 300 per cent in Japan
over the next decade, 200 per cent in the UK and 150 per cent in
Belgium, France, Italy and the US.[20] Some prefer to use net debt ratios,
rather than gross, on the grounds that governments have assets that
can be set against their debts. But the BIS authors argue convincingly
that such assets are difficult to value and may not be easy to sell in a
crisis.

The key issue is that governments have a number of stakeholders – creditors, taxpayers and benefit recipients. To get out of the current mess, one of these sets of stakeholders must pay. Creditors might not get their money back in real terms; taxpayers might pay more; or benefits might be cut. A combination of all three outcomes is also possible. As Arnaud Mares of Morgan Stanley put it, 'The question is not whether they [governments] will renege on their promises, but rather upon which of their promises they will renege, and what form the default will take.'[21]

The sheer scale of these debts is worrying for a number of reasons. It may be true that every liability is also an asset, but as we have seen throughout this book, the interests of debtors and creditors have often come into conflict. The main problem is that debt regularly needs to be refinanced, or rolled over. Every time that happens, the creditors have to believe the debtors are good for their money; it is like a regular vote of confidence. And loss of confidence is contagious. If one debtor defaults (perhaps because the creditor will not extend the loan), lenders may fear that other debtors will follow suit. The higher the ratio of debt-to-GDP, the worse this potential problem becomes. Say each crisis involves the default of one-in-ten debtors; at a 100 per cent debt-to-GDP ratio, this puts 10 per cent of output at risk. At 400 per cent of GDP, 40 per cent of output is in danger.

The second problem was outlined in the last chapter. A lot of debt is secured against asset values. If debtors have to sell assets to repay loans, the price of those assets will fall, lowering the collateral of all lenders. The value of the debt is fixed; the value of the assets is variable. The danger is a debt-deflation spiral, first described by Irving Fisher in the 1930s,[22] in which falling prices depress activity. Consumers never spend today on the grounds that goods will be cheaper tomorrow.

Fisher described a process with nine links. Debt liquidation leads to distress selling, followed by a contraction of the deposit currency, a fall in prices, a greater fall in the net worth of businesses, a decline in profits, falls in output and employment, resulting in loss of confidence, hoarding and disruptions to interest rates. As prices fall 'each dollar of debt still unpaid becomes a bigger dollar' Fisher wrote, since 'the liquidation of debts cannot keep up with the fall of prices it causes'. He added that 'the very effort of individuals to lessen their burden of debts increases it, because of the mass effect of the stampede to liquidate in swelling each dollar owed . . . The more the debtors pay, the more they owe.'

A third problem concerns the identity of the creditors and the debt-ors. As was seen in the last chapter, certain nations in the developed world (most notably America) now owe money to the developing world (most notably China). For a country used to dominating global politics, this puts America in a rather uncomfortable position. What if the Chinese used their new-found financial power against them? The Chinese also have to worry about what will happen if America defaults.

Even if the government does not default on the debt, then servicing the debt may still be very expensive. Interest costs may eat up a lot of the annual budget, leaving less money to spend on more useful things like schools and roads. To meet those higher costs, the government may well increase taxes, and higher taxes have a depressing effect on economic activity. Policies that favour creditors over debtors may favour the rich over the poor. But a policy of favouring debtors may end up sending capital elsewhere.

In a follow-up paper to their book studying sovereign debt defaults, Professors Reinhart and Rogoff find that a country's rate of economic growth starts to deteriorate once the debt-to-GDP ratio passes 90 per cent of GDP.[23] This paper has attracted a lot of criticism.[24] Correlation does not imply causality. It could be that debt-to-GDP ratios rise rapidly when countries get into economic trouble (i.e. GDP falls faster than debt rises). The most likely adverse economic impact of high government debts would come from the 'crowding out' of private-sector investment; the government would absorb all of the nation's savings, leaving nothing for business. On that basis, however, the annual deficit, not the stock of debt, should be the key criterion.

Despite the criticisms, it seems likely that countries with high debt-to-GDP ratios will have high deficits as well (because of the interest burden). It also seems likely that countries with high debt-to-GDP ratios will have a higher level of government spending as a proportion of GDP. Studies suggest that the higher the level of government spending, the slower the growth rate; one study[25] finds that, for every one percentage point rise in spending, relative to GDP, growth falls by 0.12–0.13 per cent.

Slow growth and high debts are not a very appealing combination, especially given the demographic problems of the developed world, which will be the subject of the next chapter.

11

Bequeathing Our Debts

'For I, the Lord thy God am a jealous God, visiting the iniquity of the fathers upon the children unto the third and fourth generation of them that hate me.'

Deuteronomy 5: 9

The rapid rise in human population is a fairly recent phenomenon. It was not until around 1800 that the global population passed the 1 billion mark, but the 2 billion mark was reached in the 1920s, and 3 billion by the 1960s. Remarkably the number of humans has more than doubled since then and was scheduled to reach 7 billion in late 2011. Is it any coincidence that this period of population expansion was also a period of rapid economic growth? Each person is both a potential producer of goods and a consumer. The link is not automatic; China was a miserably poor country until the late 1970s thanks to its government's misguided economic policies. But while rapid population growth may bring its problems, a shrinking in population is likely to be even more of an issue.

Demographic trends are not set in stone but they tend to be quite slow to change. Current UN projections indicate that the pace of population growth is set to slow. After more than doubling in the second half of the twentieth century, global population is set to rise by only 50 per cent in the first half of the twenty-first.

That is still a pretty rapid rate of growth. But the key issue for the Western world is the distribution of that increase. Nearly all the growth will come in the developing world. According to an analysis by Deutsche Bank, the population of the developed world will grow just 3 per cent between 2010 and 2050.[1] That is as close to static as makes no difference. Moreover, within that total some countries are expected to see sharp falls in population; a phenomenon not seen since the Black Death in the fourteenth century. Japan will have 25 million fewer people by 2050, a loss of 20 per cent; Russia will lose 24 million, or 17 per cent; Germany 11.6 million, or 14 per cent.

The composition of those populations will also be changing. The number of elderly people (those aged over sixty-five) in the developed world will rise from around 197 million to 334 million between 2010 and 2050. As a proportion of the total, that is a rise from 16 to 26 per cent. For the world as a whole, the elderly proportion will rise from 7.6 per cent to 16.2 per cent. By the middle of the century, around a billion people will be over sixty-five, an age that has traditionally been associated with retirement.

The median Briton was thirty-four years old in 1980 and almost forty years old by 2009. By 2050, he or she is forecast to be forty-two and a half. The median American age has risen from thirty in 1980 to thirty-six and a half in 2009 and will be almost forty-two by 2050. Thanks to China's one-child policy, the median Chinese person is on his or her way from being twenty-two in 1980 to forty-five by 2050.

BABY BUST

These figures are only forecasts. We must be conscious that demographic trends can change unexpectedly. Even Keynes got this wrong. In a 1937 lecture, he declared that

We know much more securely than we know almost any other social or economic factor relating to the future that, in place of the steady and indeed steeply rising level of population which we have experienced for a great number of decades, we should be faced in a very short time with a stationary or declining level.[2]

At the time, the government actuary was predicting a British population of 34 million by the year 2000. The post-war baby boom duly followed.

Just as that boom caught observers by surprise, there could be a sudden rise in the birth rate in the developed world or, on a less cheerful note, a disease that culls the ranks of the elderly, to confound the forecasts. But two developments are well established. The first trend is for prosperity to be linked with declining birth rates. This has been true of the developing as well as the developed world. Poor people tend to have more children for prudential reasons. For a start, infant mortality is higher for those with low incomes. They may need four children to be certain that two will survive into adulthood. In addition, poor people often rely on their children to help them work the land and support them in old age.

Around the world, women take the chance of better education and access to birth control to have fewer children. If they go to university, women get married later and have children later, eating into their period of maximum fertility. In the developed world, the ability to have a career gives women an economic freedom that they did not have in the nineteenth century, when most were dependent on a husband's income (in 1911, 90 per cent of British wives did not have paying jobs).[3]

In addition, children are an economic burden, not an asset, in rich countries. They cost money to bring up, are not allowed to work by law and remove women from the workforce during some of their peak earning years. Nor is it now usual for children to support their parents in their old age; state benefits are designed to do that.

The fertility rate in Europe, measured by the number of children per woman, has fallen from an average of 2.58 in the period from 1960 to 1965, to 1.41 in 2000–05. This is well below the 2.1 'replacement rate' calculated by demographers (the figure is higher than 2 to account for infant and childhood mortality), although it does appear to have stabilized. Japan has seen a similar decline, from 2.02 to 1.29. The US is in a rather better position. Its birth rate has dropped, but only from 3.31 to 2.04, and it has benefited from a steady flow of immigrants.

The second development is improved longevity. European life expectancy at birth has increased by almost ten years since 1950. Global life expectancy at birth has risen from fifty-eight years in 1970–75 to sixty-seven years at present and is forecast to reach seventy-five years by 2045–50. In the developed world, life expectancy at birth should reach eighty-two years by the middle of the century. The trend seems inexorable: Japan is already at this level and is on its way to eighty-seven years by 2050. This improvement is down to a number of factors: better nutrition; the development of antibiotics which have cut deaths from disease; a decline in manual labour which had previously shortened the lives of male workers; and a reduction in smoking.

All these demographic changes have profound consequences for economic growth. Such growth comes from two main sources: a rise in the workforce, and an improvement in the output each worker can produce – in other words, productivity. If the workforce is static or shrinking, productivity will have to make all the running.

Therefore growth will be much slower, short of some technological miracle that will improve our productivity quickly. But relying on that is like counting on a lottery win to improve your finances. Furthermore, elderly people consume a lot of nursing care, an activity that is unlikely to result in a lot of productivity gains. The more 'efficient' the care becomes, the less it may be valuable. The whole point of care is the time spent with each patient.

The size of the UK's pensionable age population is projected to increase from 11.8 million in 2008 to 15.6 million in 2033. The rate of increase is slowed by the planned rise in the state pension age, particularly for women. But even if they can't retire, not all of these people will find work. The number of people aged sixty and over is projected to increase from 13.6 million to 20.6 million over the same period, or from 22 per cent of the total population to nearly 29 per cent. The numbers of people aged over eighty-five will more than double, from 1.3 million to 3.3 million. These very old people will almost certainly not be working.

In terms of the burden on the British taxpayer, the key ratio is that of workers to dependants, which includes children and the elderly. By 2033, there will be just 1.52 people of working age for every dependant; in 2008, the ratio was 1.64. The baby boomers are moving through the population profile rather as a python absorbs his dinner. If the boomers are defined as those born between 1946 and 1964, they entered the workforce from the 1960s to the 1980s and reached their peak earning power (deemed to be between the ages of thirty-five and fifty-four) between the 1980s and 2000s. The first baby boomers are now reaching sixty-five, but many will have been winding down their careers from the early 2000s onwards.

Things look even worse if you consider the ratio of workers to retirees. Retirees are a bigger burden on the state than children, thanks to healthcare and pension promises. The number of workers per retiree was 4.3 in 1970, 3.6 in 2010, but will fall to 2.4 in 2050. In America, there were 5.3 workers per retiree in 1970, 4.6 in 2010, and there will be 2.6 in 2050. By 2050 France will have 1.9 workers per retiree, Italy 1.5 and Japan just 1.2.

Meanwhile, the retirement age has failed to keep step with increased life expectancy. The first government pension scheme was devised by Otto von Bismarck, the German Chancellor, in 1889; he set the retirement age at sixty-five, at a time when life expectancy at birth was forty-five. (This figure was pushed down by infant mortality. Many people did make it into old age, including Bismarck himself, who died aged eighty-three.) But the second half of the twentieth century saw a steady increase in the life expectancy of those who made it to sixty-five. Improved healthcare probably made the difference. For example, those who suffered heart attacks achieved a much higher recovery rate. In Britain, the average sixty-five-year-old male in 1950 could expect to live for another twelve years; by 2008, life expectancy for such men had increased to twenty-one years. The state pension age remained unchanged over that period, so that the average retirement period had increased by 75 per cent.

The obvious way to approach this problem is to increase the retirement age so that people spend longer in the workforce. The period of idleness needs to be shortened; in France, the extreme example, men spend ten years longer in retirement than they did in 1970. Some of these 'lost years' need to be reclaimed. If the ratio of retirement years to life expectancy had stayed at its 1970 level, then the average OECD worker would already be retiring at seventy.[4]

In any case, a healthier population can be economically active for a longer period. To some extent, this is already happening; visit a Wal-Mart in the US and you are likely to be greeted by some cheerful grandpa figure as you enter the store. By paying taxes, such people are reducing the burden on the rest of the population, as well as keeping themselves busy.

However, changes in the official retirement age are likely to be slow. In part, this is down to fairness. If you are already sixty-three, postponing your retirement age by a couple of years is a little sudden. You may not be able to replace your anticipated retirement income at such short notice. So changes are announced well in advance to allow people time to prepare. At the time of writing, the British pension age was being raised to sixty-eight, but not until 2044. Even if the process is accelerated, it will not have a dramatic impact on the size of the workforce in the short term.

Pushing through even these modest increases will require a degree of flexibility on the part of employers and employees. With notable exceptions (like Wal-Mart and the British DIY retailer, B&Q) employers have proved reluctant to take on older staff, apparently regarding them as inflexible and difficult to train. Employers will have to learn to take advantage of the life experience of older workers. Workers may also have to learn to accept lower salaries as they get older, unlike the traditional approach of rewarding seniority. And they may also have to adopt a 'portfolio' approach to work, in which they take on a series of part-time jobs. Nevertheless, working longer will be a lot easier in some professions than others. Office workers may find it easy to continue working until they are sixty-seven; firemen and police officers will find it less so.

So the underlying problem is that fewer workers will have to support more retirees. Deutsche Bank reckons the key thirty-five to fifty-four cohort will shrink by 14 per cent in the developed world by 2050 and by 24 per cent in Europe.[5] This will be partly offset by the reduced numbers of economically dependent children. But many countries, including Japan, Italy, Germany and France, will have more elderly people in 2050 than they will have in the prime thirty-five to fifty-four cohort.

In France, President Sarkozy's proposal to increase the minimum pension age from sixty to sixty-two caused widespread protest in 2010. Its demographics are better than those of several other European countries but the trend is still dreadful. The number of workers aged between fifteen and sixty-four (the available working population) rose by 128 per cent between 1910 and 1950; it is set to fall by 5 per cent over the next forty years. Over that same period, the number of people aged over sixty-five will rise by 71 per cent.

The result is likely to be a strain on government finances. State pensions are an obvious example of such obligations, but the elderly also need a lot more healthcare than the young. A report by Standard & Poor's, the ratings agency, forecast that, if policies are unchanged, the median advanced country's budget deficit will rise from 4.7% of GDP to 7.5% in 2020, 9.7% in 2030 and 24.5% by 2050.[6] Age-related spending would absorb 27% of the typical advanced economy's GDP by 2050. That will push up the median advanced country's debt-to-GDP ratio to 78% by 2020, 112% by 2030 and 329% by 2050.

Of course, it is very hard to imagine that countries will be allowed, either by the markets or their voters, to let things deteriorate so far. But the required adjustments will be very great; S&P reckons that the median advanced country will have to shrink its deficit by around 8.4 per cent of GDP to prevent the problem from getting out of control.

That, however, highlights a policy dilemma. From the point of view of long-term sustainability, the sooner the deficit is cut the better. But a government that raises taxes and slashes spending at a time when the global economy is weak risks sending the domestic economy back into recession. That could make the financial position worse if GDP falls faster than the debt burden is cut. In addition, governments that tackle the debt burden aggressively may become electorally unpopular, and lose office. Furthermore, in the modern world, it is easy for the most talented people to move abroad to avoid a heavy tax burden.

THE UNRECOGNIZED LIABILITIES

As was noted in the last chapter, politicians have also made promises to workers in the public sector that are very large indeed. To understand this, we will have again to dip into the murky world of pensions. State pensions (those paid to all people over a certain age) are not the biggest issue. Instead, the problem is with those people who have worked for the government in the civil service, police force, healthcare system and so on.

In many countries, and in particular Britain and America, public-sector workers are offered a pension linked to their final salary. This will be based on a formula, according to which each year of service buys a proportion of their pay. Take, for example, a sixtieth scheme. Every year of service buys one-sixtieth of final salary, so a forty-year career earns the employee a two-thirds pension. After the inflationary experience of the 1970s, such pensions were usually given a degree of index-linking, so the pension keeps up, at least in part, with prices. There may also be benefits for any surviving spouse and coverage of healthcare costs.

How does the employer pay for that promise? It is complicated. Some pension schemes operate on a pay-as-you-go basis, taking in money from employees in the form of contributions and paying it out to retirees. Some build up a fund through annual contributions by themselves and by the workers. The proceeds are then invested to help build up a sum big enough to meet the pensions.

The pay-as-you-go approach is a clear example of a pyramid scheme. A constant supply of new workers is needed to pay for the benefits of the retirees. Indeed, one needs more workers than retirees since employee contributions (usually between 3 and 10 per cent of salary) are much smaller than benefits. When pension schemes are first established, a high ratio of workers-to-retirees is natural. But as time passes, the economics of the plan start to deteriorate. When benefits start to outweigh contributions in a public-sector scheme, the taxpayer has to pick up the shortfall.

It might seem as if a funded public-sector final salary plan is a much more sensible approach. It might even save the taxpayers money. Tax revenues would be expected to grow in line with economic output or GDP. But the government might hope that the pension fund can earn a higher return than GDP growth by investing in equities and other risky assets.

By and large that is what pension funds, both public and private, have tried to do over the last fifty years. They believed that equities would deliver better returns than other assets, particularly bonds and cash, over the long run. That allowed them to ride out short-term periods of stock market volatility such as during 1987 or 2000–02, when the dot.com bubble burst. This bet seemed reasonable in theory. Equities should deliver a long-term return because they are more risky and because one would expect companies to earn a return greater than their cost of finance (the return on bonds or cash). After all, if companies did not earn a decent return, then the economy would be in serious trouble. The bet also seemed to work in practice during the period 1982–2000 when equity markets were booming.

But deciding on the contribution rate needed to fund a final salary pension plan involves a lot of assumptions. What will employees earn by the time they retire? How long will they live? If their benefits are index-linked, what will the level of inflation be after they retire? What will be the return on the fund?

If a high return on the fund is assumed, the investments appear to be doing all the work. Many companies used the bull market of 1982–2000 to take a contributions holiday. The temptation is just as great for government bodies as it is for private-sector companies. In New Jersey, for example, Governor Jim Florio increased the assumed rate of return on the pension fund in 1992; this allowed him to lower the contribution rate and balance the state budget. His successors further eased the accounting assumptions and increased the benefits. As a result, by the middle of 2010, the state pension fund had a deficit of $173 billion, or 44 per cent of the state's GDP, a figure three times its official debts.[7] This problem was replicated all over America. According to one calculation, the individual states had a collective pension deficit of $3.2 trillion, equivalent to a quarter of all federal debt.[8] Some states could run out of the money needed to pay their pensions by the end of this decade.

How was this huge figure calculated? Not by using the assumed rate of return. Such an approach encourages pension plans to take on more risk. The more risky assets they buy, the lower their liabilities appear to be. But this is taking a punt with public money.

In the private sector, a pension plan that takes big risks might conceivably bankrupt the company. If that happens, workers will not receive all the promised benefits (some countries have set up funds to insure company benefits, but that is another story).[9] Governments (national and local) cannot wriggle out of their pension promises so easily. Even if the investments fail to deliver the expected returns, the benefits must still be paid by the taxpayer. In other words, *the size of the liabilities is independent of the assets meant to fund them.* If I receive a £1,000 tax bill, I may choose to fund it by putting £40 on a horse at 25-to-1 odds. But if the horse fails to win, the taxman will still want his money.

A pension promise by the government is like a debt; a commitment to pay the recipient a set sum of money after a set period of time. The government could fund the scheme either by giving all employees bonds that will mature at set points in their retirement, or by offloading the pension promise to a private-sector company. It would have to borrow the lump sum needed to fund this deal. In either case, it is clear that the key measure is the government's cost of borrowing. It is that rate that should be used to discount the liabilities.

This makes states' pensions promises very expensive. The Bank of England regards its pension scheme as the equivalent of an issue of index-linked debt, since employees' benefits are inflation-linked when they retire. So the bank buys index-linked bonds to fund its pension scheme.[10] The cost was 55 per cent of payroll in 2011, and that is far more than most state pension schemes put aside.

The problem has been hidden because of the way that pension schemes have been accounted for. Gradually, however, it will become apparent as the cash cost of paying benefits starts to rise. In the US, where almost all states have balanced budget amendments, any increase in contributions will have to be financed by higher taxes or cuts in services.

In Britain, the biggest public-sector pension schemes operate on a pay-as-you-go system. Employers are 'charged' a notional contribution from their budgets but this has been too low. The Treasury is set to increase the top-up cost of financing pensions from £4 billion in 2010–11 to £9 billion in 2014–15, at a time when the government is struggling to trim the deficit. Using the government bond yield as the discount rate, the total state-sector pension liability of the British government in late 2010 was £1.2 trillion, almost as much as the country's entire GDP.[11] This bill is not due straight away. Nevertheless, it is money that has to be met over the long term. The cost might be bearable if the rest of government finances were in good shape. But, of course, that is most definitely not the case.

Governments are slowly taking steps to reduce the pensions cost. Such measures, understandably, will be opposed by the trade unions, which are stronger in the public than the private sector. This will lead to much conflict in coming years. Apart from extending the retirement age, governments may decide to pursue other reforms, such as changing the pension rights of new staff. These people may be offered so-called 'defined contribution plans', as are common in the private sector. Under such plans, employers contribute money but provide no guarantee as to the eventual pension; it is all up to the performance of the assets in the portfolio. In essence, the employee rather than the employer bears the investment risk.

Another option is to move workers to a career-average rather than final-salary scheme. Final-salary schemes favour the senior staff in an organization, whose pay rises as they get promoted. This increases the expense for the employer. Most staff, however, tend to increase their wages in line with inflation. Switching to a career-average pension would not cost low-paid workers much but would save employers money.

The pension burden can also be cut by reducing the extent of inflation-linking. Britain has already made this move, announcing that public-sector pensions will increase in line with the consumer price index, rather than the retail price index. The former tends to rise by around 0.7 per cent a year less than the latter. This change may reduce the government's pension bill by 10 per cent or so.

Indeed the proposed British pension reforms for the public sector involved a combination of different measures – as well as a change in inflation-linking, the government also planned to make public-sector workers retire at the state pension age (rather than at sixty), switch them to career-average schemes and increase the level of their contributions. This quadruple whammy prompted a strike in late June 2011 and further disputes looked inevitable.

In the US, the costs of ageing fall under the general heading of 'entitlements', in particular Social Security and Medicare. Social security, the pension plan, is technically a funded scheme but only in the sense that the trust fund invests in Treasury bonds. Since such bonds are simply a promise to pay by a future government, this funding approach is the equivalent of saving for college fees by putting an IOU in your biscuit tin. Benefits are still dependent on future taxpayers.

Medicare is the cost of funding health treatment for the elderly. This is very expensive; the US spends twice as much as a proportion of GDP on healthcare without any benefit to longevity. Analysis by KPCB, a venture capital firm, found it had been underfunded by $1.9

trillion over the last 45 years. Annual payments per beneficiary had risen 26-fold since 1966. Lifetime healthcare costs for the average American are $631,000, of which the government pays almost half.

As the population ages, this spending is set to accelerate. If one adds in Medicaid (health spending on the poor) then entitlements will absorb the entire projected federal budget by 2025. Very little has been done to try to reduce the growth of these spending plans.

A NEW ATTITUDE

An ageing population does not just affect government debt. Think of this population shift in terms of the ability to service, and the willingness to take on, debt. By and large, retirees are dependent on income derived from three sources: state benefits, their own savings, and an employment-linked pension. Once the employee retires, none of those sources is likely to generate significant income growth. Keeping up with inflation is about the best the elderly can hope for.

So why would the elderly take on, or be granted, debt? A creditor could not be confident that a retired person's cashflow would improve sufficiently to repay both capital and interest. The elderly are unlikely to want to gear up to buy bigger houses. Indeed, normally they will seek to be trading down to smaller places as their children will have left home. (Some will seek to borrow against the security of their houses in order to generate cashflow.)

The life-cycle theory of investing suggests that people save different amounts at different ages. They save little, and borrow more, when they are young; save most when they are middle aged; and run down their savings when they retire. On this basis, there should have been a surge in the savings rate in the 1990s and 2000s as the baby boomers moved into the forty-five to fifty-five age range.

The odd thing about American baby boomers, however, is that they did the opposite. The savings rate was very low, by historic standards, between 1990 and 2010. Some commentators warned that this would be a source of future trouble, but free-market economists argued that the savings rate was being understated, since the capital gains made by the baby boomers on their houses and shares were not being counted. Those economists were surely right as to the motivation behind this phenomenon. Baby boomers did assume that, as they were getting wealthier, they did not need to save out of their income. But capital gains are not permanent, and indeed equity gains were reversed from 2000–02, and property gains from 2007–09.

For the economy as a whole, savings made out of income are important in providing the funds for investment that will stimulate future growth. Capital gains are the early recognition of that future growth; the house or share price goes up because people expect wages or profits to rise in future. But by themselves, those capital gains do nothing to create such wage or profit increases. In 2007, fewer than half of all Americans aged fifty-five and over had savings of more than $100,000.[12] Using the old rule of twenty (you need a capital sum twenty times your desired income), that translates into a pension of less than $5,000 a year.

The requirements of the elderly have further implications. As they seek to live off their savings, they will be selling their assets, particularly their houses. This is a familiar process. But in the past, the selling generation has been smaller than the buying generation. This has allowed the elderly to realize their assets at a higher price than they bought them. But with more people in the retired category than in the peak earning age category, asset sales will drive prices down. That will be a great disappointment for the elderly, of course. But it will also be a problem for those of working age who have mortgages; more of them will end up in negative equity. Demand for housing as an investment (second homes, buy-to-let) will surely decline.

Over the long term, one would expect the value of houses to rise in line with GDP. During the boom years, they rose considerably faster. So house prices will face a double whammy from the older generation's asset sales. The natural rate of house price rises will slow, as GDP growth slows. And the average value of houses should, at least, fall back to its historic relationship with GDP, as the elderly fund their retirements.

The current period of low interest rates, if sustained, also makes life difficult for the elderly. If they are already retired, and they hold a significant proportion of their assets in cash deposits, their incomes will already have declined. But life is just as difficult for those approaching retirement. They need to build up a capital sum that can generate the income they require in retirement. If interest rates are 5 per cent, a capital sum of $200,000 will generate an income of $10,000; if rates are 2 per cent, then the income will be just $4,000. If the potential retiree is targeting an income of $10,000 he or she will have to save a lot more – $500,000 would be required. That is a big ask.

Worse still, the effort to generate that sum will be made more difficult by low interest rates. The potential retiree will have to save more out of his or her income, since returns are doing less of the work. Low rates thus act as a way of encouraging saving – a nice paradox. Incidentally, it doesn't make any difference whether the retiree is saving on his own behalf or through a company scheme. The same principles will apply.

In short, not only will growth be slower but the tax burden will be greater, as governments pay the interest on previously accumulated debt and meet the social costs of elderly benefits. Truly are the sins of the fathers being visited on their children. Ever since governments took on debt, younger generations have had to pay the debts of the old. But the key difference of the last 300 years has been that each generation has been bigger than the last. The ageing of the developed world means this is no longer the case. The Ponzi scheme is running out of suckers.

ENERGY

There is another factor that could constrain future global growth which is unrelated to demography. This is a much more controversial issue and readers should bear in mind that many experts will reject the idea out of hand. The concept is that economic activity depends on the efficient use of energy, and energy efficiency is on the decline.

Think back to the eighteenth century and the miraculous change in economic activity that saw the industrial and agrarian revolutions, and a population boom. Until that point, economic growth had been pathetically slow over the long term by modern standards, less than 1 per cent a year. Mankind had been caught in a Malthusian trap, where any rise in human population outstripped food supplies and caused famine that led the population to decline again.

What changed human activity, and why was this process led by Britain, a rain-swept island on the north-west European coast? A number of explanations for the British exception have been advanced, including the Protestant faith, constitutional monarchy, a legal system that protected property rights, the reinvestment of profits from slave trading, and so on. However, it is clear that three things had to happen virtually at once. New industries had to find finance, markets and labour. People had to come off the land to work in industry. That means agriculture had to be more efficient, producing more food with fewer workers. The population could then grow, creating bigger markets for industries to tap into, allowing them to employ more workers, and so on.

The key factor may well have been energy. For much of man's history, he had depended on his own labour and that of his animals. But a steam engine could do the work of many men or horses. Man's traditional fuel source – wood – was a diminishing resource; Britain had cleared its big forests as ruthlessly as any modern Amazonian logger. Coal made a huge difference. It could be dug out of the ground in apparently unlimited supplies; the industry was still one of Britain's biggest employers in the 1950s.

According to the writer Adam Ridley,[13] in 1830 alone Britain consumed the coal equivalent of 15 million acres of forest, or three times the size of Wales. Coal powered the country's factories and its trains and heated its cities. Later on, oil took over as the engine of economic growth, providing the fuel for every form of transport. Once again, it was remarkably cheap, relative to the human and animal labour it replaced. In the twentieth century, oil-based products were used to make the fertilizers that improved crop yields and fed the rapidly growing global population.

Think of all economic activity as a form of embedded energy. I type this sentence on a laptop powered by electricity; its components of metal and plastic required energy to create them; it sits on a table made from wood cut down with a power saw, transported by diesel-fuelled lorry and crafted in a factory dependent on power and light. It takes energy to cook my food, transport me to work, manufacture my clothes and so on.

Imagine the effort involved if I had to hunt or grow my own food, sew my own clothes, write my manuscripts with a quill pen and deliver them by hand, etc., etc. Think of all the modern conveniences that would not exist without this energy use – the washing machine, tumble drier, microwave, refrigerator, CD player and radio. All of these would seem like magic to an observer from Jane Austen's world.

The use of coal expanded economic activity because it was much more efficient. The energy mankind got out of using it was vastly greater than the energy put into discovering it and using it. Think of the economy as a company and the use of coal and oil as an enormous boost to profit margins. Just as that company would grow inexorably, so did the global economy on the back of cheap energy.

Naturally enough, mankind used the easiest sources of energy first. After trees, we exploited the coal and oil that were nearest the surface, or cost less to refine. Saudi Arabia is so rich because its oil is so cheap to extract; a few dollars per barrel.

Some people think the Saudi oil reserves have been overstated and that we have already reached maximum global oil production – peak-oil theory, as it is known. Certainly, individual areas have peaked, including the North Sea fields between Britain and Norway. Others argue that it is all a matter of price. High prices will create the incentive to find and exploit new reserves. But the new reserves that have been found in recent years are either expensive to exploit (under the Atlantic near Brazil, for example) or in politically difficult places. This point is highly significant. The higher extraction costs are passed on by exploration companies to consumers: that has been one factor driving up energy prices in recent years. At the time of writing, oil trades in a range of $90–$100 a barrel; a decade earlier $20–$30 would have been the typical price. In terms of our earlier equation, we have to put in a lot more units of energy to extract the same amount of utility. The profit margins of the global 'company' have declined.

Some numbers may help. The oil deposits found in the 1930s produced about 100 times as much energy as they took to exploit; in the 1970s, the ratio was around 30 to 1.[14] But Canadian tar sands require a lot of heat and energy to refine; one estimate suggests they only produce 70 per cent more energy than it costs to extract them, or a ratio of 1.7 to 1.[15] Biofuels may be even worse.

Why does this matter? We are accustomed to improvements in productivity; creating more output with fewer inputs. Think of Moore's Law, where the capacity of a microprocessor doubles every eighteen months. That has allowed computers to be smaller and much more powerful than the room-sized devices, filled with whirring tapes, which were the staple of 1960s science-fiction films.

But gains in overall productivity will be much harder to achieve if energy use is less efficient. The effects could be enormous. As energy becomes more expensive to extract, its price will go up. Higher oil prices have often been associated with recessions, in the 1970s and again in 2008 and 2009. Consumers are forced to spend more on heat and fuel and thus have less money over to spend on everything else.

Adam Lees, an investment banker who has studied the issue, thinks energy spending may rise from around 5 per cent of GDP to 20 per cent. If he is right, a lot of modern life will have to change. Fuel costs will make it impractical for commuters to drive to work from distant suburbs; they will have to live nearer their jobs or take public transport. Air conditioning may become prohibitively expensive, making some parts of the world unbearable to live in. Intercontinental flights may once again be reserved for the rich. The costs of re-engineering the economy may be huge and will create lots of redundant property; economic output will be further affected.

Higher energy prices flow through to everything. They affect all aspects of life, from the transport of food from farm to shop and home, to the energy needed to make the steel that forms the structure of office buildings and the aluminium that goes into cars. As we saw in 2008, when the oil price is high, farmers have the incentive to switch corn production into ethanol use, and that puts upward pressure on food prices. Indeed, the fertilizers used to improve crop yields require much energy to produce.

Of course, some new sources of more efficient energy may emerge that will solve the problem. Cheap solar power is one possibility; another is nuclear fusion, which would involve less waste than the current fission-based process. Shale gas is being exploited in the US but the process of extracting it, known as fracking, is highly controversial. It involves drilling a hole deep underground and pumping in water, sand and chemicals. This creates fissures in the rock that allow the gas to escape. But the process has been linked to contamination of the water supply and even earth tremors in the affected areas; France banned the technique in 2011.

Even if such technologies become more widespread, it would be foolish to underestimate the benefits mankind has received over the centuries from having sources of energy that we just had to dig out the ground. These benefits will not be easily replicated. And none of the above discussion has anything to do with global warming, which may also have its own effects on output in the form of extreme weather events and crop destruction.

To sum up, higher energy prices are likely to be a further strain on both the finances and growth rate of the developed world. Just when the ageing of the population suggests that the West needs a productivity boost to deal with its debt problem, the energy sector is likely to deliver a productivity decline.

12

Paying the Bill

'Every country in the world owes money, but to who? Who does everybody in the world owe money to? And why don't we just kill the bastard and relax?'
Tommy Tiernan, *Michael Macintyre's Comedy Roadshow*,
BBC1, broadcast 9 October 2010

Over thousands of years, the nature of money has changed and the economic ties that bind us to each other, in the form of debt, have multiplied. When Lehman Brothers and AIG collapsed in the autumn of 2008, the effects were felt around the world. Within weeks, industrial production was collapsing in countries as far apart as Taiwan and Brazil.

These international repercussions were a dramatic indication of the importance of the financial system and of the key role that confidence plays. The local supermarket takes our pounds, dollars and euros because they believe the paper has value and can be passed on to someone else; we deposit our money in the bank because we believe it will always be there. Without that confidence, a modern society could not function.

At root, this confidence depends on our belief in the state. We require the state to maintain the value of our money (or at least to prevent it from eroding too quickly); and to enforce our debt contracts in courts of law. The banks may regard themselves (and indeed, reward their staff) as private-sector institutions, but at heart, as we saw in 2008, the state stands behind them. When the state fails to maintain the value of money, as it did in the Weimar Republic and in Zimbabwe, chaos ensues. Similarly, when creditors cannot enforce their rights, economies stagnate through a lack of investment. When the state allows the banks to collapse, as the US did in the 1930s, the result is a depression.

But the state also has another key role. It has to be able to fund itself at a reasonable rate. And that in turn requires creditors, foreign and domestic, to believe that its economic policy is sound and that its taxpayers have the capacity to pay those debts back. Thanks to the crisis of 2007 and 2008, some countries have reached the stage where creditors no longer have that belief.

Now any writer on the subject of debt has to recognize that the alarm bells have been sounded many times before. The nineteenth-century historian Thomas Macaulay commented wryly on how the size of the national debt had regularly been prophesied as a crippling burden for Britain, yet the country grew ever more prosperous. *Business Week*, the US magazine, carried the headline 'Is the Country Swamped with Debt?' all the way back in 1949.

What makes this crisis different in scale is the interaction with the international monetary system. The combination of paper money and the adoption of floating exchange rates, in the developed world at least, facilitated a massive increase in the volume of debt. While individual countries can recover from debt crises, global debt crises are much more dangerous. The problems experienced in the 1930s – the debt/deflation spiral, the paradox of thrift – have returned.

Let us start with some simplified sums. Assume that a country has government debt equivalent to 100 per cent of its GDP, or annual output. And let us assume that the average interest rate on its debt is 5 per cent. This means the government pays out 5 per cent of economic output in interest payments. If the economy is growing at just 4 per cent a year, it is going to be impossible to get the debt total down, unless the government runs what is called a primary surplus of revenues over expenditures (a primary surplus excludes interest payments).

This is where the tricky bit comes in. If the government attempts to slash spending in order to generate a primary surplus, the economy may well go into recession (i.e. GDP will fall). As a result, the debt-to-GDP ratio will initially rise. Investors will note this development with alarm and demand a higher interest rate on government debt. In turn, this will require a higher primary surplus if the debt is to be eliminated, requiring further austerity measures, and so on and so on. This is the 'debt trap' mentioned earlier in the book.

By May 2011, Greece was in precisely this trap, with a debt of around 150% of GDP and bonds that yielded 24% at three years and 16% at ten. Greece was spending 6.4% of GDP on interest payments in 2011, a figure that was set to rise to 7.9% by 2013. Only the rescue package from the EU, carrying an interest rate of 4.2% (down from an initial 5.2%), was keeping it going. Even this rate will require Greece to run a primary surplus just to stabilize the debt-to-GDP ratio, let alone bring it down. This is a recipe for permanent austerity. That month, Lombard Odier, the Swiss private bank, calculated that on the basis of trend GDP growth and prevailing real debt yields, the amount of fiscal tightening needed just to stabilize the debt-to-GDP ratio was 9.7% of GDP in Ireland, 8.8% in Greece and 7.8% in Portugal.

Greece had thus reached the stage where its debt is not acceptable to global investors, and it had to piggyback on the creditworthiness of its neighbours. Investors simply do not believe that the Greek government, on its own, can repay its creditors in full.

There is an irony here in that money continues to circulate in the Greek economy and there seems no risk of hyperinflation. But that, of course, is because the Greeks adopted the euro as their currency. So the substitution effect that sometimes occurs in stricken economies, when the local currency is replaced by dollars, has happened already. However, Greece's adoption of the euro prevents the country from reducing the debt burden by the time-honoured devices of inflation or devaluation.

Greece is stuck. Were it to leave the euro and re-adopt the drachma, its debt problem would get worse, not better, since its debts are denominated in euros. A 30 per cent drachma devaluation would simply increase the cost of repaying euro debt. So devaluation would also require default. Leaving the euro might make Greek goods more competitive, but Greece has few industries that would be able to take advantage. Worse still, leaving the euro might annoy other European countries and deprive Greece of their support. Any hint of euro departure would cause Greek depositors to try and move their money to banks elsewhere in the euro-zone to avoid a 30–40 per cent hit to their savings; the result would be a run on the banks.

Rescheduling the debt would also damage the banks, which are among the biggest holders of Greek government debt. So a default by the government would require a recapitalization of the banks. But where would the money come from? Default would probably cut Greece off from private-sector lending, at least in the short term. That would require continued austerity. Default might also impose pain on other European banks, and on official lenders such as the European Central Bank. It would spark concern that other countries might follow suit, leading to a European-wide sell-off.

European countries have discussed ways in which a longer-term solution to the debt crisis could be found. One approach would be for an EU-wide body, like the EFSF, to issue debt on behalf of all countries. Such debt would be guaranteed by all countries on behalf of all countries up to a certain limit, say 60 per cent of GDP. Any country debt beyond that level would not carry the guarantee, and would be priced accordingly. (Such a scheme would be similar to the Brady bond system set up after the Latin American debt crisis.)

This ingenious solution faces two obstacles. The first is that it represents a subsidy from strong countries, like Germany, to weaker ones since the former will effectively be lending their credit rating to the latter. German voters might not like this. The second obstacle is whether it is plausible to create a second, high-risk tier of government debt (the portion above the 60% of GDP). Wouldn't Europe be forced to support such debt in a crisis, just as they dropped the original 'no bailout' clause for the euro?

An even more daring idea is to turn the monetary union into a fiscal one, so that Greece and Portugal can be aided with subsidies from the centre, just as Washington sends money to Arkansas and Mississippi. Many voters would be highly reluctant to hand over sovereignty to Brussels. However, European leaders have ignored the voters before.

The problems of Greece are at the extreme end of the range for sovereign countries. The plight of the rest of the developed world is less urgent, but is still ominous. Britain and the US have gross debt-to-GDP ratios of 89% and 101% respectively but are still able to borrow at a very cheap rate, even though the US has lost its AAA rating from Standard & Poor's. The US needs a fiscal tightening of 7 per cent of GDP to stabilize its debt level, according to Lombard Odier – far more than seems politically feasible.

AGGREGATING THE PROBLEM

What do we do, as individuals, when we want to repay debts? We spend less. That, as was clear in the Great Depression, can be a problem for individual countries. But it can also be a problem at the global level. When countries want to reduce their debt levels, they will want to export more and import less. But by definition, they cannot all do so.

That is why one must dismiss the argument that the debt crisis is just a trade-off between borrowers and creditors. Optimists say that if borrowers fail to repay, they are relieved of an obligation. The money that would have been spent on servicing the debt can be used elsewhere. And if borrowers do pay the money back, their disposable income may be cut but the income of the creditor rises. Money is not destroyed.

However, this process does not take place in a political or economic vacuum. The identities of the borrowers and creditors matter. Domestic creditors tend to be well off, and international creditors are by definition those with more foreign-exchange reserves. So debt repayment transfers money from the poor to the wealthy. The marginal propensity to consume of wealthier individuals and countries will be lower than that of indebted countries. In other words out of every £100 of income, the wealthy spend less than the poor would tend to spend.

Global demand growth and thus economic growth will be slower in a period of debt repayment, or deleveraging as it is called. Money is transferred out of the pockets of the feckless and into the pockets of the canny. Like a shopper confronted with a post-Christmas credit-card bill, the world will be forced to cut back for a while.

And this is the benign version of what might happen. It is far more likely that many debtors will be unable to repay. The first category of defaulters consists of those borrowers whose incomes fall, making it impossible for them to make interest payments. The second category consists of those borrowers who had secured their debts against an asset which has fallen in value. In such circumstances, both the borrower and the creditor lose out. The borrower's wealth is less than it was and so is the creditor's. They have discovered, like the clients of Bernie

Madoff, that part of their wealth was illusory. The result could be a substantial fall in living standards, rather than just sluggish growth.

THE LONG VIEW

As this book has explained, the world has seen cycle after cycle in which money and debts have expanded. These cycles are initially self-reinforcing as the extra money begets confidence, as in John Law's experiment in the early eighteenth century. That is because one of Law's insights was correct. Money is a medium of exchange as well as a store of value. The expansion of the money supply can act to encourage trade, at least for a while. Conversely a shortage of official money can discourage trade, and often leads to the development of alternative forms of payment.

It is worth recapping the history of money and debt from previous chapters. The Industrial Revolution was a decisive point in human history for all sorts of reasons. From the eighteenth century onwards, economic growth accelerated from its previous glacial pace and the population of the world grew rapidly. Better communications and transport, such as shipping, allowed for more trade.

At this stage, money was still based on precious metals. This burst of prosperity faced a potential constraint in the form of the limited nature of gold and silver supplies, at that time the sole basis of money. By luck (or perhaps because necessity drove exploration), vast new sources of gold were discovered in the course of the nineteenth century, in California and South Africa.

The system faltered in the early twentieth century as the First World War led to the suspension of the gold standard and the massive issuance of paper money. The international economy proved unable to return to pre-war normality because of the burden of international debts, in particular reparations. In addition, the war had swept away political elites and led to the widespread adoption of democracy. That complicated the task of dealing with the debt problem. Creditors tried to insist sound money was restored in the form of exchange rates fixed to gold, but the burden of debt repayment fell on the real economy, involving mass unemployment. This proved politically unacceptable and the gold standard was abandoned.

The inter-war period also produced German hyperinflation, which showed the terrible consequences if government were allowed unfettered control over the money supply. Towards the end of the Second World War, the leading countries agreed on a new system, under which currencies were linked to the dollar, which was itself linked to gold. By this stage, economic activity had far outstripped the supply of precious metals. There was simply not enough gold in the world for the metal to be used in everyday transactions. Even the inter-war attempt to restore the gold standard had only involved the idea of paper money that was backed by gold reserves. Under Bretton Woods, only central banks were entitled to convert paper into gold; this was a claim on the US, which had most of the reserves.

If the post-1945 settlement weakened one of the pillars of sound money – gold – it demolished the other: the notion of a balanced budget. European countries moved over to a welfare-state model, followed at a slower pace by the US, through Lyndon Johnson's Great Society reforms.

The Bretton Woods system of fixed exchange rates just about worked for twenty-five years, dependent on the control of capital flows and that international investors had confidence in US economic policy. But the system broke up in the 1970s. From that point, the final link with gold was removed and the ability of governments to run deficits, on both the trade and budget accounts, was vastly increased. Money and debt exploded.

The initial result was an inflation problem in the 1970s, but from the 1980s onwards, this extra money seemed to flow into the asset markets. Helping to constrain the rise in consumer prices was the entry into the global economy of China and the former communist states of the old Soviet Union, technological advances, and the greater role of women in the workforce, all of which improved productivity. But the model depended on rising asset prices and rising populations to service the higher debt levels. Like a shark, it had to keep swimming forward to survive. For much of the developed world, the model broke in 2007–08.

Central banks then faced the problem of reconciling their twin aims of safeguarding the value of the currency and protecting the financial system. They claimed that there was no conflict – that monetary easing was needed to offset the risk of recession as well as to rescue the banks. A G20 meeting of global leaders, held in London in April 2009, agreed on a co-ordinated stimulus package. The biggest pick-me-up, measured as a proportion of GDP, was delivered by the Chinese.

However, if the answer to our economic problems is to hold interest rates near zero, and for governments to spend far more than they take in taxes, mankind would surely have discovered this solution long ago. Life cannot be that easy.

WHERE DO WE GO FROM HERE?

The financial crisis of 2007–08 was definitely a turning point in global economic policy, but even from the vantage point of 2011, it was not clear in which direction policy was heading.

The rescue of the banks caused a great degree of cynicism, especially among those who remembered the arguments advanced back in the 1980s that 'lame duck' industries such as mining and steel should not be rescued, and who noticed the change of tune when the powerful banking sector was in trouble. Issues of fiscal probity also seemed to be forgotten. As Joseph Stiglitz, the Nobel prize-winning economist, remarked: 'When the banks said they needed hundreds of billions of dollars, all worries about the size of the deficit were shunted aside.'[1]

Stiglitz even sees the collapse of Lehman Brothers as a moment to rival the fall of the Berlin Wall;[2] in this case, it was the free market capitalist model that was undermined. To critics like Stiglitz, the US could no longer claim that its financial system was the best allocator of capital. The rival Chinese approach, with governments controlling the banks and restricting the flow of international capital, looked much more appealing to developing countries. The price paid for letting the banks roam free looked simply too great.

One might have assumed that such a crisis for capitalism would provide a political bonanza for left-wing parties. But it was not to be. True, Barack Obama was elected US President in November 2008 when the crisis was at its height, but in the elections of autumn 2010, the tide swung back to the Republicans. In September 2011, right-wing parties were in power in Britain, France, Germany and Italy, while the left-wing government in Spain staring at defeat in scheduled elections. The old temptation to blame economic crises on outsiders emerged again; far-right parties made progress in Finland, Sweden and the Netherlands.

Perhaps this was because, while voters may have detested the bankers that caused the crisis, they were unconvinced that left-wing governments had the answer, especially if higher taxes were required. Despite the rhetoric of politicians and academics, the 'neo-liberal' revolution was limited in scope. For all the efforts of Mrs Thatcher, the size of the British state did not shrink very much under her administration. When she took office in 1979, public spending was 44.6 per cent of GDP; five years later, it was 47.5 per cent. Only then, thanks to an economic boom, did spending fall, to 39.4 per cent of GDP in the year she left office. When the Conservatives lost power completely in 1997, spending was around 40 per cent of GDP (and by the time Labour's Gordon Brown lost power in 2010, public spending's share of national income was back where it had been in 1979).

The Keynesian approach was tempered rather than eliminated. It was generally accepted that politicians should not try to balance the budget during recessions, as some did in the 1930s with disastrous results. Instead, the 'automatic stabilizers' should be allowed to work. As tax revenues fell and social spending rose, the budget would naturally go into deficit.

In the mind of economists like Paul Krugman, governments have done too little in response to the financial crisis, rather than too much. The risk is of a repeat of the 1930s. So governments should simply keep spending to support the economy and worry about the debt burden later. The most important thing is to restore economic growth. With the right level of growth, deficits can quickly disappear, as governments found in the 1990s. However, opponents of Krugman argue that a debt crisis is not solved by adding more debt. The net result will be to burden our children and to increase government involvement in the economy, a step that will only slow growth in the long run.

After the 2010 congressional elections, the US government was divided between Republicans, who were opposed to increases in taxes, and Democrats, who disliked reductions in spending. The immediate effect in late 2010 was a compromise deal with President Obama that cut taxes for everyone, without any countervailing spending reductions.

That deal only made the debt problem worse. A cynical view is that Americans have revived their preference for monetary expansion over tax-raising that dates back to the Revolutionary war. The dichotomy was summed up in the debate over the extension of the debt ceiling that occurred in the summer of 2011. The trigger for the crisis was a requirement for Congress to approve any increase in the Federal debt limit, dating back to the First World War. Traditionally, this was treated as a formality; after all, the government was borrowing money to find policies that Congress had already voted for. But the Republicans, spurred on by their tea party supporters, saw this as a chance to impose some budget discipline on President Obama. They refused to support a ceiling extension unless it was accompanied by spending cuts. Nor would they agree to tax increases as part of the package. The stand-off hung over the financial markets and the global economy like the sword of Damocles: had the debt ceiling not been extended, the US government would have had to choose between paying its workers, benefit recipients or creditors. A deal was done at the last minute, although the details of the planned cuts were offloaded onto a mixed committee of Republicans and Democrats that seemed unlikely to reach agreement.

The crisis was quickly followed by the downgrading of US debt. The US ought to have no problems in repaying its debt, at least in nominal terms; its debt is issued in its own currency which it can create at will. But the crisis showed that while the US might be able to repay, it could, for political reasons, be unwilling to do so. It is far from clear that the US electorate understands the dilemma it faces: if it wants to reduce its debt burden, it must tackle its cherished entitlement programmes.

The day of reckoning has merely been postponed.

THE UNHOLY TRINITY

So what are the likely long-term consequences of the debt crisis? Realistically, there are three: inflation, stagnation and default. Some will argue that economies can escape from the crisis by rapid growth. That is roughly how countries reduced the debt burdens after the Second World War, although a fair degree of inflation helped as well.

But as the last chapter argued, many Western nations are unlikely to achieve that growth because of population constraints. The next few years will not see a second baby boom, nor are Western societies likely to make the kind of productivity gains that result from taking men out of uniform or converting industry from armaments to civilian production. Higher energy prices will only add to our difficulties. We can hope for some massive gain from alternative energy (cheap solar power, for example) but we cannot count on such a change. Developed nations are being forced to compete with China and India for scarce (or at least, more expensive to develop) energy resources. The effect, for those of us in Europe, America and Japan, is akin to a tax increase.

Muddling through is possible for some countries, but not for all. The risk is that more countries fall into the debt trap that has ensnared Greece, Ireland and Portugal.

INFLATION

So let us turn to our three less palatable outcomes and start with inflation. This book has shown that paper money systems have always led to rapid inflation in the past. Indeed, we have already had fairly rapid inflation since the link with gold was dropped in 1971. Could we return to 1970s-style double-digit inflation rates?

High inflation is a very tempting option for governments that have trouble balancing their books. Economist Peter Bernholz, who made a study of hyperinflation, stated: 'There has never occurred a hyper-inflation in history which was not caused by a huge budget deficit of the state.'[3] The key ratio, in his view, is when the deficit equals 40 per cent of annual government revenues. In 2011, the British and American governments had deficits of around 25 per cent of revenues; if a deterioration in their finances continued, they would come within hailing distance of Bernholz's threshold.

Many of those who worry about inflation point to a talk given by Ben Bernanke back in 2002, well before he became the US Federal Reserve's chairman. The speech, entitled 'Deflation: Making Sure It Doesn't Happen Here',[4] drew on Bernanke's acknowledged expertise as an economist who had studied the Great Depression, and it was made in the context of an early deflation scare that followed the collapse of the late 1990s bubble in technology stocks and a brief US recession. Bernanke also examined the experience of Japan, which was well into a long period of economic stagnation and mild deflation.

One or two sentences look rather embarrassing with the benefit of hindsight. 'A particularly important protective factor in the current environment is the strength of our financial system,' he said. 'Despite the adverse shocks of the past year, our banking system remains healthy and well-regulated and firm and household balance sheets are for the most part in good shape.' Admittedly, Bernanke spoke before the worst excesses of the housing boom, but his words still seem complacent.

Bernanke went on to explain the key problem of deflation for central banks, the zero interest rate bound. Interest rates cannot be forced below zero. You cannot charge people for the privilege of holding money on deposit since they will simply keep the money at home instead. As a result, Bernanke pointed out, 'When the nominal interest rate has been reduced to zero, the *real* interest rate paid by borrowers equals the expected rate of deflation, however large that might be.' Real in this sense means the inflation (deflation) adjusted cost of funds. So if deflation is running at 10 per cent, 'someone who borrows for a year at a nominal interest rate of zero actually faces a 10 per cent *real* cost of funds, as the loan must be repaid in dollars whose purchasing power is 10 per cent greater than that of the dollars borrowed originally'. Drawing from history, Bernanke cited the problems of the farmers championed by William Jennings Bryan. He then discussed the best ways of heading off deflation: by allowing inflation to be low but positive, by regulating the banks well, and by heading off any drift towards deflation with aggressive rate-cutting. But what if, despite all those precautions, the central banks came up against the zero rate bound, as indeed they have since 2009?

In a famous passage, Bernanke declared that

the US government has a technology, called a printing press (or today, its electronic equivalent), that allows it to produce as many US dollars as it wishes at essentially no cost. By increasing the number of US dollars in circulation, or even by credibly threatening to do so, the US government can also reduce the value of a dollar in terms of goods and services, which is equivalent to raising the prices in dollars of these goods and services. We conclude that, under a paper money system, a determined government can always generate higher spending and hence positive inflation.[5]

He explicitly recognized that such a move would probably result in dollar depreciation. 'A striking example from US history is Franklin Roosevelt's 40 percent devaluation of the dollar against gold in 1933–34, enforced by a program of gold purchases and domestic money creation,' he said.

The devaluation and the rapid increase in money supply it permitted ended the US deflation remarkably quickly. US CPI inflation went from –10.3% in 1932 to –5.1% in 1933 to +3.4% in 1934. The economy grew strongly, and by the way, 1933 was one of the best years of the century for the stock market. If nothing else, the episode illustrates that monetary actions can have powerful effects on the economy, even when the nominal interest rate is at or near zero, as was the case at the time of Roosevelt's devaluation.[6]

Of course, a sharp dollar decline would be very bad news for overseas creditors owning dollar-denominated Treasury bonds. As Albert Edwards, a strategist at French bank Société Générale remarked, this would be 'default in all but name'. Some commentators have dubbed Mr Bernanke 'Helicopter Ben', ever since his reference to a remark by Milton Friedman that the Fed could create inflation by simply dropping money on the population from a helicopter. But there are a number of questions over whether a deliberate policy of increasing inflation could ever be carried out.

The first question concerns the reaction of investors. They will not stand idly by if they believe a government is deliberately trying to create inflation to reduce the real value of their debt.[7] They will demand higher interest rates when that debt is refinanced. Those higher debt costs will place a further strain on government finances at a time when deficits are already high. Many countries have also issued index-linked debt, in which the repayment value of the bonds rise directly in line with prices, so inflation would not help to eliminate the burden of repayment on that portion of the debt at all.

If investors are completely rational, they will demand the same real rate of interest, whatever the level of inflation. So if they demand a nominal rate of 2 per cent when inflation is zero, they will insist on getting an interest rate of 12 per cent when inflation is 10 per cent. Given that many developed countries have debt-to-GDP ratios approaching 100 per cent, this is a real problem; the annual interest bill could surge to more than 10 per cent of GDP. Money intended for defence, or social spending, would have to be diverted to interest payments.

Of course, some debt is long-term. Investors in ten-year and thirty-year bonds would be unable to do anything except sell in response to the inflation strategy. So countries could effectively cheat some long-term creditors. However, a lot of countries have relatively short debt-maturity profiles. In the case of America, the average debt rolls over in less than five years. Any benefits from rapid inflation would be ephemeral.

Capital Economics, an independent research group, conducted an exercise to calculate which countries would be best placed to benefit from a deliberate inflationary strategy. They looked at the amount of inflation-linked debt the country had issued, the size of the annual deficit and the average maturity of the debt. Britain was bottom of the list. Although its average debt has a maturity of thirteen years, it had a very large budget deficit (as of 2010–11) and a high proportion of index-linked debt. The US was not much better placed. Ironically, the country best placed to inflate away its debt was Germany, but because of the Weimar example, it was the least likely to do so.

A second issue for central banks in trying to create inflation is how they would do so. Mr Bernanke's helicopter analogy remains, so far, just a flight of rhetorical fancy. Would a central bank have the courage to attempt anything similar in the face of what would probably be widespread political opposition? In August 2011, Rick Perry, a leading candidate for the Republican presidential nomination, described the prospects of another round of monetary easing by the Federal Reserve as 'almost treasonous'.

There are less dramatic alternatives. Governments could issue tax rebates, funded by the central bank, in the form of coupons. These coupons would have a 'spend by' date to prevent them from being saved, with the aim of pushing up spending in the short term. Or the central bank could announce an inflation target of 4–5 per cent, thereby creating the incentive for consumers to spend money before the value of their savings is eroded.

QE or not QE?

Instead, central banks have gone down the Bernanke route via 'quantitative easing' (QE), a concept referred to a number of times in this book. This involves the central bank buying assets from the private sector, and creating a credit at the seller's bank. This is not as crude as actually printing money, but in essence it differs only in scale from the tactics of the Reichsbank during the Weimar Republic or from medieval monarchs who debased their coinage. More money is created.

The idea was threefold. First, there would be more money sitting in the banks, which they would then be able to lend out to businesses and individuals. Secondly, the central bank's purchases will force down bond yields, making it cheaper for people to borrow money. And thirdly, the low level of yields on government bonds would encourage investors to buy riskier assets such as equities and corporate bonds. The resulting increase in share prices would boost investor, and thus, consumer, confidence, reviving economic activity.

As far as the Fed was concerned, QE was just an extension of its traditional activities. One of the ways that central banks have influenced short-term interest rates is by buying and selling short-dated government debt or treasury bills. QE was just transferring the tactic to longer-term debts.

But did it work? The evidence has been very mixed. An analysis by Capital Economics showed that bond yields fell, and the money supply expanded, shortly after the Federal Reserve began using QE in late 2008. But by the time the Fed paused its programme, Treasury yields were back at the levels prevailing when it started, and the size of the money supply was slightly lower. After the Fed stopped the programme, yields fell and money supply rose, the opposite of what might have been expected. Clearly, QE was not the only factor driving the markets.

The Fed launched another round of easing in November 2010, declaring that it would buy $600 trillion of bonds by the middle of 2011. The idea was greeted with rapture by the equity markets, indicating that this wealth effect might be the most significant of QE's potential growth-boosting mechanisms. Certainly, it seemed more reliable than the impact on bond yields; within a month of the launch of QE2, as it became known, the crucial ten-year bond yield was half a percentage point higher than when the Fed announced the programme.

This raised a number of issues. If the main impact of QE2 was on equity, rather than bond, prices, was the Fed simply providing a subsidy to the stock market? If so, this appeared to be a repeat of the 'Greenspan put' – the idea that the Fed underwrote share prices. Arguably, this is not the Fed's proper role and creates the danger that the market will collapse if the Fed withdraws its support.

Another possibility is that QE has proved more successful in reflating the economies of the developing world than the developed. Countries which peg their currency to the dollar effectively import US monetary policy, since investors are enticed by the prospect of higher returns with reduced currency risk. Inevitably, a currency peg also means that interest rates in the pegged countries cannot diverge too far from each other (unless, like the Chinese, you have extensive capital controls).

In 2010, many developing countries found themselves dealing with rising inflation rates, driven by higher commodity prices. In some cases, they also experienced sharply higher property prices and booming equity markets. The danger is that QE, as it did in John Law's day, might lead to asset bubbles, albeit not in the country of origin. The policy also attracted criticism from other countries which felt the US was trying to drive down its currency and grab a larger share of world trade. If you create more dollars, then you would expect the price (exchange rate) of the dollar to fall.

Quantitative easing could be seen as the ultimate triumph of debtors' over creditors' interests. Governments are creating money to allow borrowers to settle their debts. However, QE has also come under attack from a different direction, on the grounds that it is an unproven tactic that is unlikely to work. In Japan, QE was used on and off in the early years of the twenty-first century. Japanese bond yields were already low, so there was little benefit to be gained from this factor. And the money supply expanded, but it did not lead to a borrowing spree; the money created was simply hoarded as cash deposits.

Perhaps the tactic will not work, because everyone can see that it is a conjuring trick. 'Printing money and extending credit do not create wealth', wrote Lee Quaintance and Paul Brodsky, two hedge fund managers.[8] 'If they did, all the world's problems could be solved with a few computer keystrokes. At best, expanding money and credit merely redistributes wealth. At worst, they may temper its creation.'

The tricky part for a central bank pursuing QE is to know when to stop. If the effect of QE is to drive down yields, then yields might rise as soon as the programme is abandoned, jeopardizing the recovery. This view was taken by Bill Gross, co-head of PIMCO, the world's largest manager of bond funds. In March 2011, he wrote that 'nearly 70% of the annualised [bond] issuance since the beginning of QE2 has been purchased by the Fed', adding that just as 'at the end of a typical chain letter, the legitimate corollary question is – who will buy Treasuries when the Fed doesn't?'[9] Ironically, Gross turned out to be wrong. When the Fed stopped buying bonds in June 2011, yields fell. But that was because investors became worried about the possibility of a return to recession – hardly a sign that QE had been a success.

A further problem is that the central bank will eventually want to sell the bonds it owns. Unless it has eliminated the budget deficit by that stage, private investors will be asked to buy not just the usual amount of bonds, but the backlog being offloaded by the central bank. The bond market could suffer indigestion. Some suspect that, as a result of this constraint, central banks may never get round to reducing their bond holdings.

If one thinks back to the early eighteenth century, John Law's scheme also amounted to quantitative easing, as it involved the creation of money, which was used to buy stock in the Mississippi Company, which was then used to buy government debt. The British South Sea bubble was a similar scheme; the company bid for the right to take over the national debt, relying on speculative interest in its shares to make the plan work. These schemes did not last very long, because of their Ponzi-like nature, and because the newly created money tended to leak into other speculative propositions, including a plan to drain the bogs of Ireland and turn lead into silver.[10]

Japan's experience also raises the question of whether it is as easy for central banks to generate inflation as Mr Bernanke suggested. Rather than look at the money supply as the determinant of inflation, many economists talk of the 'output gap' between potential and actual economic activity. Inflation, they argue, only occurs when economic activity is buoyant. Employers are competing for raw materials and labour, pushing up commodity prices and wages. When there is spare capacity, inflation cannot occur. Producers offload their goods at reduced prices, like a department store in the January sales. Workers accept lower wages in an attempt to escape the misery of unemployment.

The recession of 2007–08 was relatively severe, reducing US output by around 3 per cent and British and German production by around 6 per cent. Inflation will not occur, argue most economists, as soon as this lost output is restored. That is because the economy has a tendency to grow over the long term, perhaps by 2 per cent or so in Britain and Germany and by 3 per cent in the US. So, significant inflation will not occur until economies regain both the lost output and the trend growth that would have occurred in normal years.

In other words, if British output was 100 at the start of the recession, it fell to 94 over the course of just over a year. To get back to 'normal' in two years, it would need to grow to a bit over 104; i.e., the original 100 plus two years of trend growth. And if it takes three years to recover, it will need to grow to 106, and so on. As a result, a recession has to be followed by several years of above-trend growth before rapid inflation can resume.

There are potential criticisms of this approach. The first is that we do not know what the trend rate of growth of an economy should be; we can only judge it in retrospect. History suggests that the trend can change over time. It is possible that the credit crunch resulted in a permanent reduction in the level of potential output and that all those people trained as real estate agents and house builders might never be usefully re-employed.

If these criticisms are right, and we don't know the trend growth rate, we can't know the size of the output gap. And thus we can't know when inflation is about to become a threat. In the long run, inflation may very well be the result of the response of world governments to the debt crisis. But we may try out some alternative scenarios before we get there.

STAGNATION

What about stagnation? Japan provides a clear example of this outcome. The private sector has been bogged down with debt taken on during the great boom period of the 1980s. Much of that debt was secured against property, which has fallen 30–40 per cent in price. Nominal GDP growth has been weak for the best part of twenty years and in late 2010, the stock market was a quarter of its end-1980s level. Japan has been stuck in the doldrums despite its use of QE, and a near-zero interest rate policy. Fiscal stimulus has been used extensively, leaving Japan with gross debt of 200 per cent of GDP in 2011.

Monetary policy has failed to revive activity in Japan. As Richard Koo points out in his book, *The Holy Grail of Macro Economics: Lessons From Japan's Great Recession*,[11] economists had previously thought that if you cut interest rates low enough, people would always borrow. With rates at 0.5 per cent, businesses would surely be able to find profitable projects that earned more. But Japan showed that was not necessarily the case. In Koo's view, Japan suffered a balance-sheet recession, in which companies found that their assets were worth less than their debts. The last thing they wanted was to borrow any more. Instead, low interest rates simply made it easier for them to service, and eventually reduce, their debts.

Japan is also an example of an ageing society, one where the retired cohort is growing faster than the working population, and where the overall population is starting to shrink. That has weighed on its economic growth.

The optimists will argue that the Japanese did too little, too late; that their banks were slow to restructure and that their demographics were worse than those of America. But as Chapter 11 showed, the demographics of Western Europe are very poor indeed, with several countries facing the prospect of declining populations and even more declining workforces. In the absence of a sudden surge in productivity, shrinking workforces must mean slower growth.

The Japanese example may instead show that government policy has little impact once debt ratios get too high. The private sector simply does not want to borrow, even at zero interest rates. It has lost the confidence required to borrow in the hope of future income growth.

A further problem may lie in the nature of the boom. Economists of the Austrian school, such as Friedrich Hayek and Ludwig von Mises, argued that credit booms contained the seeds of their own busts. Businesses invest on the basis of their expected return versus their cost of capital. When central banks hold the interest rate at too low a level, many more projects appear to be profitable and are duly financed. Over the long run, this causes increased competition, driving down profits. Banks start to fear for the security of their money, and call in the loans. Businesses duly collapse.

The problem is that capital has been misallocated. A classic example was Ireland during its housing boom. The country's banks lent a lot of money to property developers to build houses, on the back of interest rates that were very low relative to the growth rate of Ireland's GDP (this was a function of Irish membership of the euro-zone). During the boom, Irish GDP growth looked very healthy because Irish workers were being employed to build houses. The taxes they paid also boosted government revenues, encouraging politicians to push up spending; public-sector wages rose by 90 per cent between 2000 and 2008.

But the housing boom was unsustainable. Many of the properties stand empty and may never be occupied. So while GDP growth may have looked healthy in the boom years, Ireland was wasting its wealth. The Austrians would argue that there is nothing to be done about this except to let prices and wages fall to adjust to the new reality. By implication, a period of stagnation is inevitable. 'The sad fact is that the original, illusory boom did not herald the start of a new prosperity, but gulled businesses into wasting precious resources on bad investments. No subsequent efforts can change that historical fact, nor its malign effects', wrote Eamonn Butler of the Institute of Economic Affairs.[12] The argument in this book has echoes of the Austrian school. Interest rates were held at too low levels in the 2000s, encouraging speculation in equities and property. This did lead to a misallocation of capital, including an over-concentration of resources in the finance sector. In some parts of the Western world (although not in Germany), this focus has been at the expense of investment in the manufacturing sector. The tricky bit is accepting the Austrians' conclusion that the only option is to let the crisis blow itself out. It seems to be a counsel of despair.

Author Richard Duncan argues that deflation is the inevitable result of the trade imbalances of the last forty years.[13] In essence Americans have been buying goods on credit, and will no longer be able to afford to do so. Meanwhile Asian countries have expanded production massively to serve the American consumer market. As that demand falters, the world will be stuck with excess capacity, causing producers to slash prices.

A related argument is that the developing world is forcing down the price of manufactured goods and pushing up the price of commodities. For the developed world, this represents a deterioration in the terms of trade; what we consume is going up in price and what we produce is falling in price. The effect is a reduction in the West's standard of living, making a deflationary debt crisis more likely.

The historical experience is that economic growth tends to be slower in the wake of a debt crisis. Reinhart and Rogoff found that output falls by more than 9 per cent on average and the unemployment rate rises by seven percentage points.[14] Economies have to spend several years making up the lost ground.

One could argue that the low interest rates prevailing round the world are a sign that this forecast is playing out. Low rates and low growth go together. The cost of capital and the return on capital tend to be the same level. If the rate of growth were consistently higher, then more capital would be invested to take advantage of the opportunity; the demand for more capital would push up interest rates. So it is significant that low rates are not causing a surge in borrowing. It is a sign that the corporate sector is pessimistic about the growth outlook.

If this is the case, the Western world has followed an incredibly flawed strategy. As the developed world aged, it should have taken advantage of the shift in economic power to the developing world. It should have built up a pool of savings and invested in emerging market companies, government debt and so on, just as a prospective pensioner will build up a retirement fund. The West could then have used the income from such savings to supplement its standard of living.[15]

But building up a pool of savings would have required the West to run a long series of current account surpluses so it could accumulate assets in the emerging world. Instead, with notable exceptions such as Germany, the West has been in deficit. It owes the emerging world money, not the other way round. It is as if a sixty-year-old man were to go on a five-year spending spree before his retirement, without any consideration of how he would pay off the credit-card bill.

Stagnation will also impact on the financial sector, and will affect the attitude of workers towards their pension needs. If growth will be slow, and recessions more frequent than they were, then using leverage to bet on markets will be much less attractive. That is because the returns in good years will be lower and the risk of being wiped out in bad years will be greater.

An example may help. Say that the average market return in the good years was 12 per cent and the cost of financing was 7 per cent. But the market experiences a 30 per cent fall once in every ten years. An investor who borrowed four times his capital (i.e. $4 million on top of $1 million) would make a return of $600,000 in a good year, minus a financing cost of $280,000 for a net return of $320,000, or 32 per cent on his capital. Once in every ten years, however, he would be wiped out as a 30 per cent fall on $5 million ($1.5 million) would be more than his capital reserves (although if he worked for a bank or a hedge fund, he might regard this as a decent bet).

Compare that with a low-return world, where the cost of financing is, say, 5 per cent and the average return 6 per cent, and there is a 20 per cent market fall every five years. Using the same gearing as the first example, the investor will earn just $100,000 in a good year, but get wiped out every five.

The ramifications of this shift will be huge but they will not all occur straight away. It will take years of falling or flat asset prices for investors to realize they are not a one-way bet. Eventually, a house will be just a place to live and not the basis for an investment strategy. Whether to rent or buy will be a lifestyle choice (do we want to tie ourselves down in one place? Are we willing to wait for a landlord to repair the property and replace the white goods?) rather than a financing decision.

Stagnation may only be an interim alternative to our other two options, inflation and default. Eventually, electorates may refuse to contemplate further stagnation and opt to erode the debt, in real or nominal terms.

DEFAULT

The problem with debt is that things seem great when you first borrow the money and you get the extra spending power. But when the point comes to paying the debt back, your spending power will fall. The borrower has to hope their income has grown in the meantime – their wages, in the case of individuals, profits, in the case of companies and GDP, in the case of countries. If this has not happened, borrowers will struggle to repay the debt. This can happen at the private level – as with those American homeowners who can no longer afford their mortgage payments – and at the national level, through sovereign default.

There is only a very rudimentary system for dealing with sovereign debt defaults. If you or I fail to keep up payments on a car loan, the finance company can have the vehicle repossessed. Short of military action, there is no certain way of forcing a country to cough up. (In the nineteenth century Britain imposed a protectorate on Egypt as a way of safeguarding its interests as a creditor; the US did something similar in Haiti in 1915.) The best that creditors can do is cut off the country from access to further borrowings. After a few years, however, new creditors are usually willing to start lending, albeit at a higher rate.

The default of Argentina in 2001 was a particularly messy example of the latter. Years later, the country had still not settled with its creditors. That inspired the IMF to come up with a plan to deal with sovereign defaults, along the lines of the Chapter 11 system that governs corporate bankruptcies in the US. The problem with any such plan is that it involves a sovereign nation giving up power to a multinational body, a step countries are understandably reluctant to take.

The underlying reality is that one cannot expect countries to transfer significant proportions of their income to foreigners, year in and year out, unless they are under occupation. Sooner or later, voters will rebel. The rights of the creditors are very hard to enforce, and will not be enforced. Once debt gets beyond 100 per cent of GDP or so, then the annual cost of service will probably be more than 5 per cent of GDP and will weigh heavily on government budgets.

The temptation to default will be great, especially if it is perceived that the money is owed to greedy foreigners. In Greece there is much dislike of the troika – the IMF, European Commission and European Central Bank – that is imposing the austerity plan. Indeed, in any debt crisis, it is likely that irresponsible lenders are as much to blame as irresponsible borrowers.

Whether debt is owed internally or externally is important. The former is less of a problem. Japan's huge debt burden is owed largely to its own citizens, and it is coping better with a much bigger debt-to-GDP ratio than Greece. In their study, Reinhart and Rogoff found 250 defaults on overseas debts since 1800 and just 80 on domestic debts.[16]

Defaulting on domestic debt is a momentous decision. It means punishing savers, who may well be elderly and have no means of replacing their lost income. It means that the government is likely to have to pay more to borrow in future. And it may well result in the failure of the domestic banks.

The banks are locked in embrace with their governments like two drowning men, each dragging down the other. Often the domestic banks are big holders of government debt since such safe assets are deemed to bolster the balance sheet. So a government default may cause some banks to bear heavy losses or even go bust. A wave of defaults across Europe would be particularly threatening, as banks in healthy countries would still be in danger.

However, not everyone accepts this book's argument that sovereign defaults are likely. In an IMF staff paper of September 2010, Carlo Cottarelli, Lorenzo Forni, Jan Gottschalk and Paolo Mauro argue that default is 'unnecessary, undesirable and unlikely'.[17] Since the authors attempt to demolish the argument why default is likely, it is worth tackling their paper head on. Their first point is that debtor countries will be able to make the required fiscal adjustments (i.e. cut their deficits). The authors say there have been forty occasions in the past three decades when countries have achieved budget adjustments of 7 per cent of GDP. Furthermore, default would be pointless since it would require substantial fiscal adjustment anyway; defaulting countries are shut out of the financial markets and so have to balance their budgets.

The obvious retort to this point is that individual countries may be able to balance their budgets in a crisis: a good example was Canada in the mid-1990s. But Canada was tightening its fiscal policy at a time when the US, its neighbour and biggest customer, was booming. This time round, lots of developed countries are trying to restrain their budgets and reduce their debts at the same time. Even the US is unlikely to pursue further largescale fiscal stimulus. So there is no sugar daddy to act as a source of demand.

The second argument in the paper is that the average interest rate on sovereign debt is actually quite low, and will not cripple government budgets. But we have seen in the cases of Greece and Ireland that rates can rise very sharply when investors start to panic. And even what look like low yields by historic standards can be crippling if the economy is stagnant. However, the authors are right to mention, as was explained in Chapter 10, that a number of dynamics are at work; what matters is the maturity of the debt, the proportion owned by foreigners, the interest rate relative to GDP growth, the starting ratio of debt-to-GDP and so on.

A further IMF staff argument is that, while the fiscal adjustment needed to bring sovereign finances back into order will be detrimental for economic growth, a debt default or restructuring will be equally damaging.

However, in the circumstances of economic crisis in which default might occur, it is not clear that rational economic arguments will hold sway. The political unpopularity involved in paying 'greedy' creditors will overwhelm other issues. We know this to be the case because Reinhart and Rogoff have compiled dozens of examples of sovereign defaults. Indeed, Professor Rogoff wrote in 2010 that the troubled euro-zone countries

face the prospect of a lost decade, much as Latin America experienced in the 1980s. Latin America's rebirth and modern growth-dynamic really only began to unfold after the 1987 Brady plan orchestrated massive debt write-downs across the region. Surely a similar restructuring is the most plausible scenario in Europe.[18]

Admittedly, it seems highly unlikely that the British or American governments will formally default, not least because they retain the option of depreciation. That, of course, is partial default, at least as far as foreign investors are concerned.

Within nations, it is quite possible that there might be a lot of defaults in the private sector – at the consumer level, on credit cards and mortgages and at the corporate level, on private-equity loans and junk bonds. Such defaults may ripple through the system, as they did in 2007 and 2008, because of the linkages between banks and debt issuers.

As of September 2011, private-sector defaults have been kept in check by the low level of interest rates, which had reduced the nominal debt-service burden. But were the economy ever to return to normal (or were governments to aim for the inflationary option), rates would have to rise. That would put many borrowers in a tricky position. The only way that rates could stay at 2011 levels for an extended period would be in the stagnation scenario described above. It would be a zombie-like existence for many debtors.

Which of these three scenarios will occur? Alas, it is very difficult to know for sure but in a sense, it doesn't matter. The key point is that the debt is unlikely to be repaid in real terms, i.e. in the form of money with the same purchasing power as when it was lent. Any of the three outcomes described above – inflation, stagnation or outright default – is likely to result in a crisis at some stage.[19] This crisis will be at least as severe as the one in 2008, with falling markets, troubled banks and corporate bankruptcies. In the past, such crises have often resulted in a fundamental reordering of the international economic system. That will be the subject of our final chapter.

13

A New Order

*'The US government has to come to terms with the painful
fact that the good old days when it could just borrow its way
out of messes of its own making are finally gone.'*

Xinhua, Chinese news agency

When the world economy heads into crisis, the international currency
system often changes. It did so in the First World War when gold
convertibility was abandoned. It changed in the 1930s' Depression as
countries went off the gold standard. And it happened again in the
1970s as the Bretton Woods system collapsed. The system breaks down
either because the debtors cannot, or will not, meet their obligations,
or because creditors fear they are not being repaid in sound money.
This time round, the first symptom has appeared in the euro-zone; the
second will emerge in the China/America relationship.

Why won't the current arrangement of floating exchange rates in
the developed world and managed rates in the developing world
survive? To find the answer, we have to go back to the way the world
worked before 1971. Exchange rates against the dollar were pegged
and governments were limited in the extent that they could run persistent budget or trade deficits by the need to appease creditors.

If there is a fundamental theme of this book, it is that there are no
easy answers in economics. Fixing the value of a currency, as creditors
tend to prefer, only works for a time. When economic fundamentals
are out of whack, a fixed exchange rate builds up trouble. The examples of Greece and Argentina show that fixing the currency of a weak
economy to that of a strong one is an error unless the weak economy

undertakes fundamental reform to improve its competitiveness and tackle any financial imbalances (such as runaway public spending). William Jennings Bryan thought he had an easy answer – to expand the volume of money, or allow the currency to depreciate. This can work if there is too little money in circulation or if the exchange rate is overvalued. Over time, however, such a policy will inevitably lead to higher inflation or higher borrowing costs as creditors demand compensation for their loss in purchasing power.

The rationale for floating exchange rates is that they allow currencies to find their own level. The burden of economic adjustment can thus fall on the exchange rate, and not on economic output or indeed employment. But floating rates have been much more volatile than their supporters expected. At times, they have overshot their fundamental value (judged by relative prices), leading to problems of speculative bubbles and uncompetitive export sectors. This overshoot may have been because portfolio investment, not trade, has driven currency markets. But deliberate interference by governments has also played its part. While governments have paid lip service to the concept of floating rates, the market has not always been allowed to find its level.

Quantitative easing is a modern version of Bryan's philosophy. Central banks are creating more money, a tactic which will (other things being equal) drive down their exchange rate.[1] QE is a direct attempt to reduce the income of creditors by cutting the bond yield.[2]

Creditors have been dicing with danger ever since the breakdown of the Bretton Woods system. After 1971, countries were free to depreciate their currencies at will. Many duly did so. Nations also ran budget and trade deficits for extended periods, undermining their long-term creditworthiness.

But creditors have been given several crumbs of comfort. After suffering big losses in the 1970s, investors were reassured by events in the 1980s and early 1990s. First central banks, led by Paul Volcker of the US Fed, showed themselves willing to tackle inflation. And secondly, real interest rates were high, compensating creditors for their earlier losses. As a result, investment returns were high as bond yields fell from their late 1970s peaks.

From the late 1990s onwards, however, the main investors in government bonds were not retail investors or professional fund managers, looking to maximize returns. Instead they were central banks and sovereign wealth funds in Asia and the Middle East, looking to park the foreign exchange reserves earned through accumulating current account surpluses. Such buyers have been relatively indifferent to yield.

Nevertheless, eventually even the patience of those investors must wear thin. By the autumn of 2011, government bond yields were very low round the world, leaving investors very vulnerable to inflation, currency depreciation or default. The European crisis has shown that government bonds are not the risk-free asset that they had been assumed to be.

OPTIONS FOR CHANGE

So how might the system change? Much of the discussion concerns whether the US dollar will be replaced as the global reserve currency by the Chinese renminbi, or whether it will simply be one of a range of reserve currencies including the euro, renminbi and yen.

The global reserve currency is the currency that forms the biggest proportion of the holdings of central banks. More broadly, however, it is also the one most likely to be accepted by merchants in other countries; if you are a tourist in Africa, you will be better off trying to buy goods with dollars than pounds or yen.

In my view, the debate about whether the dollar will be replaced by the renminbi is a bit of a red herring. Such a shift may eventually occur but it is likely to take a long time. As of 2010, 60 per cent of all foreign exchange reserves were denominated in dollars, giving the US currency a critical mass.[3] Investors are still comfortable with holding it; at times of crisis, the dollar is regarded as a safe haven despite the country's fiscal problems. After all, sterling was still being used as a reserve currency in the mid-twentieth century long after Britain's relative economic decline had become apparent.

The choice of reserve currency involves many factors. The US's political, military and economic pre-eminence have undoubtedly boosted the dollar's status. But it is also important that investors, and other central banks, can easily realize their dollar holdings if they have to – in other words, that the US market is highly liquid. All commodities are still priced in dollars and the US currency is used in around 86 per cent of all foreign-exchange transactions. Nor do investors fear that the US will arbitrarily try to seize their holdings. The rule of law is well established in the country, and President replaces President without a hitch (hanging chads aside). About $500 billion of US currency circulates outside the home country.[4]

This confidence is the result of many decades of practical experience. Even if China allows the renminbi to become convertible (it has set a target date of 2015 for the switch), it will take a long time for its markets to become anything like as liquid as those in the US. And it will take even longer for international investors to become confident that a Communist-led government will always respect their rights.

Even if the dollar steadily falls in value against the renminbi, as seems likely, it will still have attractions as a reserve currency. Indeed, currency depreciation goes with the territory of being a reserve currency. In a sense, this dates back to the Triffin dilemma outlined in Chapter 5: for a currency to be used internationally there must be lots of it circulating abroad. For that to happen, however, a country must run a deficit so its currency builds up in the accounts of overseas merchants. And if the deficit becomes too large, confidence in the currency will eventually decline.

Some talk of a basket currency, such as the special drawing right or SDR, replacing the dollar. When the G20 countries attempted to revive the global economy in early 2009, they agreed on a new issue of SDRs to boost global liquidity. To date, however, SDRs lack the vital ingredient of liquidity. They comprise less than 5 per cent of global reserves and no private company has issued bonds denominated in the currency.[5]

China will eventually become the world's largest economy, if current trends continue, in the 2020s, and its foreign-exchange reserves already give it significant power as a creditor nation. But even if foreigners wanted to hold the renminbi instead of dollars, there are constraints on them doing so. And removing the constraints would probably cause the renminbi to soar, something the Chinese are keen to avoid.

If it seems unlikely that the next ten years will see a renminbi standard replacing a dollar standard, what about a new Bretton Woods agreement? An arrangement on the scale of the 1944 system would be very difficult. In a sense, it was only possible because of the limited number of participants and the urgency of wartime. Much of Europe was under Nazi occupation and could not take part; the Soviet Union had little intellectual input; and the developing world was consulted on a fairly cursory basis. The Americans were in charge, but listened to Keynes out of respect for his intellect.

A modern agreement would have to get consensus from America, China, the EU, India, Brazil and so on. This would be tricky. But there could be a less formal arrangement than the Bretton Woods regime. In November 2010, Robert Zoellick, a former US Treasury official who runs the World Bank, wrote of a scheme that would see countries agree on structural reforms to boost growth, forswear currency intervention and build a 'co-operative monetary system'.[6] This system 'should also consider employing gold as an international reference point of market expectations about inflation, deflation and future currency values'.

Some saw this mild suggestion as a call for a return to the gold standard. It is hard to see the standard returning, save in the desperate circumstances of Weimar-style hyperinflation. Even an alternative approach, based on a basket of commodities, seems unlikely to be accepted. There is a case for gold as a store of value over the very long term (although it let its enthusiasts down during the 1980s and 1990s). But there is simply not enough gold for it to play its part as money's other key function, as a medium of exchange.

But before we dismiss all the ideas for reform, we should remember that the world operates under what some call a Bretton Woods II regime, with the Americans buying Chinese goods and the Chinese supplying the finance. The implication of this process is everlasting US trade deficits and an ever greater investment by the Chinese people in US government debt. As Herb Stein, an economic adviser to President Nixon, proclaimed: 'that which cannot go on forever must stop'.

The system may have suited the Chinese up till now because they were eager to find manufacturing jobs for their rural population. But at some point the Chinese may feel the need to do something else with their trillions of reserves. Already they are looking to diversify by acquiring natural resources in the developing world. They have also criticized the US for its economic policy, calling on the Americans to limit their deficit. This criticism reached a new pitch after the downgrading of US government debt in August 2011. The official news agency, Xinhua, said that 'The US government has to come to terms with the painful fact that the good old days when it could just borrow its way out of messes of its own making are finally gone. China, the largest creditor of the world's sole superpower, has every right to demand the United States address its structural debt problems and ensure the safety of China's dollar assets. International supervision over the issue of US dollars should be introduced and a new, stable and secured global reserve currency may also be an option to avert a catastrophe caused by any single country.'

Despite the rhetoric, an outright Chinese abandonment of the dollar is out of the question. They already own so much in the way of US government debt that any indication of their intention to sell would cause a plunge in bond prices. As has been the case so often in this book, the fates of creditor and debtor are locked together. So the answer might be some kind of managed deal, with the Chinese agreeing to let their currency rise and to limit their current account surplus while the Americans agree to tackle their deficit. The currencies would trade in a range while the deficit would have a target.

This would be akin to the European Exchange Rate Mechanism that existed from the late 1970s to the 1990s. The ERM was plagued by recurrent crises as countries struggled to keep their currencies within the set bands. A global system would obviously face the same pressures. Indeed, they might be worse. The French and German economies have more in common than those of the US and China. But remember that we are choosing between imperfect systems, and the current system has helped create the debt crisis that weighs on the global economy.

Tim Geithner, the US Treasury Secretary, hinted at such a deal in October 2010, suggesting a limit on current account surpluses of around 4 per cent of GDP. A G20 meeting of finance ministers nodded mildly in the direction of this proposal, saying that 'persistently large imbalances, assessed against indicative guidelines to be agreed, would warrant an assessment of their nature and the root causes of impediments to adjustment'.[7]

Moving from that fairly bureaucratic statement to something more concrete will not happen overnight. Neither the Chinese nor the Americans will want to accept constraints on their behaviour.

The Chinese will change tack if they believe such a shift is in their own interest. This might be because they face losses on their government bond holdings or because they wish to shift to a consumption-based, rather than an export-led, model to court domestic popularity.

To some, the idea that America would accept constraints on the independence of its economic policy might seem a fantasy. It is hard enough for a President to get his plans through Congress, let alone get approval for a set of policies dictated from abroad. The US gets an enormous benefit from its ability to denominate its debt in its domestic currency, allowing it to depreciate some of its debt burden away. Losing that right, even partially, would be a heavy cost to bear.

As a result, one would only expect a new system to arise as part of a further crisis. It could be a funding problem, in which the US Treasury was unable to raise money on reasonable terms. Or it could result from a plunge in the dollar, leading to inflationary fears. Indeed, quantitative easing could go horribly wrong, as it did in the Weimar Republic. Suddenly, all the newly created money (much of which is sitting idly in the banking system) could wash back into the global economy, driving up prices.

Remember also that Western countries have used up a lot of their policy options. In the middle of 2011, interest rates were 1 per cent or below almost across the board. Further fiscal stimulus looked unlikely. And the potential impact of quantitative easing was far from clear.

In a speech in October 2010, Mervyn King, the governor of the Bank of England, called for a 'grand bargain' between the major players in the world economy.[8] 'The risk is that unless agreement on a common path of adjustment is reached, conflicting policies will result in an undesirably low level of world output, with all countries worse off as a result,' he said. 'The need to act in the collective interest has yet to be recognized and, unless it is, it will only be a matter of time before one or more countries resort to trade protectionism.'

The fundamental problem is the imbalance between the saving and the spending nations. In a sense, the situation resembles that of the late 1920s when the Americans and French owned a huge proportion of the world's gold reserves; this time it is the Asian and OPEC countries that have too much squirrelled away. What should naturally happen in such circumstances is for the exchange rates of the surplus nations to appreciate. This should eliminate the trade imbalances and reduce the drain on the deficit countries. Goldman Sachs reckoned that, as of late 2010, emerging market currencies needed to appreciate by around 20 per cent against the dollar.[9]

But countries have been attempting to hold their currencies down, either by intervening in the markets or by imposing capital controls. A classic example was the Swiss franc, traditionally seen as a safe haven from Europe's financial problems. Its currency rose so fast that the Swiss National Bank intervened to cap its level against the Euro in September 2011. The SNB said it could buy 'unlimited' foreign currency with Swiss francs, effectively using QE to drive down its exchange rate. But all currencies cannot fall; some must rise and risk deflation in the process. The risk, as Mervyn King stated, is of a backlash in the developed world in which tariffs are imposed in an effort to protect jobs, thereby repeating the mistakes of the early 1930s. This would hurt both the developed and the developing economies.

The irony is that America finds itself advocating a policy that Keynes favoured in the 1940s, but Washington rejected. Keynes argued that the problem with the inter-war monetary system was that all the costs of adjustment fell on the debtor countries, and that the creditor countries should also have to change policies. It was not until the Americans became debtors that they adopted Keynes's view. But now of course they are in no position to impose their view on the Chinese.

The Asian current-account surpluses arose, in part, as a form of insurance against the risks of economic and financial instability. But they have long surpassed any plausible insurance needs. They now represent a claim on other countries' assets; claims that currently earn low returns and seem unlikely to be repaid in full. This seems a bit of a waste.

Martin Wolf of the *Financial Times* argues that developing countries need the confidence to run current-account deficits without putting them at risk of speculative attacks.[10] This may require the belief that the IMF will provide finance, if needed, without the sort of onerous conditions imposed in the late 1990s on debtor countries. In turn, this may require reform of the IMF, which has been dominated by the developed nations since 1944. In an ideal world, the managing directorship of the IMF would no longer be a sinecure for European politicians.[11] However, when Dominique Strauss-Kahn was forced to resign from his job as head of the IMF after his arrest on sexual assault charges he was quickly replaced by another French politician, Christine Lagarde. The emerging countries were unable to defeat the deal in the face of support for Lagarde from both Europe and the US.

THE OUTLINES OF A SYSTEM

Any target for exchange rates, or current-account surpluses, would have to be flexible. Fixed exchange rates require either subordination of monetary policy or capital controls to be effective. The Chinese, who already restrict investment, might favour capital controls, but it is hard to see the US, with its huge financial services industry, agreeing to a worldwide restriction.

However, there is one factor that might persuade the US government to change its mind – its debt burden. As has already been discussed, reducing debt via an austerity programme is unpalatable, and outright default is almost unthinkable. But governments did manage to reduce their debt burdens after the Second World War, under the auspices of the Bretton Woods system.

In a March 2011 paper, Carmen Reinhart and Belen Sbrancia argue that the success of this debt-reduction programme was down to 'financial repression'.[12] Domestic investors such as pension funds were forced to lend to governments through regulations that restricted their investment freedom; the interest rate on this debt was then held at artificially low levels. The result was that real (after inflation) interest rates were negative for roughly half the time between 1945 and 1980; investors were coerced into losing money. Reinhart and Sbrancia reckon this policy may have reduced debt-to-GDP ratios by between three and four percentage points a year.

It is not too much of a stretch to see the Basle III rules, agreed after the 2007–08 crisis, as a step down the road to financial repression. Banks are being forced to hold more capital, a policy that will lead them to own more government bonds. Pension funds also own more government bonds these days under the guise of 'liability matching'. As Reinhart and Sbrancia remark, financial repression may re-emerge in 'the guise of prudential regulation'. Russell Napier, a financial historian, takes a similar line, writing:

> It is time to bring back capital controls. Only with such controls can government debt burdens be inflated away. With capital controls, private savings can be more easily forced into public sector debt. It was capital controls that ensured the UK's gilt yields could be below its inflation rate in the 1970s.[13]

The post-1945 rules were difficult to evade thanks to the imposition of capital controls. In those days, payments took time to process, and rules were easier to enforce; British tourists were even limited in the amount of sterling they could take abroad.

Now money can be moved with the click of a computer mouse. And even back in the 1960s, ways were found round the rules; multinational companies could always find ways of switching profits from country A to country B by allocating costs in ingenious ways. They would be even better at following such strategies today, since they already manage their tax affairs via such devices.

Nevertheless, the tide is shifting in the direction of capital controls. Various developing countries are already trying to control the inflows into their currencies; Brazil twice raised taxes on bond investors in 2010. Restricting capital flows may even be a vote-winner, given the unpopularity of the finance sector in the wake of the crisis. Many European politicians have always disliked speculators and have sought restrictions on their ability to affect exchange rates, government-bond yields and commodity prices. It has only been the resistance of the Anglo-Saxon powers (America and Britain) that may have stopped international restrictions. But if Britain and America ever become the target for speculative attacks, rather than the host nations for speculators, they may change their tune.

Long-held ideological convictions are often sacrificed on the altar of expedience. Think of how many unlikely things happened in 2008. Some of the grandest names on Wall Street either went bust or were close to doing so. A right-wing Republican president allowed the government to take equity stakes as part of the rescue. Global leaders agreed to co-ordinate fiscal policies. Developed world interest rates were cut to unprecedented levels.

Perhaps such a deal could be sweetened by having the Chinese agree to let their currency appreciate by up to 10 per cent a year, making it seem as if the Chinese had given way to American pressure for a more flexible exchange rate.

How would such a managed exchange-rate system work? After all, it eventually proved impossible to keep exchange rates pegged under Bretton Woods. But the system did work for a quarter of a century. If an exchange-rate peg gives speculators a tempting target, the answer will be to curb the speculators. Again, if it is the Chinese who are setting the rules, such a move seems more likely. They regard Western governments as being foolish for allowing their economic policies to be at the mercy of the markets.

If Britain set the terms of the gold standard, and America set the terms of Bretton Woods, then the terms of the next financial system are likely to be set by the world's biggest creditor – China. And that system may look a lot different to the one we have become used to over the last thirty years.

Now there are plenty of objections to this argument, not least that China is not as dominant a creditor as America was after the world wars. The Japanese and the OPEC countries are also substantial owners of government debt. Nevertheless, China is by far the most important of the creditors in political and military terms, and it is hard to imagine a new system emerging that does not meet with Chinese approval.

A further objection is that the Chinese are passive participants in international debates and are unlikely to take the lead. But the same was true of America in the years before the First World War. Even after the war, the US retreated into an isolationist phase, refusing to join the League of Nations, which made international co-ordination much more difficult in the inter-war years. Eventually, America realized it was in its own interests to ensure that the international trade and financial systems operated smoothly.

The same is true of China today. As has already been noted, it has followed an export-led economic model, shifting its rural population into manufacturing industries on the coast. To keep those factories ticking over, it needs its customers in the West to be prosperous. In addition, having invested so much of its reserves in Western government bonds, it has an interest in ensuring that the US and Europe are not consumed by a financial crisis.

In any case, I am not suggesting that the Chinese are about to remake the system next week or next year. After the gold standard collapsed in the early 1930s, it took another decade, and a world war, before Bretton Woods was agreed. Bretton Woods collapsed in 1971, but order was not really restored to the financial system until the 1980s.

However, eventually, if Chinese power grows as fast as many commentators expect, theirs will be the largest economy in the world, with the largest population and a dominant position in the world's largest continent, Asia. The developed world has mortgaged its future with a foolish bet on asset prices and an excessive reliance on the finance sector. Like Mr Micawber, it is left waiting for something to turn up to rescue it from its plight.

Something will turn up but it may take ten or fifteen years and it will not necessarily be to the West's liking. A new order will emerge. And, like so many of the goods sold in Western supermarkets, it will be made in China.

PAPER PROMISES

In the last forty years, the world has been more successful at creating claims on wealth than it has at creating wealth itself. The economy has grown, but asset prices have risen faster, and debts have risen faster still. Debtors, from speculative homebuyers to leading governments, have made promises to pay that they are unlikely to meet in full. Creditors who are counting on those debts to be repaid will be disappointed.

Clearing up the mess will be a long, slow process. It will involve many false starts, as occurred during the banking crisis of 2008 and as we have already seen in the European sovereign debt crisis. The debts may be repaid in inflated money, or devalued currency; they may be passed on to other governments with a greater capacity to repay; or they may result in outright default.

Breaking those paper promises will result in economic turmoil, as both debtors and creditors suffer. This is a crisis as severe as those that resulted in the end of the gold standard in the 1930s or the end of fixed exchange rates in the 1970s. The global economy is changing; for many in the West, it will not be for the better.

Notes

INTRODUCTION

1. John Taylor, *An Inquiry into the Principles and Policy of the Government of the United States*, first published 1814.
2. The issues are summarized in an essay by Quentin Taylor at http://www.usagold.com/gildedopinion/oz.html.
3. Paul Krugman, 'Mugged by the moralizers', *New York Times*, 31 October 2010.

1. THE NATURE OF MONEY

1. 'North Korea's currency revaluation', Banyan's notebook, Economist.com, 2 December 2009.
2. 'N Korea executes two over bungled currency reform', Agence France-Presse, March 2010.
3. H. Montgomery Hyde, *John Law: The History of an Honest Adventurer*, London, 1969.
4. Ibid.
5. A pyramid scheme named after a 1920s fraudster in which the ability to pay returns to old investors depends on taking money from new investors. Much more on this later in the book.
6. Quoted in Janet Gleeson, *The Moneymaker*, London, 1999. The philosopher's stone was sought after by alchemists and could turn base metal into gold. It appears in the British title of the first Harry Potter book; for American readers, it was thought the term 'philosopher' was too off-putting and the term 'sorcerer's stone' was used instead.
7. Quoted in Gleeson, *The Moneymaker*.
8. Meyrick Chapman, *Don't Be Fooled Again: Lessons in the Good, Bad and Unpredictable Behaviour of Global Finance*, Harlow, 2010.

9. Quoted in Glyn Davies, *A History of Money: From Ancient Times to the Present Day*, Cardiff, 2002.

10. J. K. Galbraith, *Money: Whence It Came, Where It Went*, 2nd edn, London, 1995.

11. Davies, *A History of Money*.

12. Ibid.

13. Charles Kindleberger, *A Financial History of Western Europe*, London, 1984.

14. Galbraith, *Money*.

15. Davies, *A History of Money*.

16. Kindleberger, *Financial History*.

17. James Macdonald, *A Free Nation Deep in Debt: The Financial Roots of Democracy*, Princeton, 2003.

18. One could, of course, slash all prices relative to gold but this would be a fearsomely complex process, requiring all debts and incomes to be cut as well.

19. Kindleberger, *Financial History*.

20. Roger Bootle, *The Death of Inflation: Surviving and Thriving in the Zero Era*, London, 1996.

21. Davies, *A History of Money*.

22. Goldsmiths were not the first banks. Earlier banks were often successful merchants whose credit was regarded as sound. Trade was often financed by 'bills of exchange' – the promise by one merchant to pay another. A shrewd merchant could buy these bills at a discount. If that discount was greater than his cost of borrowing, he could make money from the trade. In effect, he had become a bank.

23. Quoted in Peter Bernholz, *Monetary Regimes and Inflation: History, Economic and Political Relationships*, Cheltenham, 2003.

24. Davies, *A History of Money*.

25. Many people are both creditors and borrowers. But wealth is usually fairly concentrated, so the creditor/rentier class is a minority.

26. A modest amount of inflation is fine, which is why central banks tend to target a rate of 2% or so. But once annual inflation passes 5% or so, and certainly when it reaches double digits, problems emerge.

2. IGNORING POLONIUS

1. James Macdonald, *A Free Nation Deep in Debt: The Financial Roots of Democracy*, Princeton, 2003.

2. Sidney Homer and Richard Sylla, *A History of Interest Rates*, 4th edn, New York, 2005.

3. Macdonald, *A Free Nation*.

4. Charles Kindleberger, *A Financial History of Western Europe*, London, 1984.

5. Virginia Cowles, *The Great Swindle: The Story of the South Sea Bubble*, London, 1960.

6. Hilaire Belloc, *Usury*, London, 1931.

7. Homer and Sylla, *Interest Rates*.

8. Ibid.

9. Plutarch, *Life of Lucullus*.

10. Homer and Sylla, *Interest Rates*.

11. Ibid.

12. Ibid.

13. Ian Mortimer, *The Perfect King: The Life of Edward III, the Father of the English Nation*, London, 2006.

14. Macdonald, *A Free Nation*.

15. Carmen Reinhart and Kenneth Rogoff, *This Time Is Different*, Princeton, 2009.

16. All quotes from Ron Chernow, *Alexander Hamilton*, London, 2004.

17. From ibid.

18. Homer and Sylla, *Interest Rates*.

19. One might raise the objection that the debtor is making no such rational calculation, that he or she is unable to wait to get his or her hands on the desired goods. This is a problem of deferred gratification. But the creditor has to be sure that the debtor will be able to repay, so the system still depends on the prospect of growth.

20. Lendol Calder, *Financing the American Dream: A Cultural History of Consumer Credit*, Princeton, 1999.

21. Ibid.

22. Some economists think that Keynes was wrong about this, on the grounds that saving must always equal investment. So businesses would be able to go on an investment spree, if savings boom. But Keynes said that businesses needed confidence or 'animal spirits' to invest, which they might lack during recessions. Planned savings could thus be larger than planned investment. Some savings would be hoarded, the equivalent of keeping cash under the mattress, and thus not invested by entrepreneurs.

3. GOING FOR GOLD

1. China favours a fixed exchange rate and economic expansion. But it is a bit of a special case, choosing to undervalue its rate to boost its exports. The normal policy dilemma was that faced by Britain in 1931 or the US in 1971 – letting down creditors, by devaluing, or damaging the economy.

2. Roger Bootle, *The Death of Inflation: Surviving and Thriving in the Zero Era*, London, 1996.

3. Sidney Homer and Richard Sylla, *A History of Interest Rates*, 4th edn, New York, 2005.

4. John Maynard Keynes, *The Economic Consequences of the Peace*, London, 1919.

5. Barry Eichengreen, *Golden Fetters: The Gold Standard and the Great Depression 1919–1939*, Oxford, 1995 and *Globalizing Capital: A History of the International Monetary System*, Princeton, 2008.

6. Filippo Cesarino, *Monetary Theory and Bretton Woods: The Construction of an International Monetary Order*, Cambridge, 2006.

7. J. K. Galbraith, *Money: Whence It Came, Where It Went*, 2nd edn, London, 1995.

8. Glyn Davies, *A History of Money: From Ancient Times to the Present Day*, Cardiff, 2002.

9. Walter Bagehot, *Lombard Street*, first published 1873, reissued New York, 1999.

10. Peter Bernholz, *Monetary Regimes and Inflation: History, Economic and Political Relationships*, Cheltenham, 2003.

11. Figures from James Macdonald, *A Free Nation Deep in Debt: The Financial Roots of Democracy*, Princeton, 2003.

12. Figures from Harold James, *The End of Globalization: Lessons from the Great Depression*, Cambridge, Mass., 2002.

13. Quoted in Liaquat Ahamed, *Lords of Finance: 1929, the Great Depression and the Bankers Who Broke the World*, London, 2009.

4. MONEY AND THE DEPRESSION

1. Liaquat Ahamed, *Lords of Finance: 1929, the Great Depression and the Bankers Who Broke the World*, London, 2009.

2. John Maynard Keynes, *The Economic Consequences of the Peace*, London, 1919.

3. Quoted in Ahamed, *Lords of Finance*.

4. Ibid.

5. See http://freetheplanet.net/articles/106/interim-report-of-the-cunliffe-committee-1918.

6. Indeed, in his personal life, Churchill could never balance a budget and was frequently in debt.

7. John Maynard Keynes, *The Economic Consequences of Mr Churchill*, London, 1925.

8. Barry Eichengreen, *Golden Fetters: The Gold Standard and the Great Depression 1919–1939*, Oxford, 1995.

9. Keynes, *Economic Consequences of Mr Churchill*.

10. Filippo Cesarino, *Monetary Theory and Bretton Woods: The Construction of an International Monetary Order*, Cambridge, 2006.

11. Richard Duncan, *The Corruption of Capitalism*, Hong Kong, 2009.

12. Barry Eichengreen and Peter Temin, 'Fetters of Gold and Paper', *Vox EU*, 30 July 2010.

13. Quoted in Eichengreen, *Golden Fetters*.

14. Cesarino, *Monetary Theory*.

15. David Howell, *MacDonald's Party: Labour Identities and Crisis 1922–1931*, Oxford, 2002.

16. Diane B. Kunz, *The Battle for Britain's Gold Standard*, London, 1987.

17. Quoted in Austen Morgan, *J. Ramsay MacDonald*, Manchester, 1987.

18. Ibid.

19. Because one event occurred before another, the former must have caused the latter.

5. DANCING WITH THE DOLLAR

1. Quoted in Armand van Dormael, *Bretton Woods: Birth of a Monetary System*, New York, 1978.

2. Quoted in ibid.

3. Quoted in ibid.

4. Quoted in Filippo Cesarino, *Monetary Theory and Bretton Woods: The Construction of an International Monetary Order*, Cambridge, 2006.

5. Quoted in van Dormael, *Bretton Woods*.

6. Charles Kindleberger, *A Financial History of Western Europe*, London, 1984.

7. Quoted in David Marsh, *The Euro: The Politics of the New Global Currency*, New Haven, Conn., 2008.

8. Interview with Fred Hirsch, 1965.

9. Robert Triffin, *Gold and the Dollar Crisis*, New Haven, Conn., 1960.
10. Tim Congdon, 'America's Deficit, the Dollar and Gold', World Gold Council Research Study No. 28, 2002.
11. Marsh, *The Euro*.
12. Cesarino, *Monetary Theory*.

6. PAPER PROMISES

1. Milton Friedman, *Studies in the Quantity Theory of Money*, Chicago, 1956
2. Tim Congdon, 'America's Deficit, the Dollar and Gold', World Gold Council Research Study No. 28, 2002.
3. Martin Wolf, *Fixing Global Finance: How to Curb Financial Crises in the Late 21st Century*, rev. edn, New Haven, Conn., 2010.
4. David Marsh, *The Euro: The Politics of the New Global Currency*, New Haven, Conn., 2008.

7. BLOWING BUBBLES

1. Jeremy Grantham, 'Night of the Living Fed', GMO *Quarterly Letter*, October 2010.
2. Carmen Reinhart and Kenneth Rogoff, *This Time Is Different*, Princeton, 2009.
3. Richard Duncan, *The Dollar Crisis*, rev. edn, New York, 2005; Richard Duncan, *The Corruption of Capitalism*, Hong Kong, 2009.
4. Clearly this is a simplified example. Some people would have bigger deposits, some smaller.
5. Willem Buiter, 'Housing Wealth Isn't Real Wealth', www.economics-ejournal.org/economics/journalarticles/2010-22.
6. Russell Roberts, 'Gambling with Other People's Money: How Perverted Incentives Caused the Financial Crisis', Mercatus Center, George Mason University, May 2010.
7. In the modern era, he would have described his business as postal arbitrage.
8. It doesn't take much analysis to work out that the average person cannot gain from such schemes. If each person puts in $1,000, then the return of the average person must be $1,000. But the last layer of investors must lose.
9. Of course, multinational companies can earn money overseas and rise above the national economy. But the analysis must be true at the global level.

10. Charles Kindleberger, *Manias, Panics and Crashes: A History of Financial Crises*, 4th edn, New York, 2000.

11. In his books *The Dollar Crisis* and *The Corruption of Capitalism*.

12. A put gives the owner the right to sell an asset at a set price. It is bought by investors to protect themselves against sharp price falls.

13. Roberts, 'Gambling with Other People's Money'.

14. 'What Has – and Has Not – Been Learned About Monetary Policy in a Low Inflation Environment? A Review of the 2000s'. Speech by Richard H. Clarida to the Federal Reserve Bank Conference, 21 October 2010.

15. For up-to-date figures, see www.irrationalexuberance.com.

16. Quoted in the *Wall Street Journal*, 25 February 1993.

17. 'Farewell to Cheap Capital? The Implications of Long-term Shifts in Global Investment and Saving', McKinsey Global Institute, December 2010.

18. The figures are based on ten mature economies and four developing economies (Brazil, China, India and Mexico).

19. This argument relies on the discounted cashflow approach to valuation. The value of an asset is equal to the future cashflows, discounted to allow for the time value of money. A lower discount rate thus means a higher present value. This argument is a little short-sighted, however. Low real rates should be a sign of low expected growth. So to the extent that the discount rate falls, expected future cashflows should fall as well.

20. Grantham, 'Night of the Living Fed'.

8. RIDING THE GRAVY TRAIN

1. J. K. Galbraith, *Money: Whence It Came, Where It Went*, 2nd edn, London, 1995.

2. Lawrence Mishel, 'CEO-to-Worker Pay Imbalance Grows', Economic Policy Institute, June 2006.

3. Ian Dew-Becker and Robert Gordon, 'Where Did the Productivity Growth Go? Inflation Dynamics and the Distribution of Income', National Bureau of Economic Research, Working Paper 11842.

4. Edward N. Wolff, 'Recent Trends in Household Wealth in the United States: Rising Debt and the Middle Class Squeeze', an update to 2007 Working Paper no. 589, Levy Economics Institute, March 2010.

5. Raghuram Rajan, *Fault Lines: How Hidden Fractures Threaten the World Economy*, Princeton, 2010.

6. 'Finance, Financial Sector Policies and Long-Run Growth', by Asli Demirguc-Kunt of the World Bank and Ross Levine of Brown University.

7. Adair Turner, 'What do banks do? Why do credit booms and busts occur and what can public policy do about it?' in 'The Future of Finance', LSE report, 2010.

8. Andrew Haldane, 'The $100 Billion Question'. Comments given at the Institute of Regulation & Risk in Hong Kong, 30 March 2010.

9. Russell Roberts, 'Gambling with Other People's Money: How Perverted Incentives Caused the Financial Crisis', Mercatus Center, George Mason University, May 2010.

10. Haldane, 'The $100 Billion Question'.

11. Jim Reid, 'Fundamental Credit Special', privately circulated research note, July 2010.

12. Piergiorgio Alessandri and Andrew Haldane, 'Banking on the State', Bank of England, November 2009.

13. 'Still Vulnerable: It Looks Too Early to be Buying Financial Stocks', *The Economist*, 17 April 2008.

14. If you have capital of £100 million and earn a return of 10%, shareholders get £10 million. If you borrow another £900 million at a cost of, say, 5%, and still earn a return of 10% on the bigger balance sheet, shareholders get £55 million.

15. Alessandri and Haldane, 'Banking on the State'.

16. Luc Laeven and Fabian Valencia, 'Systemic Banking Crises: A New Database', IMF Working Paper No. 08/224, 2008.

17. Simon Johnson and James Kwak, *13 Bankers: The Wall Street Takeover and the Next Financial Meltdown*, New York, 2010.

18. Quoted in John Cassidy, 'What Good is Wall Street?' *New Yorker*, 29 November 2010.

19. Bob Woodward, *Maestro: Greenspan's Fed and the American Boom*, New York, 2001.

20. Admittedly, that would be very difficult in the case of the European Central Bank. Its mandate was set by treaty.

21. Michiyo Nakamoto and David Wighton, 'Citigroup Chief Stays Bullish on Buy-outs', *Financial Times*, 9 July 2007.

22. Quoted in Nick Leeson, *Rogue Trader*, London, 1996.

23. Pablo Triana, *Lecturing Birds on Flying: Can Mathematical Theories Destroy The Financial Markets?*, New York, 2009.

24. Nassim Nicholas Taleb, *The Black Swan: The Impact of the Highly Improbable*, London, 2008.

25. Peter Thal Larsen, 'Goldman Pays the Price for Being Big', *Financial Times*, 13 August 2008.

26. Andrew Haldane, 'Why Banks Failed the Stress Test', 9–10 February 2009.

27. Interview with the author, 25 October 2010.

9. THE CRISIS BEGINS

1. Tim Congdon, *The Debt Threat*, Oxford, 1989.
2. Peter Warburton, *Debt and Delusion*, London, 1999.
3. 'Debt and Deleveraging: The Global Credit Bubble and its Economic Consequences', McKinsey Global Institute, January 2010.
4. Scott Schuh, Oz Shy and Joanna Stavins, 'Who Gains and Who Loses from Credit Card Payments? Theory and Calibrations', Federal Reserve Bank of Boston, March 2010.
5. 'Debt and Deleveraging'.
6. J. K. Galbraith, *The Affluent Society*, 4th edn, London, 1984.
7. Elizabeth Duke, speech to the Payment Cards Center Conference, Philadelphia, December 2010.
8. 'Debt and Deleveraging'.
9. Private equity firms often get lumped together with venture capitalists, but they are quite different. A venture capitalist invests in small, often start-up companies that could have great growth potential; the investment will usually be in the form of equity, not debt. These investments have a high failure rate; the hope is that the occasional big success makes up for the many losers. By encouraging innovation, venture capital is generally seen as a much better thing for the economy than private equity; alas, it has delivered much lower returns.
10. See Peter Morris, 'Private Equity, Public Loss?', Centre for the Study of Financial Innovation, July 2010.

10. NOT SO RISK-FREE

1. Carmen Reinhart and Kenneth Rogoff, *This Time Is Different*, Princeton, 2009.
2. Alexander Sack, quoted in 'Unfinished Business: Ten Years of Dropping the Debt', Jubilee Debt Campaign, May 2008.
3. The Multilateral Debt Relief Initiative factsheet, August 2010.
4. 2010 Development Cooperation Report, OECD.
5. Elgie McFadyen, 'The Multilateral Debt Relief Initiative: Impact on Structural and Economic Development Among African Nations', Kentucky State University, April 2008.
6. Alan Beattie, 'Rich Nations Face Increased Debt Burden', FT.com, 31 October 2010.
7. Reinhart and Rogoff, *This Time Is Different*.

8. Martin Wolf, *Fixing Global Finance: How to Curb Financial Crises in the Late 21st Century*, rev. edn, New Haven, Conn., 2010.

9. Figures from the IMF at http://www.imf.org/external/np/exr/faq/greece-faqs.htm.

10. 'Threadbare: A Briefing on Ireland's Economy', *The Economist*, 20 November 2010.

11. Bennett Stancil, 'Ireland: From Bubble to Broke', Carnegie Endowment for International Peace, May 2010.

12. As I tried to explain to friends and relatives at the time, this move was a mistake. A sovereign can guarantee deposits in its domestic currency, providing it is willing to print enough money. But the Irish could not guarantee sterling deposits. Nor could it guarantee euro deposits, since it did not have a printing press for euros.

13. 'Debt and Deleveraging: The Global Credit Bubble and its Economic Consequences', McKinsey Global Institute, January 2010.

14. Dhaval Joshi, 'A Spanish Lament', privately circulated research note, December 2010.

15. 'How Banks can Undermine their Sovereign', privately circulated research note, December 2010.

16. Jason Manolopoulos, *Greece's Odious Debt: The Looting of the Hellenic Republic by the Euro, the Political Elite and the Investment Community*, London, 2011.

17. 'Will the ECB Ride to the Rescue?', privately circulated research note, December 2010.

18. Desmond Lachman, 'Can the Euro Survive?' Legatum Institute paper, December 2010.

19. Jagadeesh Gokhale, 'Measuring the Unfunded Obligations of European Countries', Cato Institute policy report no. 319, January 2009.

20. Stephen Cecchetti, M. S. Mohanty and Fabrizio Zampolli, 'The Future of Public Debt: Prospects and Implications', Bank for International Settlements, Working Papers 300.

21. Quoted in Arnaud Mares, 'Ask Not Whether Governments Will Default, But How', Morgan Stanley research note, 20 September 2010.

22. Irving Fisher, 'The Debt-Deflation Theory of Great Depressions', *Econometrica*, 1 (4), 1933.

23. Reinhart and Rogoff, in 'Ask Not Whether Governments Will Default'.

24. For a sweeping critique, see John Irons and Josh Bivens, 'Government Debt and Economic Growth: Overreaching Claims of Debt "Threshold" Suffer from Theoretical and Empirical Flaws', Economic Policy Institute briefing paper no. 271, July 2010.

25. Antonio Afonso and Davide Furceri, 'Government Size, Composition, Volatility and Economic Growth', School of Economics and Management, Technical University of Lisbon, working paper ISSN 0874-4548, January 2008.

11. BEQUEATHING OUR DEBTS

1. 'Global Demographics – From Golden to Grey, Long-Term Asset Return Study', Deutsche Bank, 10 September 2010.
2. Quoted in David Willetts, *The Pinch: How the Baby Boomers Took Their Children's Future – And Why They Should Give it Back*, London, 2010.
3. Ibid.
4. Martin Neil Baily and Jacob Funk Kirkegaard, 'US Pensions Reform: Lessons from Other Countries', Peterson Institute for International Economics, 2009.
5. 'Global Demographics'.
6. 'Global Aging 2010: An Irreversible Truth'.
7. Eileen Norcross and Andrew Biggs, 'The Crisis in Public Sector Pension Plans: A Blueprint for Reform in New Jersey', http:://mercatus.org/pensions.
8. Robert Novy-Marx and Joshua Rauh, 'Public Pension Promises: How Big Are They and What Are They Worth?' http://papers.ssrn.com/sol3/papers.cfm?abstract_id=1352608.
9. And another potential liability for the government.
10. There is an irony here. If the Bank of England fails in its mission to control inflation, its employees will be extremely well protected.
11. 'Reforming Public Sector Pensions: Solutions to a Growing Challenge', The Public Sector Pensions Commission, July 2010.
12. 'USA Inc.: A Basic Summary of America's Financial Statements', February 2011.
13. Figures from George Magnus, *The Age of Aging: How Demographics Are Changing the Global Economy and Our World*, New York, 2009.
14. Adam Ridley, 'Don't Dismiss the Materialist Explanation', Cato Unbound, 8 October 2010.
15. Tim Morgan, 'Dangerous Exponentials: A Radical Take on the Future', research note for Tullett Prebon, June 2010.
16. Andrew Lees, 'In Search of Energy', in *The Gathering Storm*, edited by Patrick L. Young, New York, 2010.

12. PAYING THE BILL

1. Joseph Stiglitz, *Freefall: Free Markets and the Sinking of the Global Economy*, rev. edn, London, 2010.

2. Ibid.

3. Peter Bernholz, *Monetary Regimes and Inflation: History, Economic and Political Relationships*, Cheltenham, 2003.

4. The full speech is available at www.federalreserve.gov/BOARDDOCS/SPEECHES/2002/20021121/default.htm.

5. Ibid.

6. Ibid.

7. But they might be forced to if governments impose capital controls. See the final chapter.

8. Writing in *The Gathering Storm*, edited by Patrick L. Young, New York, 2010.

9. 'Investment Outlook', March 2011, www.pimco.com.

10. Virginia Cowles, *The Great Swindle: The Story of the South Sea Bubble*, London, 1960.

11. Richard C. Koo, *The Holy Grail of Macroeconomics: Lessons from Japan's Great Recession*, rev. edn, New York, 2009.

12. Eamonn Butler, 'Ludwig von Mises – A Primer', IEA Occasional Paper 143, 2010.

13. Richard Duncan, *The Corruption of Capitalism*, Hong Kong, 2009.

14. Carmen Reinhart and Kenneth Rogoff, *This Time Is Different*, Princeton, 2009.

15. This policy might not have worked. Emerging markets might not have wanted to absorb so much foreign capital, and might have imposed restrictions on foreign investment; or the money might have flowed into speculative activity, as it did in the 1990s, and been lost. Still, there is the example of Norway, which has used its oil wealth to build a pool of assets to safeguard the interests of future generations.

16. Reinhart and Rogoff, *This Time Is Different*.

17. Carlo Cottarelli, Lorenzo Forni, Jan Gottschalk and Paolo Mauro, 'Default in Today's Advanced Economies: Unnecessary, Undesirable and Unlikely', September 2010. An IMF staff paper is not the official position of the fund itself.

18. Kenneth Rogoff, 'The Euro at Mid-crisis', Project syndicate website.

19. Inflation eventually results in a currency crisis or in a deep recession if the central bank attempts to bring it back under control. Stagnation leads to political discontent, making default more likely.

13. A NEW ORDER

1. Clearly, all countries cannot drive down their exchange rate via QE, although there can be a ripple effect; if one central bank uses QE for this purpose, others might be tempted to follow. Many commentators cited QE as a reason to buy gold in 2009 and 2010; if most countries are keen to drive down the value of paper money, then gold's appeal increases.

2. Of course, if yields on existing debt fall, prices go up, something that is good news for creditors. But the rise may only be in local currency terms; foreign creditors may still suffer a loss once the exchange rate is taken into account. And debt is being refinanced all the time so the income on new debt falls.

3. Barry Eichengreen, *Exorbitant Privilege: The Decline of the Dollar and the Future of the International Monetary System*, Oxford, 2010.

4. Ibid.

5. 'The Global Monetary System: Beyond Bretton Woods 2', *The Economist*, 6 November 2010.

6. Robert Zoellick, 'The G20 Must Look Beyond Bretton Woods', *Financial Times*, 8 November 2010.

7. Martin Wolf, 'Current Account Targets are a Way Back to the Future', *Financial Times*, 3 November 2010.

8. 'King Says G-20 Needs Grand Bargain to Avert Protectionism', *Bloomberg*, 20 October 2010.

9. 'Seoul Food: The Search for Global Balance', *Global Economics Weekly*, 3 November 2010.

10. Martin Wolf, *Fixing Global Finance: How to Curb Financial Crises in the Late 21st Century*, rev. edn, New Haven, Conn., 2010.

11. A long-standing deal has seen Americans head the World Bank and Europeans the IMF.

12. Carmen Reinhart and Belen Sbrancia, 'The Liquidation of Government Debt', NBER Working Paper 16893, March 2011.

13. Russell Napier, 'Bretton Woods on Speed', CLSA research note, November 2010.

Bibliography

Some suggestions for further reading:

Acharya, Viral and Richardson, Matthew, eds, *Restoring Financial Stability: How to Repair a Failed Financial System*, New York, 2009.

Ahamed, Liaquat, *Lords of Finance: 1929, the Great Depression and the Bankers Who Broke the World*, London, 2009.

Baily, Martin Neil and Kirkegaard, Jacob Funk, *US Pension Reform: Lessons from Other Countries*, Washington, DC, 2009.

Barbera, Robert J., *The Cost of Capitalism: Understanding Market Mayhem and Stabilizing Our Economic Future*, New York, 2009.

Belloc, Hilaire, *Usury*, London, 1931.

Bernholz, Peter, *Monetary Regimes and Inflation: History, Economic and Political Relationships*, Cheltenham, 2003.

Bootle, Roger, *The Death of Inflation: Surviving and Thriving in the Zero Era*, London, 1996.

Calder, Lendol, *Financing the American Dream: A Cultural History of American Debt*, Princeton, 1999.

Cesarino, Filippo, *Monetary Theory and Bretton Woods: The Construction of an International Monetary Order*, Cambridge, 2006.

Chapman, Meyrick, *Don't Be Fooled Again: Lessons in the Good, Bad and Unpredictable Behaviour of Global Finance*, Harlow, 2010.

Chernow, Ron, *Alexander Hamilton*, London, 2004.

Congdon, Tim, *The Debt Threat*, Oxford, 1989.

Corden, W. Max, *Too Sensational: On the Choice of Exchange Rate Regimes*, Cambridge, Mass., 2002.

Cowles, Virginia, *The Great Swindle: The Story of the South Sea Bubble*, London, 1960.

Davies, Glyn, *A History of Money: From Ancient Times to the Present Day*, Cardiff, 2002.

Dormael, Armand van, *Bretton Woods: Birth of a Monetary System*, New York, 1978.

Duncan, Richard, *The Dollar Crisis*, rev. edn, New York, 2005.

— *The Corruption of Capitalism*, Hong Kong, 2009.

Eichengreen, Barry, *Golden Fetters: The Gold Standard and the Great Depression 1919–1939*, Oxford, 1995.

— *Globalizing Capital: A History of the International Monetary System*, Princeton, 2008.

— *Exorbitant Privilege: The Decline of the Dollar and the Future of the International Monetary System*, Oxford, 2011.

Galbraith, J. K., *The Affluent Society*, 4th edn, London, 1984.

— *Money: Whence It Came, Where It Went*, 2nd edn, London, 1995.

Gleeson, Janet, *The Moneymaker*, London, 1999.

Homer, Sidney and Sylla, Richard, *A History of Interest Rates*, 4th edn, New York, 2005.

Howell, David, *MacDonald's Party: Labour Identities and Crisis 1922–1931*, Oxford, 2002.

Hyde, H. Montgomery, *John Law: The History of an Honest Adventurer*, London, 1969.

James, Harold, *The End of Globalization: Lessons from the Great Depression*, Cambridge, Mass., 2002.

Johnson, Simon and Kwak, James, *13 Bankers: The Wall Street Takeover and the Next Financial Meltdown*, New York, 2010.

Kazin, Michael, *A Godly Hero: The Life of William Jennings Bryan*, New York, 2006.

Keynes, John Maynard, *The Economic Consequences of the Peace*, London, 1919.

— *The Economic Consequences of Mr Churchill*, London, 1925.

Kindleberger, Charles, *A Financial History of Western Europe*, London, 1984.

— *Manias, Panics and Crashes: A History of Financial Crises*, 4th edn, New York, 2000.

Koo, Richard C., *The Holy Grail of Macroeconomics: Lessons from Japan's Great Recession*, rev. edn, New York, 2009.

Kunz, Diane B., *The Battle for Britain's Gold Standard*, London, 1987.

Lewis, Hunter, *Where Keynes Went Wrong: And Why World Governments Keep Creating Inflation, Bubbles and Busts*, Edinburg, Va., 2009.

Lowenstein, Roger, *While America Aged: How Pension Debts Ruined General Motors, Stopped the NYC Subways, Bankrupted San Diego and Loom as the Next Financial Crisis*, New York, 2009.

— *The End of Wall Street*, New York, 2010.

Macdonald, James, *A Free Nation Deep in Debt: The Financial Roots of Democracy*, Princeton, 2003.

Mackay, Charles, *Extraordinary Popular Delusions and the Madness of Crowds*, Ware, 1995.

Magnus, George, *The Age of Aging: How Demographics Are Changing the Global Economy and Our World*, New York, 2009.

Manolopoulos, Jason, *Greece's Odious Debt: The Looting of the Hellenic Republic by the Euro, the Political Elite and the Investment Community*, London, 2011.

Marsh, David, *The Euro: The Politics of the New Global Currency*, New Haven, Conn., 2008.

Morgan, Austen, *J. Ramsay MacDonald*, Manchester, 1987.

Rajan, Raghuram, *Fault Lines: How Hidden Fractures Threaten the World Economy*, Princeton, 2010.

Reid, Michael, *Forgotten Continent: The Battle for Latin America's Soul*, New Haven, Conn., 2007.

Reinhart, Carmen and Rogoff, Kenneth, *This Time Is Different: Eight Centuries of Financial Folly*, Princeton, 2009.

Shiller, Robert J., *Irrational Exuberance*, Princeton, 2000.

Skeel, David A. Jr, *Debt's Dominion: A History of Bankruptcy Law in America*, Princeton, 2001.

Skidelsky, Robert, *John Maynard Keynes: Fighting for Freedom 1937–1946*, London, 2001.

— *Keynes: The Return of the Master*, London, 2009.

Sorkin, Andrew Ross, *Too Big to Fail: Inside the Battle to Save Wall Street*, London, 2009.

Stiglitz, Joseph, *Freefall: Free Markets and the Sinking of the Global Economy*, rev. edn, London, 2010.

Taleb, Nassim Nicholas, *The Black Swan: The Impact of the Highly Improbable*, London, 2008.

Warburton, Peter, *Debt and Delusion: Central Bank Follies that Threaten Economic Disaster*, London, 1999.

Willetts, David, *The Pinch: How the Baby Boomers Took Their Children's Future – and Why They Should Give It Back*, London, 2010.

Wolf, Martin, *Why Globalization Works: The Case for the Global Market Economy*, New Haven, Conn., 2005.

— *Fixing Global Finance: How to Curb Financial Crises in the Late 21st Century*, rev. edn, New Haven, Conn., 2010.

Young, Patrick L., ed., *The Gathering Storm: How to Avoid the Next Crisis from the Minds that Predicted the Crunch*, New York, 2010.

Zuckerman, Gregory, *The Greatest Trade Ever: The Behind-the-Scenes Story of How John Paulson Defied Wall Street and Made Financial History*, New York, 2009.

Index